TRADITION AND REVOLUTION

TRADITION AND REVOLUTION

Dialogues with J. Krishnamurti

Edited by
Pupul Jayakar
Sunanda Patwardhan

Website on the teachings of J.Krishnamurti
www.jkrishnamurti.org

Published by

Krishnamurti Foundation India
Vasanta Vihar, 124 Greenways Road
Chennai – 600 028.
E:mail : publications@kfionline.org
Website : www.kfionline.org

Second Edition
Reprinted 1999, 2003, 2013

Philosophy/Religion
ISBN 81-87326-07-7

Cover design: Deepa Kamath

Printed by

The Indcom Press
393 Velachery Main Road
Vijayanagar, Velachery
Chennai - 600 042

CONTENTS

PREFACE

These dialogues, the majority of which are on ancient Indian philosophical themes, were first published in 1972 and have subsequently been reprinted several times. In offering a second edition, we hope to introduce new readers to the characteristic style of spiritual inquiry that Krishnamurti was able to nourish. The participants in these dialogues were not professional philosophers but people who were trying to rediscover the Indian philosophical past and, in some important sense which cannot be identified with scholarship, renew that past. In their attitude to the past, they were more like poets rediscovering a familiar language rather than like literary scholars anxious to get at the historical truth. The preface to the first edition of the book provides the clue to what the participants were seeking.

PREFACE TO THE FIRST EDITION

Since 1947 J. Krishnamurti, while in India, has been regularly meeting and holding dialogues with a group of people drawn from a variety of cultural backgrounds and disciplines—intellectuals, artists, *sannyāsis*. During these years, the methodology of investigation has richened and taken shape. What is revealed in these dialogues, as if through a microscope, is the extraordinary fluid, vast and subtle mind of Krishnamurti and the operational process of perception. These dialogues are not, however, questions and answers. They are an investigation into the structure and nature of consciousness, an exploration of the mind, its movement, its frontiers and that which lies beyond. It is also an approach to the way of mutation.

There has been in these dialogues a coming together of several totally varied and differently conditioned minds. There has been a deep challenging of the mind of Krishnamurti, a relentless questioning that has opened up the depths of the human psyche. One is witness not only to the expanding and the deepening of the 'limitless', but also to the impact on the limited mind. This very inquiry leaves the mind flexible, freeing it from the immediate past and from the grooves of centuries of conditioning.

In these dialogues, Krishnamurti starts his questioning from a totally tentative position, from a state of 'not-knowing', and, therefore, in a sense, he starts at the same level as the participants. During the discussion, various analytical inquiries are made which are tentative and explorative. There is a questioning without seeking immediate solutions: a step by step observation of the processes of thought and its unfolding—a movement of penetration and withdrawal, every movement plunging attention deeper and deeper into the recesses of the mind. A delicate wordless communication takes place; an exposure of the movement of negation as it meets the positive movement of thought. There is a 'seeing' of fact, of 'what is', and the mutation of 'what is'. This is again perceived from various directions to examine its validity.

The nature of duality and non-duality is revealed in simple language. In that state of questioning, a state when the questioner, the experiencer, has ceased, in a flash, 'truth' is revealed. It is a state of total non-thought. Krishnamurti says:

> The mind, which is the vessel of movement, is completely quiet when that movement has no form, no 'me', no vision. In it there is no memory. Then the brain cells undergo a change. The brain cells are used to movement in time; they are the residue of time. And time is movement within the space it creates as it moves.
>
> When there is no movement, there is a tremendous focus of energy. So mutation is the understanding of movement, and the ending of movement in the brain cells themselves. (Dialogue 6)

The revelation of the instant of mutation, of 'what is', provides a totally new dimension to the whole field of intellectual and religious inquiry.

There may be repetition in the dialogues, but they have not been eliminated, because to do so would have inhibited the understanding of the nature of consciousness and the method of inquiry.

We feel that these discussions will be of major assistance to those seeking a clue to the understanding of the self and of life.

New Delhi
May 11, 1972

PUPUL JAYAKAR
SUNANDA PATWARDHAN

THE FLAME OF SORROW

Dialogue 1

K: What does sorrow mean in this country? How do the people in this country meet sorrow? Do they escape from sorrow through the explanation of *karma*? How does the mind in India operate when it meets sorrow? The Buddhist meets it in one way, the Christian in another way. How does the Hindu mind meet it? Does it resist sorrow, or escape from it? Or, does the mind rationalize it?

P: Are there really many ways of meeting sorrow? Sorrow is pain—the pain of someone dying, the pain of separation. Is it possible to meet this pain in various ways?

K: There are various ways of escape, but there is only one way of meeting sorrow. The escapes with which we are all familiar are really the ways of avoiding the greatness of sorrow. You see, we use explanations to meet sorrow, but these explanations do not answer the question. The only way to meet sorrow is to be without any resistance, to be without any movement away from sorrow—outwardly or inwardly—and to remain totally with sorrow, without wanting to go beyond it.

P: What is the nature of sorrow?

K: There is personal sorrow, the sorrow that comes with the loss of someone you love—the loneliness, the separation and the anxiety for the other. With death there is also the feeling that the other has ceased to be, and that there was so much that one wanted to do. All this is personal sorrow. Then there is that man, ill-clad, dirty, with his head down; he is ignorant, ignorant not merely of book-knowledge, but deeply, really ignorant. The feeling that one has for that man is not pity, nor is it an identification with that man—it is not that one is placed in a better position than he is and so feels pity for him, but that there is within one the sense of the timeless weight of sorrow in man. This sorrow has nothing personal about it. It exists.

P: While you have been speaking, the movement of sorrow has been operating within me. There is no immediate cause for this sorrow, but it seems like a shadow, always with man. He lives, he loves, he forms attachments, and everything ends. Whatever be the truth of what you say, in us there is such an infinitude of sorrow. How is it to end? There appears to be no answer. The other day you said that in sorrow there is the whole movement of passion. What does it mean?

K: Is there a relationship between sorrow and passion? Is there such a thing as sorrow without a cause? We know the sorrow which is cause and effect. My son dies; in that is involved my identification with my son: my wanting him to be something which I am not, my seeking continuity through him. When he dies all that is denied, and I find myself completely emptied of all hope. In that there is self-pity, fear; in that there is pain which is the cause of sorrow. This is the lot of everyone. This is what we mean by sorrow.

Then there is also the sorrow of time, the sorrow of ignorance, the ignorance of one's own destructive conditioning; the sorrow of not knowing oneself; the sorrow of not knowing the beauty that lies at the depth of one's being and the going beyond.

Do we see that when we escape from sorrow through various forms of explanation, we are really frittering away an extraordinary happening?

P: Then what does one do?

K: You have not answered my question: Is there a sorrow without a cause? We know sorrow and the movement away from sorrow.

P: You have talked of sorrow free of cause and effect. Is there such a state?

K: Man has lived with sorrow from immemorial times; he has never known how to deal with it. So he has either worshipped it or run away from it; they are both the same movement. My mind does not do either, nor does it use sorrow as a means of awakening. So what takes place?

P: Our knowledge is a product of our senses. Sorrow is more than that; it is a movement of the heart.

K: I am asking you: What is the relationship between sorrow and love?

P: They are both movements of the heart.

K: What is love, and what is sorrow?

P: Both are movements of the heart—one is identified as joy and the other as pain.

K: Is love pleasure? Would you say that joy and pleasure are the same? Without understanding the nature of pleasure, there is no depth to joy. You cannot invite joy; joy happens. The happening can be turned into pleasure. When that pleasure is denied, there is the beginning of sorrow.

P: At one level it is so, but it is not so at another level.

K: As we said, joy is not a thing to be invited; it happens. I can invite pleasure, I can pursue pleasure. If love was pleasure, then love could be cultivated.

P: We know that pleasure is not love. Pleasure may be one manifestation of love, but it is not love. Both sorrow and love emerge from the same source.

K: I asked: What is the relationship between sorrow and love? Can there be love if there is sorrow?—sorrow being all the things that we have talked about.

P: I would say yes.

K: In sorrow there is a factor of separation, of fragmentation. Is there not also a great deal of self-pity in sorrow? What is the relationship of all this to love? Has love dependency? Has love the quality of the 'me' and the 'you'?

P: But you talked of passion—

K: When there is no movement of escape from sorrow, then love is. Passion is the flame of sorrow, and that flame can only be awakened when there is no escape, no resistance—which means, sorrow has in it no quality of division.

P: In that sense, is that state of sorrow any different from the state of love? Sorrow is pain. You say that when one is in pain, and there is no resistance, no movement away from pain, the flame of passion emerges. Strangely, in the ancient texts *kāma* (love), *agni* (fire) and *yama* (death) are said to be the same. They are placed on the same level; they create, purify and destroy to create again. There has to be an ending.

K: You see, that is just it. What is the quality of a mind that has understood sorrow and, therefore, the ending of sorrow? What is the quality of the mind that is no longer afraid of ending, of death?

When energy is not dissipated through escape, then that energy becomes the flame of passion. Compassion means passion for all. Compassion *is* passion for all.

New Delhi
12 December, 1970

ALCHEMY AND MUTATION

Dialogue 2

P: I was considering whether it would be worthwhile to discuss the ancient Indian attitude to alchemy and mutation, and to see whether the findings of alchemy have any relevance to what you are saying. It is significant that Nāgārjuna, one of the great propounders of Buddhist thought, was himself a master alchemist. In India, the alchemist's search was not directed so much to turning base metal into gold as to investigating certain psycho-physical and chemical processes in which, through mutation, the body and mind could be made free of the ravages of time and the processes of decay. The field of investigation included the mastery of breath, the partaking of an elixir brewed in the laboratory, a substance wherein mercury played a vital part, and a triggering of an explosion in consciousness. The action of the three led to a mutation of the body and mind. The symbolism used by the alchemist was sexual; mercury was the seed of Śiva, mica the seed of the goddess; the union of the two, not only physically and in the crucibles of the laboratory but in consciousness itself, brought into being a mutation, a state that was free of time and the processes of ageing, a state that was unrelated to the two constituents that in total union had triggered the mutation. Has this any relevance to what you are saying?

K: You are asking about the state of consciousness which is out of time.

P: In every individual one can see the male and female elements in operation. The alchemist saw the need for union, for balance. Is there any validity in this?

K: I think one can observe this in oneself. I have often observed that in each one of us there are male and female elements. Either they are in perfect balance or in a state of imbalance. When there is the complete balance between the male and the female, then the physical organism never really falls ill; there may be superficial illnesses, but deep within there is no disease which destroys the organism. This is probably what the ancients must have sought, identifying the male and the female with mercury and mica. Through meditation, through study, and, perhaps, through some form of medicine, they tried to bring about this perfect harmony.

One can see very clearly in oneself the operation of the male and female. When one or the other gets exaggerated, the imbalance creates disease—not superficial ailments but disease at the depths. I have noticed personally within myself, under different situations and climates, with different people who are aggressive and violent, that the female element takes over and becomes more prominent. This prominence of the female, the other uses to assert himself. But when there is too much of femininity around one, the male does not become aggressive but withdraws without any resistance.

S: What are the male and female elements?

K: The male is generally aggressive, violent, dominating, and the female is quiet; it is taken for submissiveness and then exploited by man. But submissiveness is really gentleness which gradually conquers the other.

When the female and the male are in complete harmony, the quality of both changes; it is no longer male or female, but something totally different. The male and female as the positive and negative are dualistic because of their very nature. Whereas the complete balance, the harmony of the two has a different quality.

It is like the quality of the earth in which everything lives, but is not of it. I have noticed this operating very often. When the whole mind withdraws from the physical environment, it is as though the mind is very far away—far away not in space and time, but in a state which nothing can touch. This state is not an abstraction nor a withdrawal, but an inward, absolute non-being. When this perfect harmony takes place, because there is no conflict, it has its own vitality. It does not destroy the other. So conflict is not only in the outer but also in the inner. And when this conflict completely comes to an end, there is a mutation which is not touched by time.

P: The alchemist called this the birth of Kumāra, of the magical child—he who never grows old, he who is completely innocent.

K: It is very interesting, but alchemy has become synonymous with so much phony magic.

P: But the alchemists, the Masters who were known as *rasa-siddhas*—the holders of the essence—maintained that what they described they had seen with their own eyes, what they recorded was not from hearsay nor from the dictation of a teacher. There is another factor of interest. A great deal of attention was paid in alchemy to the instrument, the vessel. The science of metallurgy developed out of this. One of the vessels or *yantra*s was known was the *garbha-yantra*, the womb vessel. It is a key word in alchemy. Is there such a thing as preparing the womb of the mind?

K: The moment you use the word 'preparation', it means a process in which time is involved.

P: The alchemists were also conscious that at the point of mutation, at the point of the fixation of mercury, and at the birth of the timeless, time was not involved.

K: Do not use the word 'preparation'. Let us put it this way. Is there a necessary state, a necessary background, a necessary vessel which can contain this? I should say not, because when they found the boy Krishnamurti, the people who were supposedly clairvoyant for the time being saw that he had no quality of selfishness and, therefore, was worthy of being the vessel. And I think that that has remained right through.

S: That may be so, but what about ordinary people like us? Is this a privilege given only to a very, very few, one in a thousand years or more? Or can this happen to people who are concerned with all this, who are committed to all this, who are really serious in this inquiry?

K: Certain physical factors and psychological states are necessary. Physically there must be sensitivity. Physical sensitivity cannot possibly take place when there is smoking, drinking, eating meat. The sensitivity of the body must be maintained; that is absolutely essential. Traditionally, such a body generally remains in one place supported by disciples, by the family. The body is not shocked or exposed.

Can a man who is very serious in all this, can he, with a body which has gone through the normal brutalizing effects, make that body highly sensitive? And also, can the psyche that has been wounded through experience throw off all the wounds and marks and renew itself so that there is a state in which there is no hurt? These two are essential: sensitivity and the psyche not having a mark. I think this can be achieved by any person who is really serious. You see, the womb is always ready to conceive; it renews itself.

P: Like the earth, the womb has that in-built quality of renewal.

K: I think the mind has exactly the same quality. When the earth lies fallow and the womb is empty and the mind without any movement, then renewal takes place. When the mind is completely empty, it is like the womb: pure to renew, to receive.

P: This then is the vessel, the receptacle.

K: Yes, this is the vessel; but when you use the word 'vessel' and the word 'receptacle', you must be exceedingly careful. This in-built quality of the mind to renew itself can be called eternal youth.

P: It is known as *kumāra vidyā* (the science of youthfulness).

K: So what makes the mind old? Obviously the movement of the self makes the mind old.

P: Does the self wear away the cells?

K: The womb is always ready to receive; it has the quality of purifying itself all the time. But the mind which is burdened with the self—friction is the self—has no space to renew itself. When the self is so occupied with itself and its activities, the mind has no space in which to renew itself. So space is necessary, both physical space and space for the psyche. How does this go with alchemy?

P: The language they use is different. They talk of mutation through union.

K: All that implies effort, friction.

P: How does one know?

K: If it implies any form of process, any form of achievement, it implies effort.

New Delhi
14 December, 1970

THE CONTAINMENT OF EVIL

Dialogue 3

P: One of the most vital problems that has concerned man is the necessity of containing evil. It appears as if at certain times in history, because of various circumstances, evil has had a wider field within which to operate. The manifestations of evil are so wide, the problems of evil so complex that the individual does not know how to deal with them. What would you say is the way of dealing with evil? Is there such a thing as evil independent of good?

K: I wonder what you mean. Do you call the bush with so many thorns evil? Do you call a serpent with poison evil? No savage animal is evil—neither the shark nor the tiger. So what do you mean by the word 'evil'?—Something harmful? Something that can bring tremendous grief, something that can bring great pain, something that can destroy or prevent the light of understanding? Would you call war evil? Would you call the generals, the rulers, the admirals evil because they help to bring about war, destruction?

P: That which thwarts the nature of things can be called evil.

K: Man is brutal. Is he evil?

P: If he is thwarting, if he, through malignant intention, does certain things—

K: I was just wondering what that word 'evil' means. What does evil mean to an intelligent mind, to a mind that is aware of all the horrors in the world?

P: Evil is that which diminishes consciousness, that which brings darkness.

K: Fear, sorrow, pain do that. Would you say that evil is the encouragement of fear? Is evil a means to further sorrow? Is evil the social conditioning which perpetuates war? All these limit consciousness and create darkness and sorrow. Evil, according to the Christian idea, is the devil. Does the Hindu have any idea of evil?

If he has an idea of evil, what would it be? Personally I never think of evil.

Would you say that in the flowering of goodness there is no evil at all, that this state does not know evil? Or, is evil an invention of the mind which breeds fear and projects the good?

P: May I say something? If you go down deep into the recesses of the human mind, into the history of mankind, there has always been the sorcerer, the witch who subverts the laws of nature, who brings fear and darkness. It is one of the strangest elements in the human mind. It is because of this terrible fear of the unknown, of the darkness without limit, without end, which prevails through history, that the human being has cried out for protection; a cry that echoes through human consciousness. This is the unknown, unnamed matrix of fear. It is not enough to suggest that it is fear; evil is all that and more.

K: Are you saying that deep in man, in the inner recesses of the mind, there is the fear of the unknown, of something which man cannot touch or imagine? Being afraid so deeply, he demands protection of the gods, and anything that brings an awakening of that danger, any intimation of that hidden thing, he calls evil.

P: This darkness exists deep in human consciousness all the time.

K: Is evil the opposite of the good or is it totally independent of the good?

P: It is independent of the good.

K: You say that it is independent. So, is evil something that is in itself unrelated to the beautiful, to love? Against evil, man has always sought protection, as he would against an animal. There is this hidden, dark danger. Man is aware of it, he is frightened and seeks, through incantations, rituals, prayers, and so on, to put it away and be guarded against it. The bush that is so full of thorns protects itself against the animal, and the animal would call that evil as it cannot get at the leaves. Is there such a force, an embodiment of evil which is totally apart from the good, the beautiful? There is this whole idea that evil is fighting good. This evil is seen as embodied in people, and it is always fighting the good and the gentle. I ask: Is evil something totally independent of the good? You must be very careful not to become superstitious.

P: There is a demand for protection, and the mantra as spell, the *maṇḍala* as magical diagram and the *mudrā* as magical gesture were intended to provide protection against evil.

K: You see, when you go deeply into consciousness, you reach a point where the unknown appears as the dark, and you stop there because you get frightened. The mind penetrates deeply up to a point, and below that point there is the feeling of dark emptiness. Because of the darkness, you have prayers, incantations, and because of the fear of the dark, you ask for protection. Can the mind go through the darkness? Which means, can the mind not be afraid? Can it operate so that the darkness becomes light? Can you penetrate the darkness of which you are afraid, which you have named 'evil'? Can you penetrate that so completely that darkness does not exist? Then, what is evil?

P: When the ritual *maṇḍala* is drawn, the entry into the *maṇḍala* is through spell and *mudrā*. In this entry into darkness, what is the spell which will open the gates?

K: Consciousness as thought, investigates itself—its depth. As it enters it comes upon this darkness. This investigation is not a process of time. And you are asking: What is the spell or energy that will penetrate to the very bottom of the darkness?

What is that energy, and how is it to come into being? The very energy which started investigating is still there, more heavy, vital as it enters, penetrates. Why do you ask whether there is need of greater energy?

P: Because energy dries up. We penetrate up to a point and do not go further.

K: Because of fear, because of apprehension of something we do not know, we dissipate energy instead of bringing it into focus. I want to penetrate into myself. I see that entering into myself is the same movement as the movement into the outer—it is entering into space. In entering into space, there is a certain demand, a certain energy. That energy must be without any effort, without any distortion. As it enters, it gathers momentum. If it has no passage through which it can escape, it is not distorted, it becomes deeper, wider, stronger. Then you reach a point where there is darkness. And how does one enter that darkness with this tremendous energy? (*pause*)

P: The first question with which we started was: How is evil to be contained? You have said: As one penetrates the sea of darkness, darkness is not; light is. But when there is evil in human beings, in certain situations, in certain happenings, is there any action which can contain this evil?

K: I would not put it that way. Resistance to evil strengthens evil. So, if the mind is living in goodness, there is no resistance, and evil cannot touch it. Therefore there is no containing of evil.

P: Is there only goodness then?

K: We have to go back to something else—the mind has gone into darkness and it is finished with darkness. But is there evil which is independent of all that? Or, is evil part of goodness?

You see, in nature there is the big living on the little, the bigger on the big. I would not call that evil. Is the deliberate desire to hurt another part of evil? I want to hurt you because you have done something to me. Is that evil?

P: That is part of evil.

K: Then that implies will. You hurt me and, because I am proud, I want to retaliate. Wanting-to-retaliate is an action of the will. The will to retaliate and the will to do good are both evil.

P: Again, coming back to the *maṇḍala*, evil can enter when the gateways are not protected. Here, your eyes and ears are the gateways.

K: So you are saying: When the eyes see clearly and the ears hear clearly, then evil cannot enter.

To go back, the deliberate intention, the collection of intentions, the 'thinking-it-over', which is the deep intention to hurt, is all part of the will. I think that is where evil is—in the deliberate act to hurt. You hurt me, I hurt you. If I apologise, it is finished. But if I hold, retain, deliberately strengthen a policy to hurt you, which is part of the will in man to do harm or good, then there is evil.

So is there a way of living without will? The moment I resist, evil must be on one side, and the good on the other, and there is a relationship between the two. When there is no resistance, there is no relationship between the two. And love then is an open space without any words, without any resistance; love is action out of emptiness. As we were discussing yesterday, when the male element deliberately becomes assertive, demanding, possessive, dominating, man invites evil. And the female, yielding, yielding, yielding and deliberately yielding in order to dominate, also invites evil.

So, where there is the cunning pursuit of domination, which is the operation of the will, there is the beginning of evil. We try to protect ourselves against evil. We are ourselves creating evil, and yet we draw a circle, a diagram round the doorstep of the house to seek protection from evil, and inwardly the serpent of evil is operating. Keep your house clean. Forget all the mantras; nothing can touch you. We ask protection of the gods whom we have created. It is really quite fantastic.

All these wars, all the racial hatreds, all the accumulated hatreds which man has been storing up, must result in a collected hatred, a gathered evil. The Hitlers, the Mussolinis, the Stalins, the concentration camps, the Atillas—all that must be stored, must have a body somewhere. So also, the feeling of 'Do not kill, be kind, be gentle, be compassionate'—that also must be stored somewhere.

When people try to protect themselves against evil, they are protecting themselves against the good too, because man has created these two. So, can the mind enter into darkness?—for the very entrance into it, is the dispelling of darkness.

New Delhi
15 December, 1970

THE AWAKENING OF ENERGY

Dialogue 4

P: When we were discussing Tantra, you said that there is a way of awakening energy. The Tāntrics concentrate on certain psychic centres and, thereby, release the dormant energy in those centres. Would you say that there is any validity in this? What is the way of awakening energy?

K: Concentrating on the various psychophysical centres implies, does it not, a process of time? So I would like to ask: Can that energy be awakened without a process of time?

P: The traditional way demands correct posture and an equilibrium of breath. If the body does not know how to sit erect, and how to breathe rightly, there can be no ending of thought. To bring body and breath to an equilibrium, a process of time becomes inevitable.

K: There may be a totally different approach to this problem. Tradition starts from the psychosomatic—the posture, control of the breath and, gradually, through various forms of concentration, moves to the full awakening of energy. That is the accepted way. Is there not an awakening of this energy without going through all these practices?

P: It is like the Zen Masters who say that the real master is one who puts aside effort and, yet, in Zen, to master archery a tremendous mastery over technique is necessary. It is only when there is a total mastery that effort drops away.

K: You are beginning at this end rather than at the other—this end being time, control, energy, perfection, perfect balance. All this seems to me like dealing with a very small part of a very vast field. Tradition gives great importance to the past, to breathing, to the right posture. All these are limited to a corner of the field, and through that corner you hope to have enlightenment. The corner then becomes a trick. Through some kind of psychosomatic acrobatics, it is hoped that you will capture the light, the whole universe. I do not think enlightenment is there—through one corner. It is like seeing the sky through a small window and never going outside to look at the sky. I feel that that way is an absurd way of approaching something totally vast, timeless.

P: Even you would admit that correct posture and right breathing strengthen the structure of the mind.

K: I want to approach all this quite differently. In approaching it entirely differently, it is necessary to throw out all that has been said. I see that the corner is like a candle in sunshine: the candle is being lit very carefully, in brilliant sunshine. You are not concerned with the sunshine, but work away at lighting the candle.

There are other things involved. There is the awakening of energy which has so far been dissipated. To centralize energy, to gather the whole of it, attention is involved, and also the complete elimination of time. Time and an attention which is not forced, which is not concentration, which is not centred around a part, and the gathering of energy—I think these are the fundamental things one has to understand, because enlightenment must be and is the comprehension and understanding of this vast life, the whole travail of living, dying, loving, and the going beyond it.

The traditional masters would also agree that you have to have attention to go beyond time. But they are the worshippers of the corner; they use time to go beyond time.

P: How sir? I take a posture and direct my attention. How is time involved in this?

K: Is attention the result of time?

P: No. You ask a question, and there is immediate attention. Is this attention the product of time?

K: No, certainly not.

P: Your question and my attention being there—is there time involved in that? If you would regard this as involving time, then the self-knowing process which is going on continuously also involves time. My mind twenty years ago could not have known its present quality; this state had no existence then.

K: Let us go slowly. We are trying to understand something which is out of time.

P: The tradition says: Prepare the body and the mind.

K: Through time you prepare the body and the mind to receive, to comprehend and to be free of time. Can you do this through time?

P: The tradition also posits that through time you cannot go beyond time.

K: I question that through time you can perfect the instrument. Can you perfect the instrument through time? Now, first of all, who is it that is perfecting the instrument? Is it thought?

P: It would be invalid to say only thought. There are many other factors involved.

K: Thought, the knowing of thought and intelligence are all maintained by thought. To say that thought must end and that intelligence must come into being, is again an action of thought —as is the statement that the thinker and the thought are one.

To me, the traditional approach of perfecting the instrument through thought in order to go beyond thought, the cultivation of intelligence and then going beyond time, is still within the area of thought. That is so. Therefore, in that very thought there is the thinker—the thinker who says: This must happen, this must not happen. That thinker has become the will to achievement. The will to perfect the instrument is part of thought.

P: In this circle, which you have just described, is also implied the questioning of the very instrument which is thought.

K: But the questioner is part of thought; the whole structure is part of thought. You can divide, subdivide, change, but it is all within the field of thought; and that is time. Thought is memory, thought is material; the material is memory. We are still functioning within the area of the known, and the man who is cultivating thought says that he will go to the unknown through the known, perfect the known and get enlightenment. Again, all this is thought.

P: If everything is thought, it must then be necessary to give birth to a new instrument.

K: When thought says that it must become silent and becomes silent, it is still thought. What the traditionalists do is to work within the field of thought, which is the corner of the field. But it is still the result of thought. The *ātman* is the result of thought; the *brahman*, to which man looks up, is the result of thought. The man who experienced *brahman* had nothing to do with thought—it just happened. Whereas his disciples came along and said: Do this, do that—but all that is within the field of thought.

P: Then there is no proceeding.

K: See how thought plays tricks upon itself—I must have balance, I must have the right posture in order that the life-energy flows through. Right? I say that thought is of the past; thought can create the most marvellous instruments—it can go to the moon, to Venus—but thought can never possibly touch the 'other', because thought is never free. Thought is old, thought is conditioned; thought is the whole structure of the known.

P: What do you mean by the 'other'?

K: *That* is not *it*.

P: That is not what?

K: This is within the field of time; thought is time. That is within the field of silence. Therefore, find out if sorrow can end. Come out of the corner. Find out what life is, what death means, what it means to end sorrow. If you have not come upon *this*, playing tricks upon thought has no meaning. You can awaken all the *kuṇḍalinīs*, but to what purpose? Teaching how to awaken the *kuṇḍalinīs*, or making man proficient in archery in the Zen way, or practising the various forms of Tantra are all within the bondage of time which is thought.

I see this and I also see that I am going around in circles. The circle may be higher, but it is still a circle, a bondage, which is time. So I would not touch it. I would not touch it because I see the nature, the structure and the disorder of this corner. The corner has no meaning to me —when there is the marvellous sun, all the *siddhis* or powers are like so many candles.

Can the mind, listening to this, wipe it away? The very listening is the wiping away. Then you have it. Then there is attention, love; everything is there. You see, logically this holds, whereas the other does not. The exercise of the brain is to find the true and the false, that is, to see the false as the false. You see, when the boy

Krishnamurti saw the truth, it was over; he gave up all organizations, etc. He had no training to see.

P: But you had training; you were put through a vigorous training of the body.

K: So they tell us. Because the body had been neglected, they said that if he was not looked after, he would fall ill.

P: But sir, apart from physical discipline, there were instructions as to how to bring up that boy.

K: Doing *āsanas* and *prāṇāyāma* was like combing the hair; it was all at that level.

P: It is very subtle. I am not saying that what happened had any relationship to the illumination, but it is necessary to look after the body.

K: Yes, it is necessary to keep the body healthy.

P: Sir, if I may say so, you have the way of the yogi, you look like a yogi, your body takes the pose of a yogi. You have been doing *āsanas* and *prāṇāyāma* every day for so many years. Why?

K: That is not important. It is like keeping my nails clean. It is so childish to spend years in perfecting the instrument. All that you have to do is *to look*.

P: But if one is born blind, it is only when a person like you comes and says, '*Look*', that something does happen. Most people would not understand what you were talking about.

K: Most people would not listen to all this. They would brush it aside.

B: The other is easier. It gives something, whereas this gives nothing.

K: This gives everything, if you touch it.

B: But the other is easier.

K: You see, I am terribly interested in this. How has the mind of Krishnamurti maintained this state of innocence?

P: What you are saying is not relevant; you may be an exception. How did the boy Krishnamurti come to it? He had money, organization—everything, and yet he left everything. If I were to take my grand-daughter and leave her with you, and she had no other companion but you, even then she would not have it.

K: No, she would not have it.(*pause*) Wipe out all this.

P: When you say that, it is like the Zen *koan*: the goose being out of the bottle. Did you have a centre to wipe away?

K: No.

P: So you had no centre to wipe away. You are unique and, therefore, are a phenomenon, and so you cannot tell us: I did this and so it happened. You can only tell us: This is not it. And whether we drown or not, no one else can tell us. We see this. We may not be enlightened, but we are not unenlightened.

K: I think it is tremendously interesting to see that thought is time, thought is memory and that anything that thought touches is not the real.

New Delhi
16 December, 1970

THE FIRST STEP IS THE LAST STEP

Dialogue 5

P: Yesterday you said: The first step is the last step. To understand that statement, I think we should investigate the problem of time, and whether there is such a thing as a final state of enlightenment. The confusion arises because our minds are conditioned to think of illumination as the final state. Is understanding or illumination a final state?

K: You know, when we said that the first step is the last step, were we not thinking of time as a horizontal or a vertical movement? Were we not thinking of movement along a plane? We were saying yesterday that if we could put aside the vertical and the horizontal altogether, we could observe this fact, namely, that wherever we are, whatever be the level of our conditioning, the perception of truth, of the fact, is at that moment the last step.

Take a clerk in a little office with all the misery involved in that—the clerk listens and at that moment really sees. That seeing, that perception, is the first and the last step, because at that moment he has touched truth and he sees something very clearly. The very perception brings about liberation. But what happens afterwards is that he wants to cultivate that state, he wants to perpetuate it, to turn it into a process. And, therefore, he gets caught and loses the quality of perception entirely.

What we are saying is that all methods, practices, systems imply a process, a movement from the horizontal to the vertical, towards a finality, to a point which has no movement. If there were no conceptual ideal of finality, there would be no process.

P: The whole structure of thought is built on a horizontal movement.

K: We are used to reading a book horizontally.

P: Everything has a beginning and an ending.

K: And we think that the first chapter must inevitably lead to the last chapter; we feel that all practices lead to a finality, to an unfoldment—all that is horizontal reading. Our minds, eyes and attitudes are conditioned to functioning along the horizontal, at the end of which there is finality—the book is over. You ask if truth or enlightenment is a final achievement, a final point beyond which there is nothing—

P: A point from which there can be no slipping back. I might for an instant touch the quality of *that*. A little later, thought arises again, and I say to myself: I am back in the old state. I question whether that touching had any validity at all. I put a distance, a block between myself and that state and say: If that were true, thought would not arise.

K: I perceive something that is extraordinary, something that is true; I want to perpetuate that perception, to give it a continuity so that that perception continues throughout my daily life. I think that is where the mistake lies. The mind has seen something true. That is enough. That mind is a clear, innocent mind which has not been hurt. Thought wants to carry on that perception right through daily life.

The mind has seen something very clearly. Leave it there. The next step, the leaving of it, is the final step. Because my mind is already fresh to take the next, the final step in the daily movement of life, it does not carry over; the perception has not become knowledge.

P: The self as the agent in relation to thought and in relation to seeing has to cease.

K: Die to the thought that is true. Otherwise it becomes memory, which then becomes thought, and thought asks: How am I to perpetuate that state? If the mind sees clearly, and it can only see clearly when the seeing is the ending of it, then the mind can start a movement where the first step is the last step. In this there is no process involved at all; there is no element of time. Time enters when, having seen it clearly, having perceived it, there is a carrying over and an applying of it to the next incident.

P: The carrying over is the not-seeing or the not-perceiving.

K: So, all the traditional approaches which offer a process must have a point, a conclusion, a finality. It is like saying that there are many roads to the station. The station then is a fixed point. But anything that has a finality—a final point—is not a living thing at all. Is truth a finality? Does it mean that once I am on the train, nothing can happen to me, that the train *will* carry me to my destination? That is, having once achieved truth, is everything else—your anxieties, your fears and so on—over? Or, does it work in a totally different way?

A process implies a fixed point. Systems, methods, practices all offer a fixed point, and promise man that when he achieves the end all his troubles will be over. Is there something which is really timeless? A fixed point is in time. It is in time because you have postulated it, because it has been thought over; and the thinking is time. Can one come upon this thing which must have no time, no process, no system, no method, no way?

Can this mind which is so conditioned horizontally, knowing that it lives horizontally, perceive that which is neither horizontal nor vertical? Can it perceive for an instant? Can it perceive that the seeing has cleansed, and end it? In this is the first and the last step, because the mind has seen anew.

Your question: Is such a mind ever free of trouble? is a wrong question. When you put that question, you are still thinking in terms of finality, you have already come to a conclusion, and so are back again in the horizontal process.

P: The subtlety of it is that the mind has to ask fundamental questions, but never ask *how*.

K: Absolutely. I see very clearly; I perceive. Perception is light. I want to carry it over as memory, as thought, and apply it to daily living. Therefore I introduce duality, conflict, contradiction. So I say: How am I to go beyond that?

Perception is light to this mind. It is not concerned with perception any more because if it is concerned, it becomes memory. Can the mind, seeing something very clearly, end that perception? Then the very first step is the last step here. The mind is fresh to look.

Do troubles end for such a mind? It does not ask this question. See what takes place. When I ask the question: Will this end all trouble? I am already thinking of the future and, therefore, am caught in time.

But I am not concerned. I perceive. It is over. Therefore, the mind is never caught in time. Because I have taken the first step, I have also taken the last step, *each time*.

So we see that all processes, all systems must totally be denied because they perpetuate time; through time you hope to arrive at the timeless.

P: I see that the instruments you use are seeing and listening. These are sensory movements. It is through sensory movements that conditioning also comes into being. What is it that makes one movement totally dissolve conditioning and another strengthen it?

K: How do I listen to that question? First of all, I do not know; I am going to learn. If I learn in order to acquire knowledge, from which I am going to act, that action becomes mechanical. But when I learn without accumulating, which means perceiving, listening without acquiring, the mind is always empty.

Then what is the question? Can the mind which is empty ever be conditioned? And why does it get conditioned? Can the mind which is really listening ever be conditioned? It is always learning; it is always in movement—not a movement from something towards something. A movement cannot have a beginning and an ending. It is something which is alive, never conditioned. A mind that acquires knowledge to function is conditioned by its own knowledge.

P: Is it the same instrument which is operating in both?

K: I do not know. I *really* do not know. The mind which is crowded with knowledge sees according to that knowledge, according to that conditioning.

P: Sir, seeing is like switching on a light; it has no conditioning in itself.

K: The mind is full of images, words, symbols, through which it thinks, it sees.

P: Does it see?

K: No. I have an image of you, and I look through that image; that is distortion. The image is my conditioning. It is still the same vessel with all the things in it, and it is the same vessel which has nothing in it. The content of the vessel is the vessel. When there is no content, the vessel has no form.

P: So that it can receive 'what is'.

K: Perception is only possible when there is no image—no symbol, no idea, no word, no form. Then perception is light. It is not that I see light; there is light. Perception is light. Perception is action. And a mind which is full of images cannot perceive; it sees through images and so is distorted. What we have said is true; it is logically so. I have listened to this. In the factor of listening there is no 'I'; in the factor of carrying it over, there is the 'I'. The 'I' is time.

New Delhi
19 December, 1970

ENERGY AND TRANSFORMATION

Dialogue 6

P: Science and yoga both maintain that when a living organism is exposed to tremendous energy there is a mutation. An excessive exposure to radiation, for example, leads to a mutation in the genes. It also happens, according to yoga, when thought is placed in consciousness before the fire of energy. Do you think this has meaning in terms of what you are teaching?

B: Radiation can cause deformity—there can be destructive mutation. A laser beam pierces steel and flesh; it has the power to destroy as well as to heal.

K: What would you say is human energy? What is energy in human beings? Let us keep it very simple.

P: Energy is that which makes movement possible.

B: Energy is at different levels: there is the energy at the physical level; then the brain itself is a source of energy, it sends out electrical impulses.

K: All movement, all action is energy. When does it become intense? When can it do the most astonishing things? When can it be directed to do incredible things?

P: When it is not dissipated; when it is brought into focus.

K: When does that happen? Does it happen in anger, hatred, violence? Does it happen when there is ambition, when there is tremendous desire? Or, does it happen when a poet has the urge, the vitality, the energy to write?

P: Such energy crystallizes and becomes static.

K: We know this form of energy. But the energy we know does not bring about a change in the human mind. Why? This energy becomes intense when there is fulfilment in action. When does it move to a different dimension? An artist or a scientist, using his talent, intensifies energy and gives expression to it. But the quality of his mind, of his being, is not transformed by this energy.

P: Something is missing in all this.

K: You are asking whether there is a quality of energy which transforms the human mind. Now, why does it not take place in the artist, in the musician, in the writer?

P: I think it is because their energy is one dimensional.

K: The artist still remains ambitious, greedy, a bourgeois.

S: Why do you say that greed would come in the way of energy operating? Man may be ambitious but he is also good. These are the elements which structure his self.

K: We are asking why, when man has that energy, it does not bring about a radical change.

P: Man has energy to operate in his environment, but there are large areas of his being where there is no movement of energy.

K: Man uses energy in one direction only, as he operates in only one direction; energy is dormant in one part of his existence, and is active in the other part.

P: Even man's sensory instruments are utilized partially.

K: He is a fragmented being. Why does this division take place? One fragment is tremendously active, the other does not function at all. One fragment is ordinary, bourgeois, petty. When do these fragments coalesce to become a harmonious energy, an energy which is not fragmented?

P: When the sensory instruments operate fully.

K: When does this take place? Do they operate completely when there is a tremendous crisis?

P: Not always, sir. The action of crisis can also be partial: when you see a snake you can jump into a bush of thorns.

K: When does the fragment cease to be a fragment? Are we not thinking in terms of movement, in terms of action, in terms of change? We have accepted the movement of becoming; we have accepted fragmentation. The movement of becoming is always a movement in fragments. Is there a movement which does not belong to these categories? See what happens if there is no movement at all.

P: I have always found it difficult to understand this question of yours. The nature of the very question suggests the other—the opposite.

S: One really does not know the dormant movement.

K: At the beginning we said that there was fragmentation. One fragment is very alive, and the other is not alive.

B: The energy of the artist, the whole of his being, operates in one dimension—there is non-awareness.

K: You are saying that the other fragment is not aware of itself at all.

P: The artist paints, he also has an affair with a woman. He does not see these actions as fragments.

K: We have gone beyond that. We see that he is fragmented and that he operates in fragments—one active and the other dormant. In that dormancy there is action going on—action in a minor key. We see this. Now the question is: Can this energy—

P: Can it take the sluggish part along and alter its very structure so that there is a transformation in both?

K: I may be a great sculptor, but a part of me is dormant. You ask: Can there be a mutation not only in the energy which is dormant but also in that energy which goes into the making of the sculptor? The question here is: Am I willing to accept that I may cease to be a sculptor? Because that may happen. When I go into this problem of a change in the very brain cells, it is possible I may never again be a sculptor. But it is very important for me to be a sculptor; I do not want to let that go.

P: Let us leave the sculptor. Here we are in front of you and you say: Look, this change in the structure of the brain cells may be the ending of all talent, of all significant action. We accept what you say.

K: That is right. If you are prepared to let go, then what takes place? Which means, you let go the talent, the fulfillment, the perpetuation of the 'me'. Now, when does this mutation in the brain cells through energy take place?

You see, where energy is being dissipated through talent and through other channels, energy is not completely held. When this energy has no movement at all then, I think, something happens, then it must explode. I think then the quality of the brain cells changes. That is why I asked: Why are we always thinking in terms of movement?

When there is no movement of any kind, inwardly or outwardly—no demand for experience, no demand for awakening, no seeking—then energy is at its height. Which means, one must negate all movement. When that takes place, energy is completely quiet; that is silence.

As we said the other day, when there is silence the mind is transforming itself. When it is completely fallow, when nobody is cultivating it, then it is quiet—like the womb.

The mind, which is the vessel of movement, is completely quiet when that movement has no form, no 'me', no vision, no image. In it there is no memory. Then the brain cells undergo a change. The brain cells are used to movement in time; they are the residue of time. And time is movement within the space it creates as it moves. When the mind sees this, when it sees the futility of all movement as time, all movement ceases. So when the mind denies totally all movement and, therefore, all time, all thought, all memory, there is absolute quietness—not relative quietness.

The point therefore is not how to bring about mutation, but to inquire into the structure of the brain cells. The realization that any movement from the brain cells gives continuity to time itself, puts an end to all movement. Movement is always in the past or in the future—movement from the past through the present to the future. That is all we know, and we want change in this movement: we want the movement, and yet we want change in this movement. Therefore the brain cells continue. (*pause*)

It is amazingly simple. We all want to complicate it. I do not know if you see this. Any effort to stop movement is contradiction, therefore time, and, therefore, no change at all. The seekers have all talked of a higher movement—the hierarchical movement. The question is: Can the mind deny to itself all movement? You see, as you watch your brain, there is the centre which is completely quiet and yet listening to everything that is going on—the bus, the birds. We want to stop the noise outside but keep on with the inner noise. We want to stop outer movement but carry on with the inner movement. When there is no movement, there is tremendous focus of energy. So mutation is the understanding of movement and the ending of movement in the brain cells themselves.

New Delhi
21 December, 1970

THE OBSERVER AND 'WHAT IS'

Dialogue 7

P: The problem of duality and its ending cannot be understood unless we go into the nature of the thinker and the thought. Can we discuss this?

K: How do the Hindu thinkers, the Advaita philosophers deal with this problem?

P: Patañjali's *Yoga-sūtras* postulate a state of liberation which has anchors, and a state of liberation which is without anchors. In one, the thinker is the prop; it is a state where the thinker has not ceased. In the other, there is a state where everything, including the thinker, has ceased.

The Buddhists talk of *kṣaṇa-vāda*, of time as instant, total and complete in itself, a state where the thinker has no continuity. The Advaitic philosophers talk of the cessation of duality and the attainment of non-duality. They go through a dualistic process to attain this non-dual state. Śaṅkara approaches this state of non-duality through negation (*neti, neti*). For the Buddhist philosopher Nāgārjuna, negation is absolute: If you say that there is God, he negates it; if you say that there is no God, he negates that also. Every statement is negated.

B: The Buddha says that what exists is 'the solitude of reality'; you are the result of your thoughts.

P: The Buddha, Śaṅkara, Nāgārjuna have all talked about non-duality, but non-duality has become a concept; it has not affected the structure of the mind itself. In India, for centuries, the negative approach has been discussed, but it has not affected the human mind; the brain cells have remained dualistic; they operate in time and are caught in time. Though negation and the non-dual have been posited, there is no clue to apprehending these states. Why has non-duality not affected the mind of man? Can we go into it to see whether we can discover that which will trigger the non-dual state?

B: Scientific and technological developments have affected the minds of people. Man has discovered the non-dualistic state, but it has not affected his mind nor his life.

S: If every experience leaves a mark on the brain cells, what is the impact of the state of non-duality, of oneness? Why is a mutation not taking place in the relationship between the thinker and the thought?

P: Is the mechanism which records the technological the same mechanism which *sees* or *perceives*?

K: The fragment of the brain which deals with the technological, and the fragment which records and which perceives—

P: They seem to form the ego.

K: The technological and the recording fragment, these two, make up the ego; not the perceptive part.

P: I am including the perceptive part also. The recording is concerned with both—with the technological and with the perceptual.

K: That may be a verbal explanation.

P: The core of man never seems to get affected; the essential duality between the thinker and the thought continues.

K: Do you think that there is, basically, a duality? Or, is there only 'what is'—the fact?

P: When you, sir, ask a question like that, the mind stands still and one says: Yes, it is so. Then the query starts: Am I not separate from S, from B? Though the mind says yes, it also queries a split second later. The moment you asked the question, my mind became still.

K: Why not stay there?

P: The query arises.

K: Why? Is it habit, tradition, conditioning? Is it in the very nature of the operation of the self? All that may be due to cultural imposition—to survive, to function and so on. Why bring that in when we are looking at facts, at whether there is a basic duality?

P: Are you saying that it may be a reflex action of the brain cells?

K: We are the result of our environment, of our society; we are the result of all our interactions—that is a fact also. I am asking myself: Is there a basic duality at the very core or, does duality arise only when the mind moves away from 'what is'? When I do not move away from the basic non-dualistic quality of the mind, is there duality? Does the mind create duality when it is completely with 'what is'?

I never think when I look at a tree. When I look at you, there is no division as the 'me' and the 'you'. Words are used for linguistic and communicative purposes; the 'me' and the 'you' are somehow not rooted in me. So, where does the thinker separate from thought arise if the mind remains in 'what is', remains with pain? When there is no thinking of non-pain, there is the sense of suffering—that is 'what is'; there is no feeling of wanting to be out of it. Where does duality arise? Duality arises when the mind says: I must be rid of pain. I have known states of non-pain, and I want to be in a state of non-pain. (*pause*)

You are a man and I am a woman. That is a biological fact. But is there a psychological dualism? Is there a basically dualistic state or does it arise only when the mind moves away from 'what is'?

There is sorrow—my son is dead. I do not move away. Where is the duality? It is only when I say: I have lost my companion, my son, that duality comes into being. I wonder if this is right. I have pain—physical or psychological grief. A movement away from it is duality. The thinker is the movement away—the thinker that says: This should not be, and the thinker that also says: There should not be duality.

First see the fact that the movement away from 'what is' is the movement of the thinker, who brings in duality. In observing the fact of pain, why should there be a thinker? The thinker arises when there is a movement, either backwards or forwards. The thought that I had no pain yesterday—in that duality arises. Can the mind remain with the pain? Any movement away from it brings in the thinker.

The mind is asking itself: How does this dualistic attitude towards life arise? It is not asking for an explanation of how to go beyond it. I have had pleasure yesterday; it is finished. (*pause*) Is it not as simple as that?

P: Not really.

K: I think it is. You see, this implies non-comparative observation. Comparison is dualistic; measurement is dualistic—there is pain today; there is the comparison with the non-pain of tomorrow. But there is only one fact: the pain which the mind is going through now. Nothing else exists. Why have we complicated this? Why have we built tremendous philosophies around all this? Are we missing something? Is it that the mind does not know what to do and, therefore, moves away from the fact and brings duality into being? If it knew, would it bring about duality? Is the 'what-to-do' itself a dualistic process? Do you understand?

Let us look at it again. There is pain—physical or psychological. When the mind does not know what to do, in the non-dualistic sense of doing, it escapes. Can the mind caught in the trap, in the backward and the forward movement, deal with 'what is' in a non-dualistic way? Do you understand?

So we are asking: Can pain, the 'what is', be transformed without dualistic activity? Can there be a state of non-thinking, in which the thinker does not come into being at all?—the thinker who says: I had no pain yesterday and I will not have it tomorrow.

P: See what happens to us. What you say is right. But there is a lack of something within us; it may be strength, energy. When there is a crisis, the weight of that crisis is sufficient to plunge us into a state where there is no movement away from the crisis, but in everyday life we have trivial challenges.

K: If you really understood this, you would meet these little challenges.

P: In everyday life, we have the chattering, erratic movement of the thinker operating with its demands. What does one do with that?

K: I do not think you can do anything with that. That is irrelevant. *That is the denial.*

P: But that is very, very important. That is what our minds are. One does not have the capacity to negate that.

K: Listen, there is noise outside. I cannot do anything about it.

P: When there is a crisis, there is contact. In normal living there is no contact. I go out. I can look at a tree, and there is no duality. I can see colour without duality. But there is the other—the erratic nonsense part that is continuously chattering. When the thinker sees its functioning, it starts operating on it. The great negation is to let it alone.

K: Settle the primary factor: Observe pain without moving away from it. That is the only non-dualistic state.

P: Let us speak of the chattering mind instead of pain, because that is the fact at this moment. The noise of that horn, the chattering mind—that is 'what is'.

K: You prefer this and do not prefer that, and thereby begins the whole circle.

P: The central point is the observation of 'what is' without moving away. The moving away creates the thinker.

K: The noise, the chattering, which was the 'what is', has gone,has faded away. But the pain remains. Pain has not gone. To go beyond pain non-dualistically is the issue. How is it to be done? Any movement away from 'what is' is dualistic, because in that there is the thinker operating on 'what is'. Without the dualistic movement taking place, will that transform 'what is'? Do you understand my question? That is, would the cessation of the dualistic movement transform 'what is'?

P: Is it not really a dissolution of 'what is'?

K: I know only 'what is', nothing else—not the cause.

P: That is so. One can see that when there is no movement away from pain, there is the dissolution of pain.

K: How does this happen? Why has man not come to this? Why has he fought pain with a dualistic movement? Why has he never understood or delved into pain without the dualistic movement? What happens when there is no movement away from pain—not what happens to the dissolution of pain, but what happens to the mechanism that operates? It is simple. Pain is the movement away. There is no pain where there is only listening. There is pain only when I move from the fact and say: This is pleasurable, this is not pleasurable. My son dies. That is an absolute, irrevocable fact. Why is there pain?

P: Because I loved him.

K: Look what has already happened unconsciously. I loved him. He has gone. The pain is the remembrance of my love for him. And he is no more. But the absolute fact is that he is gone. Remain with that fact. There is pain only when I say that he is no more, which is when the thinker comes into being and says: My son is no longer there; he was my companion, and all the rest of it.

S: It is not merely the memory of my son who is dead which is pain. There is loneliness now.

K: My son is dead. That is a fact. Then there is the thought of loneliness. Then there is my identification with him. All that is a process of thought and the thinker. But I have only one fact—my son is gone. Loneliness, the lack of companionship, despair, are all the result of thought, which creates duality, a movement away from 'what is'. It does not need strength or determination not to move. The determination is dualistic.

There is only one thing: the fact and my movement away from the fact, away from 'what is'. It is this which breeds bitterness, callousness, lack of love, indifference—which are all the product of thinking. The fact is my son is gone.

The non-perception of 'what is' breeds the thinker, which is dualistic action. When the mind falls again into the trap of dualistic action, that is 'what is'. Remain with that, for any movement away from that is another dualistic action. The mind is always dealing with 'what is' as noise-no-noise. And 'what is', the fact, needs no transformation because it is already 'the beyond'. Anger is 'what is'. The dualistic movement of non-anger is away from 'what is'. The movement from 'what is' is no longer anger. Therefore, once the mind has perceived, once it has had non-dualistic perception, it does not act from memory when anger arises again. The next time anger arises, that is 'what is'. The mind is always dealing with 'what is'. Therefore, the dualistic concept is totally wrong; it is fallacious.

P: This is tremendous action. The dualistic action is non-action.

K: You have to be simple. It is the mind that is not clever, that is not cunning, that is not trying to find substitutes for dualistic action, that can understand. Our minds are not simple enough.

Though we all talk of simplicity, that simplicity is of the loin cloth.

The non-dual means really the art of listening. You hear that dog barking—listen to it without any movement away from it; remain with 'what is'. (*pause*) The man who remains with 'what is', and who never moves away from it, has no marks.

P: And when marks take place, to see them taking place. One act of perception removes the mark.

K: Quite right. That is the way to live.

New Delhi
25 December, 1970

THE BACKWARD-FLOWING MOVEMENT

Dialogue 8

P: I would like to ask you about the backward-flowing movement, a state in which there is a drawing in of sight, hearing and the energies of sex. In the *Yoga-sūtra* there is a word *parāvṛtti*, which denotes the state where thought turns back upon itself. Is there such a state as the drawing in of the outward-flowing senses, and of thought turning back on itself?

K: Like a glove turned inside out? Are you saying that thought looking at itself, or swallowing itself is the backward-flowing movement?

P: What is meant by the word is a matter of experience.

K: You are asking: Is there a state in which hearing, seeing and the sensual energies draw themselves in and there is a moving backwards? What do you mean by 'backwards'? Are you saying that the hearing, the seeing and the sensual energies are withdrawing without propelling outward?

P: The normal movement of the eyes, ears and the sensual energies is an outer movement, linked with an object. Can there be a freeing of the senses from the object and a drawing-in of the senses?

K: I wonder if in the drawing-in, the no hearing, no seeing and the sensual energy not expanding, there is not a state where there is the hearing of sound, the seeing of everything, and yet a total quiet—a state of being withdrawn, where there is no desire.

P: It is not the suppression of desire.

K: Is there a state where there is the hearing of sound, the eyes seeing, objects existing and, yet, no sensuous desire? I think there is such a state, where there is sensation yet no desire. Not that one has become old, lost vitality, but there is no desire as the seeing, the touching—sensation and, out of that sensation, the wanting to possess.

P: What happens to the process of hearing when there is no naming?

K: Do you hear that siren? There is the vibration of sound and the interpretation that takes place when you hear the siren. Now, can you listen to it without any movement of memory as thought? Can you hear only the sound? Can there be no image, no naming, no interpretation? Can there be only sound? That is all. And the sound is out of silence. Because the activity of thought has come to an end, there is a hearing of sound out of emptiness. In the same way, can there be a seeing out of emptiness? I see you, I see that bottle; there is no image, no association or movement of thought because there is no image formation. So out of real emptiness, quietness, there is a seeing. Is that what you mean by withdrawing the senses?

P: My question arises out of the texts. In China and in India, the withdrawing was considered important.

K: It is simple. Are you asking: Can you look at a woman, a man or a beautiful object without desire, fulfillment or reaction? It is easy.

P: It is easy for you. See our difficulty.

K: I see a beautiful woman, a car, a child, furniture, and so on. Can they be observed without any movement for acquiring or discarding? It is very simple. It is the same for seeing and listening. I think they are one movement, not separate movements. Though the instruments of perception and hearing are separate, they are all one movement.

P: Desire existed before God; even before man came into being. The biological urge, the impetus, is based on desire. How can you take desire, which has its own propelling force, and say that it has no existence?

K: Let us be clear. I see a beautiful car, a really beautiful car—

P: Let us say I fall passionately in love; I am torn, ravaged by that desire. Can I see that person without desire operating?

K: What is it that you are trying to ask?

P: Is there an actual withdrawal of sensory perception?

K: I wonder if we mean the same thing.

P: The car and maybe even the woman can be looked at without naming. But we are loaded with questions, with problems of naming. It is not simple.

K: I wonder if the problem of naming is not related to knowledge.

P: Sir, a child is not exposed to knowledge and, yet, naming is a natural reaction. I am questioning the nature of this inward movement.

K: I am not sure I understand what you are trying to say. There is a withdrawing of sensory desires demanding fulfillment, but why do you use the word 'inward'?

P: There are practices to delve deep. With eyes and ears closed, you can delve deep inwardly. Is there any validity to delving?

K: Yes, definitely. What you call 'delving in' is to shut your eyes, to shut your ears. In that state is there a delving or is there a cessation of all movement, which appears as though you were delving in? When you really close your eyes and ears, there is no movement within or without as desire demanding fulfillment, with all its frustration. When that does take place, there is complete quietness. The moment you use the word 'delving in', a duality is implied.

P: You hear that horn. To you is there no noise at all in it?

K: No.

P: It is quite extraordinary. To you there is no noise. When you close your ears, is there no inner sound, separate from you? We hear an inner sound. Do you not hear it?

K: (*Krishnamurti closes his eyes and ears*) No. But one must be clear. When the eyes are closed, one generally sees spots. If one observes those spots, they disappear.

P: Is there not an expansion, a contraction?

K: Nothing. When I close my eyes, there is absolutely no movement of any kind.

P: That means your whole consciousness is different. When I close my eyes, there are so many patterns. To you there is no movement of sound or pattern.

K: That is why I want to go into this question of knowledge. This person has not read the *Yoga-sūtras* and the religious books, and to him there is only a complete emptiness.

P: It is not because he has not read any religious books.

K: There is no interference of knowledge.

P: The same phenomenon will not happen to anyone who is ignorant of religious literature. It cannot happen to a communist.

K: It is knowledge as pattern that interferes. The pattern is created by knowledge, experience. When there is no retention of knowledge, what happens? There is absolute quietness, no movement of the eyes, of the ears and of desire. Why do you make this out to be something special? The man who is caught in association, in ideas, in thought, in pattern, does not have an empty mind.

P: What you say is valid. There are many times when what you say is valid within me.

K: My point is this: Were those people who spoke of inward movement aware of its dualistic nature?

P: They must have been aware. The *Yoga-sūtras* say that the seer is nothing more than the instrument of seeing. They make an absolute statement like that.

K: Probably the man who perceived reality said that the seer and the seeing are one. Then the followers came along and made theories without experiencing that state.

I cannot separate the observer from the observed. When I close my eyes, there is no observer at all. Therefore, there is no inward movement as opposed to the outward movement.

P: Do you see yourself as a person?

K: If you mean the body, yes. As an ego, as a person talking on the platform, walking, climbing the hill, no.

P: Does the sense of existence, the sense of 'I am', operate in you?

K: One of the things I have never had is the sense of the 'I'. Never.

P: 'I exist' is the central core in all of us; it is the very fabric of our existence.

K: The peripheral expressions of Krishnamurti appear to suggest a person, but at the centre there is no person. I really do not know what it means. You ask whether there is a centre, the sense of 'I am', in me. No. The feeling of 'I am' is not true.

P: It is not as obvious as that. But the sense of existence, the core of the ego within us, is unexplored. There is something which holds it together, and as long as it remains, what you say has no validity for us.

K: There is no movement of the past as the 'me' in the centre, in the person. One has to go into this very carefully. As we said the other day, the first step is the last step; the first perception is the last perception; and the ending of the first perception is the new perception. Therefore, there is a total gap between the first perception and the second perception. In that interval, there is no movement of thought. There would be the movement of thought when the memory of the first perception remains, not when it is over. Can the mind not empty itself of every perception? Can it not die to every expression? And when it does, where would the root of the 'I am' be? When the mind is that, is there any movement of pattern taking place? When the eyes, ears and desire are non-existent as movement towards or away from something, why should the mind have any pattern? The seeing is the see-er—in that there is no duality. But those who make that statement into an axiom do not experience it and, therefore, it remains a theory.

P: The *sūtras* say that there are many types of liberation: Liberation by birth—some men are born that way and that is the highest form of liberation; then liberation by drugs, which is part of witchcraft; then liberation through *āsanas* and through breath control; then liberation by understanding. I have always felt that you have never been able to explain to us how liberation happened to you. Was your mind like ours and it underwent a mutation subsequently? If so, there is a possibility of seeing for oneself and transforming the self. But even that is not relevant. I see that another's seeing cannot help me to see; what I see is my own. One has to leave it there. One cannot probe further.

K: As you said, liberation is divided between those born liberated and those liberated through drugs, through yoga, through breath control and understanding. These are just explanations of a very simple fact.

P: Your mind is not like ours; that is a simple fact.

K: There are all these categories: drugs, *āsanas*, and the enormous effort involved in understanding—but I do not think it works that way at all.

P: I am not concerned with what the books say. I am very concerned when my mind chatters. In the moment of perceiving, I see that a certain withering away has taken place in me. But I am not free of the desire to end this chattering.

K: Do you really want to end it?

P: Yes.

K: Why does it not end? You see, it is very interesting: there is no ending to chattering.

P: That is what my mind refuses to see—that there is no action to end it.

K: Why? Do you want to go into it?

P: Yes.

K: First, why do you object if your mind chatters? If you want to end chattering, then the problem starts. Duality is the desire to end 'what is'. Why do you object to it? There is noise—the passing bus, the crow cawing. Let chattering go on. I am not going to resist it. I am not going to be interested in it. It is there. It means nothing.

P: This is your magnitude. If you ask me what is the greatest thing in your teaching, it is this—to be able to say to oneself, to the chattering mind: Leave it there. No teacher has said this before.

K: Which means that the peripheral influence has no meaning at the centre.

P: All teachers have talked of putting an end to chattering, to the peripheral influence.

K: Do you not see that when chattering does not matter, it is finished? It is strange how it works. I think this is the central thing which the professionals have missed. Would you say that the guru is concerned only with peripheral change?

P: No. He is concerned with central change. To you there is no difference between the centre and the periphery. Within the so-called centre there is the first and the last step. The gurus would say: Get rid of the peripheral chattering.

K: When the sun is shining, you cannot do anything about it. When it is not there, what are we to do? (*pause*) What will man make of the statement: Let it chatter? The fact is that there is no duality, and that the observer is the observed at all times. The noise of the periphery is the noise of the observer. When the observer is not, the noise is not. When there is resistance, the observer comes into existence. Can one really see that the see-er is the seeing and not accept that statement as an axiom, as an interpretation? But we see that the professionals have made that into a slogan.

Is there liberation for the man who takes drugs, who takes to breathing in and out for years? It may lead to a distorted mind. And the man who analyses and wants to understand—do you think he will find liberation? So if you deny all that, it is there on a silver platter. It is offered. That brings a tremendous aloneness which is pure, which is crystal clear.

Never repeat anything; never say anything which you do not know, which you have not lived.

New Delhi
26 December, 1970

TIME AND DETERIORATION

Dialogue 9

P: The key to your teachings appears to be in the understanding of time. The human mind, that is, the structure of the brain cells, has come to its present state with an in-built sense of time—as the yesterday, the today and the tomorrow. It is along this axis that the mind sustains itself. You appear to explode this process, to break through and, therefore, give the mind a new state of time. How is the time cycle to end?

What is your concept of time? The Buddha talks of the endless cycle of births and deaths, which is the yesterday, the today and the tomorrow, and the liberation from this cycle.

K: What is time? Is it the movement of the past through the present to the future, not only outwardly, but also inwardly from yesterday, to today and tomorrow? Or, is time that which is involved in covering physical and psychological distance?—to achieve, to fulfil, to arrive. Or, is time an ending?—as death. Or, is time the memory of pleasant and unpleasant experience? A time to learn and a time to forget—all these involve time. Time is not merely a concept.

P: We know time as a sense of duration, as clock time.

K: Time is duration, a process, a continuity and an ending. There is not only physical time, that is, time by the watch, but also psychological, inward time. Time by the watch is very clear—going to the moon requires clock time. Is there any other time?

P: We see time by the clock, the sun setting and rising. Psychological time is not different from that. If physical time has validity, my stating that I shall be tomorrow also has validity, not only physically but also psychologically. All becoming is related to the tomorrow.

K: All becoming is not only clock time, but also the *desire* to become.

P: The latter is possible only because there is a tomorrow.

K: Do you think that if there was no physical time, there would be no psychological time?

P: I question the distinction that you draw between the two—physical and psychological time.

K: I go to Madras—that needs time as today and the tomorrow. We can also see that because there is time as the yesterday, today and tomorrow, one will be different, one will change one's character, one will become 'perfect'.

P: It is easy to see that time does not bring perfection. But the nature of the movement of thought, the sprouting, is a projection in time. I question the distinction you make.

K: I know that physical time exists. Even if I do not think about tomorrow, there would be a tomorrow. Why am I sure that apart from chronological time there will be a tomorrow? It is fairly clear. This evening I will be going for a walk and between now and the walk there is an interval of ten hours. In the same way, I am something now, but I want to be something else. In that also time is involved. I am asking myself if there is such time at all. If I do not think about the walk, or about my becoming something else, is there time?

P: Certain measurements have to be made.

K: I need only physical measurement, not psychological measurement. I do not have to say: I will become that; I will fulfil; I will achieve my ideal. All that involves time. If it does not enter my consciousness, where is time? It is only when I want to change this into that, that time comes into being. I have no such desire.

P: So long as there is desire for improvement, a change for the better, which to me is a fact, there is validity to the sense of time.

K: That is, two years ago, I did not do my exercises properly. In two years, I have learnt, improved. I apply the same kind of argument to an inward process, which is, I say: I am this but I will improve in two years time.

I know only physical time, and I do not know any other time. Why do you have any other time except physical, chronological time? Why?

You see, what is really involved here is movement—the movement of improvement involves both physical and psychological time. Is there any other movement except the movement of thought? And thought which says: I have been and I will become, is time. If thought functioned only in the movement of the physical, would there be any other time? If there is no psychological being and no psychological ending, is there time? We always associate psychological time with physical time, and say: I will be. The verb 'to be' is time.

Now what happens when you do not want to do anything, one way or another?

P: What would have happened if man did not have this movement of becoming as time?

K: He would have been destroyed. So the movement of becoming was a movement of protection.

P: Then the movement of protection as time is necessary.

K: Agreed. Protection against fire is necessary; but is there any other form of protection?

P: Once you admit protection against fire, the other protection is of the same nature.

K: If the psychological is non-existent, is there need for protection?

P: What you say is true. If the other is non-existent, there is nothing to protect. But we see that there is the other.

K: You accept that there is the other; you take it for granted that there is. But is there? I need physical protection; I need food, clothes and shelter. Physical protection is absolutely necessary; nothing else. Physical protection involves time. But why should there be protection with respect to something which may not exist at all? How can you protect me psychologically? And that is what we are doing; we are doing something to protect that which does not exist; and therefore we invent time. So psychologically, there is no tomorrow; but there is a tomorrow because I need food.

P: If one sees that, in that seeing, is there the ending of time?

K: This is it. (*pause*) Shall we investigate further? Consciousness is made up of its content. Consciousness is not separate from its content. The content of consciousness is made up of time. Consciousness is time, and that is what we are trying to protect. We are using time to shield a state conditioned by time. We are trying to protect that which has no existence.

If we look at the content of consciousness, we find memories, fears, anxieties, the I-believe-I-do-not-believe—which are all products of time. And thought says: This is the only thing I have; I must protect it, shield it against every possible form of danger. What is it that thought is trying to protect? Is it words, dead memories, a formula which encourages movement, that makes it move from here to there? And is there such movement except as an invention of thought?

The movement of thought, born of memory, is from the past, even though it may appear to be free. Therefore, thought cannot bring about radical change. Therefore, it is deceiving itself all the time. When you see this, is there time at all for self-protection? If one really understood this, one's whole activity would be entirely different. Then one would protect only the physical, and not the psychological.

P: Would that not mean a state of emptiness, a meaningless emptiness inside?

K: If I only protect the physical and nothing else, obviously it is like protecting a glass. Therefore one is frightened of being empty, frightened of meaningless emptiness. But if one sees the whole thing, there is an emptiness which is tremendously significant.

S: Does time have a point at which there is an impact? How does one know the texture of time?

K: We live between regret and hope. If there is no movement, no psychological movement backwards or forwards, what is time? Is it height, which again means measurement? If there is no measurement, no movement, no backward or forward movement, no height and depth—actually no movement at all—is there time? And also, why do we give such extraordinary importance to time?

P: Because time is age, decay, deterioration.

K: Follow it up. Time is decay. I see this body, young and healthy, getting older, dying—the whole mechanism unwinding. That is all I know. Nothing else.

P: The mind also deteriorates.

K: Why should it not decay? It is part of the decaying process. I brutalize the mind in order to achieve, to succeed—which are all factors of unnatural deterioration. Then what have I left? The body grows old; I have regrets because I cannot walk up the hill anymore; the psychological struggle is coming to an end, and I am frightened. So I say: I must have a next life.

P: Does age diminish the capacity to see, to perceive?

K: No, if you have not spoilt it by scars, memories, quarrels.

P: And if you have?

K: Then you are going to pay for it.

P: Then there is no redemption.

K: At any point, the first step is the last step.

P: So time can be wiped out at any point.

K: The mind which says: Let me be aware of this whole movement, and perceives totally for one second, becomes young again for that second. But then the mind carries that over and again deteriorates.

P: The carrying over is *karma*; *karma* is also time.

K: There is past action, present action and future action. Cause is never a static thing. The effect becomes the cause. So there is a constant movement undergoing change all the time.

P: *Karma* in itself has validity.

K: I plant the seed, it will grow. I plant the seed in the woman, and the child grows.

P: So psychological time has existed as *karma*; it has reality.

K: No. Is it the real? When you look, it ceases. Let us look at this question of cause and effect. I plant a seed in the earth, and it grows. If I plant an acorn, it cannot grow to be anything but an oak. What the seed is, the bush will be, or the tree will be. I cannot change that.

S: Can the effect be changed in psychological action?

K: Yes, of course it can be changed. You have, for whatever reason, hit me physically or with words. Now what is my response to that? If I hit you back, the movement continues. But what happens if I do not react when you hit me? Because there is observing, watching, I am out of that situation.

P: I understand at that level. I set a process in motion. I observe. The process has ended. That act affects another. It is going to affect others.

K: It will affect others—your family, and the world around you.

P: The reactions arising out of my action are, in a sense, independent of my action.

K: The wave goes on.

P: The wave is *karma*: a certain energy is released which will work its consequences out unless it meets other minds which quench it.

K: The wave can only end when both of us see it at the same level, at the same time, with the same intensity. This means love. Otherwise you cannot end it.

New Delhi
27 December, 1970

DYING AND LIVING

Dialogue 10

P: There must be a way of learning how to die. To know how to die is of tremendous importance to each one of us.

K: How do the traditionalists and the professionals—by the professionals I mean the gurus, the Śaṅkarācāryas, the Ādi Śaṅkarācāryas, the yogis—answer this question?

P: Tradition divides life into various stages. There is *brahmacarya*, a stage of celibacy when, as a student, the boy learns from a guru. The second stage is that of *gṛhastha*, when a man gets married, has children, seeks to accumulate wealth and so on. He also supports the *sannyāsi* and the children, and thereby supports society. In the third stage, the *vānaprastha*, a man walks out of the pursuit of worldly things and faces the stage of preparation for the final stage which is *sannyāsa*, in which there is a giving up of name, home, identity—a symbolic donning of the saffron robe.

There is also a belief that at the moment of death, all man's past comes into focus. If his *karma*, his actions within this life, have been good, then the last thought which remains with him at the time of death continues. That is carried over into the next life. They also speak of the essential need for the mind to be quiet and fully awake at the time of death for the quenching of *karma*.

K: Will a traditional man go through all this or, is it just a lot of words?

P: Generally sir, the orthodox Hindu has the *Gītā* chanted at the time of death so that his mind cuts itself away from the immediacy of fear, of family, of wealth, etc. This does not answer my question. How is the individual to learn how to die?

K: Take a leaf in the spring—how delicate it is, and yet it has the extraordinary strength to stand the wind; in summer it matures; in autumn it turns yellow; and then it dies. It is one of the most beautiful things to see. The whole thing is a movement of beauty, a movement of the vulnerable. The leaf that is very, very tender, becomes rich, takes shape, meets summer and, when autumn comes, turns gold. There is never any sense of ugliness, never a withering away in midsummer. It is a perpetual movement from beauty to beauty. There is fullness in the spring leaf as well as in the dying leaf. I do not know if you see that.

Why cannot man live and die that way? What is the thing that is destroying him from the beginning till the end? Look at a boy of ten or twelve or thirteen—how full of laughter he is. By fourteen he becomes tough and hard; his whole manner and face change; he is caught in a pattern.

How does one learn to live and die, not just learn to die? How does one learn to live a life in which death is a part—in which the ending, the dying, is an innate part of living?

P: How is dying an innate part of life? Dying is something in the future, in time.

K: That is just it. We put death beyond the walls, beyond the movement of life. It is something to avoid, to evade, not to think about. The question is: What is living and what is dying? The two must be together, not separate. Why have we separated the two?

P: Because death is a totally different experience from life; one does not know death.

K: Is it? My question is: Why have we separated the two? Why is there this vast gulf between the two? Why do human beings divide the two?

P: Because, in death, that which is manifest becomes non-manifest; because there is an essential mystery both in birth and in death—an appearance and a disappearance.

K: Is that why we separate the two—the appearance of the child and the disappearance of the old man? Is that the reason why man has separated life from death? There is obviously a beginning and an ending: I was born, I will die tomorrow. Why do I not accept that?

P: Death involves the final cessation of the 'me'—of all that I have experienced.

K: Is that the reason for the inward division? That does not seem to be the entire reason why man has divided life from death.

P: Is it because of fear?

K: Is it fear that makes me divide the living and the dying? Do I know what living is and what dying is? Do I know the joy, the pleasure that is life, and do I regard dying as the ending of that? Is that the reason why we divide a movement called living and the movement called death? The movement which we call living—is it living? Or is it merely a series of sorrows, pleasures, despairs? Is that what we call living?

P: Why do you give it special meaning?

K: Is there any other form of living? This is the lot of every human being. Man is afraid that everything he has identified himself with will come to an end. So he wants a continuity of this thing called life—never an ending. He wants a continuity of his sorrows, of his pleasures, miseries, confusions, conflicts. He wants the same thing to go on—that there never be an ending. And the ending of all that he calls death. So now what is the mind doing in this?

The mind is confused; it is in conflict, in despair; it is caught in pleasure, in sorrow. The mind calls that living and the mind does not want it to come to an end because it does not know what would happen if it ended. Therefore it is frightened of death.

I am asking myself: Is this living? Living must have quite a different meaning than this.

P: Why? Why should it have a different meaning?

K: Living is fulfilment, frustration, and all that is going on. My mind is used to that and has never questioned whether that is living. My mind has never said to itself: Why do I call this living? Is it a habit?

P: I really do not understand your question.

K: After all, I must ask the question.

P: Why should I ask?

K: My life, from the time I am born till I die, is one eternal struggle.

P: Living is acting, seeing, being—the whole of that is there.

K: I see beauty—the sky, a lovely child. I also see conflict with my child, with my neighbours; life is a movement in conflict and pleasure.

P: Why should I question that? The mind questions only when there is sorrow, when there is a lot of pain.

K: Why not ask when you have pleasure?

P: Sir, life is not a series of crises. Crises of pain are few; they are rare occasions.

K: But I see this is happening in life. I see it happening and, therefore, question this division of living and dying.

P: You do, but others do not. We see that there is division; it is a fact to us.

K: At what level, at what depth, with what significance are you making this statement? Of course it is a fact. I am born and I will die. Then there is nothing more to be said.

P: It is not enough. The very fact that we have asked how to learn to die—

K: I say learn also how to live. Then what happens? If I learn how to live, I also learn how to die. I want to learn how to live. I want to learn about sorrow, pleasure, pain, beauty. I learn. Because I am learning about life I am learning about death. Learning is an act of purification, and not the acquiring of knowledge. Learning is purgation. I cannot learn if my mind is full. The mind must purge itself to learn. Therefore the mind, when it wants to learn, has to empty itself of everything that it has known; then it can learn.

So there is the living which we all know. There has to be first of all a learning about this daily living. Now, is the mind capable not of accumulating but of learning? Without understanding what is implied in the first act of learning, can it learn? What is implied? When I do not know, then my mind, not knowing, is capable of learning. Can the mind not know, so that it can learn about living—in which there is sorrow, agony, confusion, struggle? Can it come to it in a state of not-knowing, and so learn? Such a mind, capable of learning about life, is also capable of learning about death.

What is important is not the learning about something, but the act of learning. The mind can only learn when it does not know. We approach life with knowledge of life, with knowledge of cause, effect, *karma*. We come to life with the sense of the 'I know', with conclusions and formulas. And with these we fill the mind. But I do not know about death. I want to learn about death, but I cannot. It is only when I know learning that I will understand death. Death is the emptying of the mind of the knowledge which I have accumulated.

P: There can be learning about living in learning about death. Deep down in human consciousness there is this nameless fear of ceasing to be.

K: The nameless fear of not being. Being is knowing that I am this, that I am happy, that I had a marvellous time. In the same way I want to know death. I do not want to learn, I want to know. I want to know what it means to die.

P: So that I am free of fear.

K: If I do not know how to drive a car, I am frightened. The moment I know, it is over. Similarly, my knowledge of death is in terms of the past; knowledge is the past. Therefore I say: I must know what it means to die, so that I can live. Do you see the game you are playing with yourself, the game which the mind is playing with itself?

The act of learning is different from the act of knowing. You see, knowing is never in the active present; learning is always in the active present. The learning about death—I really do not know what that means. There is no theory, no speculation that will satisfy me. I am going to find out, I am going to learn. There is no theory, no conclusion, no hope, no speculation, but only the act of learning; therefore there is no fear of death. To find out what it means to die, learn.

In the same way, I really want to know what living is. So I must come to living with a fresh mind, without the burden of knowledge. The moment the mind acknowledges it knows absolutely nothing, it is free to learn. Free to learn about the thing that I have called living, and the thing that I have called death. I do not know what they mean. Therefore there is living and dying all the time.

There is no death when the mind is completely free of the known: the beliefs, the experiences, the conclusions, the knowledge, the saying 'I-have-suffered', and so on.

Intellectually we have carved life out beautifully according to our conditioning: To achieve God I must be celibate; I must help the poor; I must take a vow of poverty. Death says: You cannot touch me. But I want to touch death; I want to shape it into my pattern. Death says: You cannot play tricks on me. But the mind is used to tricks, used to carving something out of experience. Death says: You cannot experience me. Death is an original experience, in the sense that it is a state that *I really do not know*. I can invent formulas about death—the last thought is that which manifests itself; but they are other people's thoughts. *I really do not know*. So I am starkly frightened. Can I now begin to learn about living and, therefore, about dying?

So deny knowing—see what takes place. In that there is real beauty, real love; in that the real thing takes place.

New Delhi
28 December, 1970

BEAUTY AND PERCEPTION

Dialogue 11

P: Where is the resting place of beauty? Where does beauty reside? Obviously, the outer manifestations of beauty are observable in the right relationship between space, form and colour, and between human beings. But what is the essence of beauty? In Sanskrit texts three factors are equated—the True, the Good and the Beautiful as *satyam, śivam, sundaram*.

K: What are you trying to find out? Do you want to find the nature of beauty? What do the professionals say?

P: Traditionalists would say: *satyam, śivam, sundaram*. The artist today would not differentiate between the seemingly ugly and the seemingly beautiful, but would regard the creative act as the expression of a moment, of a perception that gets transformed within the individual and which finds expression in the action of the artist.

K: You are asking: What is beauty, what is the expression of beauty, and how does the individual fulfil himself through beauty? What is beauty? If you started as though you knew nothing about it, what would your reaction be? This is a universal problem: it was a problem for the Greeks, for the Romans, and it is still a problem for people today. So what is beauty? Does beauty lie in the sunset, in a lovely morning, in human relationships—between mother and child, husband and wife, man and woman? Does beauty lie in the extraordinarily subtle movement of thought and in clear perception? Is that what you call beauty?

P: Can there be beauty also in the terrible, the ugly?

K: In murder, in butchery, in throwing bombs, in violence, in mutilation, torture, anger, in the brutal, violent, aggressive pursuit of an idea, in wanting to be greater than somebody—is there beauty in that? Where is beauty if a man hits another?

P: In all these acts there is no beauty, but isn't there beauty in the creative act of the artist who interprets the terrible, like Picasso's Guernica?

K: So we have to ask: What is expression, what is creativity? You ask: What is beauty? Does it lie in a sunset, in the clear light of the morning, the light on the water, in relationship? And does beauty lie in any form of violence, including competitive achievement? Is there beauty *per se*, or does it lie in how the artist expresses himself? A child tortured can be expressed by an artist, but is that beauty?

P: Beauty is a relative thing.

K: The 'I' which sees, which is conditioned and which demands self-fulfilment is relative.

Now, is beauty good taste? Or, does beauty have nothing in common with it, but lies in the artist's expression and, therefore, in his fulfillment? The artist says: I must fulfil myself through expression. The artist would be lost without expression, which is part of his sense of beauty and his self-fulfilment. We ourselves try to find beauty in other people's expression, in architecture and in beautiful bridges—like the Golden Gate Bridge, or the bridges over the Seine—in modern buildings of glass and steel and in the gentleness of a fountain. We seek beauty in museums, and in a symphony.

What is amiss in the man who is seeking beauty? So, can we ask what is the inwardness, the feeling, the subtlety in the word 'beauty', so that beauty is truth and truth is beauty?

P: The expressions of other people are the only sources of beauty that are available to us.

K: What does that mean?

P: In seeing the bridge a certain quality arises within me which I call beauty. It is only in the perception of something beautiful that the quality of beauty arises in many individuals.

K: I understand that. I am asking: Does beauty lie in self-expression?

P: One has to start with what exists.

K: Which is other people's expression. Not having the perceptive eye, the strange inward feeling of beauty, I say: How beautiful that picture is, how beautiful that poem is, that symphony. Remove all that, and the individual knows no beauty. Therefore he relies, for his appreciation of beauty, on expression, on objects—on a bridge or a good chair. Does beauty demand expression, especially self-expression?

P: Can it exist independent of expression?

K: Perception of beauty is its expression; the two are not separate. Perceiving is expressing; there is no time interval at all. Seeing is doing, acting; there is no gap between seeing and doing.

I want to observe the mind that sees, where seeing is acting; I want to observe the nature of the mind that has this quality of seeing and doing. What is this mind? It is essentially not concerned with expression. Expression may come, but it is not concerned. Expression takes time—to build a bridge, to write a poem. But to the mind which sees, the mind to which perceiving is doing, there is no time at all. Such a mind is a sensitive mind; such a mind is the most intelligent mind. And without that intelligence, is there beauty?

P: What is the place of the heart in this?

K: Do you mean the feeling of love?

P: The word 'love' is a loaded term. If you are still, there is a strange feeling, a movement which takes place from this region of the heart. What is this? Is this necessary or, is it a hindrance?

K: This is the most essential part of it. There is no perception without that; mere intellectual perception is no perception. The action of intellectual perception is fragmentary, whereas intelligence implies affection, the heart. Otherwise you are not sensitive; you cannot possibly perceive. Perceiving is acting. Perceiving, acting without time is beauty.

P: Do the eyes and the heart operate at the same time in the act of perception?

K: Perception implies complete attention. The nerves, the ears, the brain, the heart—everything is at the highest quality. Otherwise there is no perceiving.

P: Is the fragmentary quality of sensory action due to the fact that the whole organism does not operate at the same time?

K: The brain, the heart, nerves, eyes, ears are never completely in attention and, as they are not, you cannot perceive.

So what is beauty? Does it lie in expression, in fragmentary action? I may be an artist, an engineer, a poet; poets, engineers, artists and scientists are fragmentary human beings. One fragment becomes extraordinarily perceptive, sensitive and its action may express something marvellous, but it is still a fragmentary action.

P: What is that state when the organism perceives violence, terror or ugliness?

K: Let us take violence in its multifarious forms—but why are you asking that question?

P: It is necessary to investigate this.

K: Is violence part of beauty? Is that what you are asking?

P: I will not put it that way.

K: You see violence. What is the response of a perceptive mind, in the sense in which we are using the word 'perceptive', to various forms of destruction, which is part of violence? (*pause*)

I've got it. Is violence a fragmentary act or is it an act of a totally harmonious perception?

P: No.

K: So you are saying that it is a fragmentary action. Fragmentary action must deny beauty.

P: You have inverted the situation.

K: What is the response of a perceptive mind when it sees violence? It looks at it, investigates it and sees it as a fragmentary action; and therefore it is not an act of beauty. What happens to a perceptive mind when it sees a violent act? It sees 'what is'.

P: To you the nature of the mind does not change as such?

K: Why should it change? It sees 'what is'. Go a step further.

P: Does the perceiving mind, observing violence which is fragmentary, and seeing 'what is', act on violence? And, in the very act of seeing, does it change its nature?

K: Wait a minute. You are asking: What is the effect of the perceiving mind when it observes violence?

P: You said: It sees 'what is'. Does it alter 'what is'? Does the perceiving mind, in the very observing of violence and seeing 'what is', act on violence and change its nature?

K: Are you asking whether the perceiving mind, in seeing 'what is', that is, the act of violence, asks: What shall I do? Is that it?

P: Such a mind does not do that, but there must be some action from the perceiving mind which changes the violence in the other.

K: The perceiving mind sees a violent act. Such an act is fragmentary. What action can there be on the part of the perceiving mind?

P: The perceiving mind sees violence on the part of x; seeing is acting.

K: But what can it do?

P: If the perceiving mind acts, it must change the violence in x.

K: Let us get this clear. The perceiving mind sees another acting violently. To the perceiving mind, the very seeing is the doing. That is a fact; perception is action. The perceiving mind sees x in violence. What is the action involved in that seeing?—the stopping of violence?

P: All those are peripheral actions. I am saying that when a perceiving mind is confronted with an act of violence, the very act of perceiving will alter the action of violence.

K: Several things are involved here. The perceiving mind sees an act of violence; the man who is acting violently may respond non-violently, because the perceiving mind is near him, close to him—and suddenly this happens.

P: One comes to you with a problem, say of jealousy. What happens in an interview with you when a confused person comes to you? In the very act of perceiving, the confusion is not.

K: Obviously that happens because of contact. You have taken the trouble to discuss violence, and something happens because of a direct sharing of the problem—there is communication. That is simple. You see a man far away acting with violence. What is the action of the perceiving mind there?

P: There must be tremendous energy from a perceiving mind, that must have some action.

K: It may act. You cannot be as certain of that as you can be in close proximity. The other may wake up in the middle of the night; he may become aware of the strange response later, depending upon his sensitivity. This may or may not be due to the perceiving mind and its impact; whereas this close communication is different. It does bring about change.

Let us come back. You were asking what beauty is. I think we can say that the mind which is not fragmentary in itself, which is not broken up, has this beauty.

P: Has it any relationship to sensory perception? If you close your eyes, your ears—

K: Even when you close your ears and eyes, because there is no fragmentation, the mind has this quality of beauty, of sensitivity. It is not dependent on external beauty. Put the instrument of such a mind in the middle of the noisiest city, what takes place? Physically it gets affected, but the quality of the mind that is not fragmented, is not affected. It is independent of the surroundings, therefore it does not concern itself with expression.

P: That is the aloneness of it.

K: Therefore beauty is aloneness. Why is there this craving for self-expression? Is that craving part of beauty—whether it is the craving of a woman for a baby, of a husband for sex in the moment of tenderness, or of the artist craving for expression? Does the perceptive mind demand any form of expression? It does not, because perceiving is expressing, is doing. The artist, the painter, the builder finds self-expression. It is fragmentary; and therefore its expression is not beauty.

A mind that is conditioned, that is fragmentary, expresses the feeling of beauty, but it is conditioned. Is that beauty? Therefore, the self which is the conditioned mind can never see beauty, and whatever it expresses must be of its quality.

P: You have still not answered one aspect of the question. There is such a thing as creative talent, the ability to put together things in a manner which gives joy.

K: The housewife baking bread, but not 'in order to'—not because of something else. The moment you do that you are lost. The speaker does not sit on the platform and speak because it gives him joy. The source of water is never empty; it is always bubbling. Whether there is pollution or the worship of water, it is bubbling; it is there.

Most people who are concerned with self-expression have self-interest. The artist, famous or otherwise, belongs to that category. It is the self which makes for fragmentation. In the absence of the self, there is perception. Perception is doing, and *that* is beauty.

I am sure that the sculptor who carved the Maheśamūrti at Elephanta created it out of his meditation. Before you put your hand to a stone or a poem, there must be a state of meditation; the inspiration must not be from the self.

P: The tradition of the Indian sculptor was that.

K: Beauty is total self-abandonment; and with the total absence of the self there is *that*. We are trying to catch that without the absence of the self; creation then becomes a tawdry affair.

New Delhi
29 December, 1970

THE PARADOX OF CAUSATION

Dialogue 12

GS: In physics we have certain unsolved problems: If the world is fully causal, you cannot change anything. If the world is not fully causal, you cannot find any laws for such a world. Either the world is causal or it is not. If you think of cause and effect as one single entity, if all the world is one and there is no separation into pieces, then of course there is no cause and effect.

If the whole universe is physical and suffers physical laws, then you have no choice. In the case of purely physical things, there are no options. Even if the soul, or whatever it is, were different from the kind of things that we are talking about, it still would have no special significance if it were subject to physical laws. You cannot say that there is no cause-effect relationship because it is not natural. You cannot also accept cause and effect because then there would be no control over it, and so what would be the point in saying that? This is the paradox. What is the way out of this paradox?

K: Are you talking of *karma*?

GS: No. The physical universe is closed; there is no movement here at all.

K: All this implies time, does it not? That is, anything put together, horizontally or vertically, is time. Cause and effect are in time. Cause becoming effect, and the effect becoming the cause are all within the field of time. Whether I move my hand up this way or move my hand that way, that is, whether the movement is horizontal or vertical, it is within the field of time. Are you asking, sir: Can we move out of time?

GS: No. The experience of a physical law is within time. One does not ask questions within that law. And what option does one have?

K: None at all. You can operate within the prison, but that would always be within the field of time; cause-effect and effect-cause are within the field of time. Memory, experience, knowledge are within time, and thought is the response of all that. If I have no memory, I cannot think; I will be in a state of amnesia. And thought is the response of memory. Thinking is within the field of time because it is put together through experience, knowledge, memory—and memory is part of the brain cells.

So thought can never move out of the field of time, because thought is never free; thought is always old. In the interval between two thoughts, one may come upon something new, and translate it in terms of time. There is a gap between two thoughts; in that interval there might be a different perception. The translation of that perception is time, but the perception itself is not of time.

GS: I have several questions to ask here.

K: Go slowly. Living in time, when thought, which is put together, tries to investigate something beyond time, it is still thought; living in time, there is nothing new. So, as long as thought and time are within the field, it is a prison; I can think it is freedom but it would be merely a conception, a formula. It is like a man who is violent and pretends he is non-violent. The whole ideological conception in this country of being non-violent and violent at the same time is a pretension.

So, as far as thought functions, it must function within the field of time. There is no escape from it at all. I can pretend that I am thinking outside time, but it is still within time. Thought is old, whether it is about the *ātman* or about the super ego; it is part of thought.

GS: Where is the way out of the paradox?

K: The intellect, thought functions there, and we are trying to find an answer here—as physicists, biologists, mathematicians, as a bourgeois or as a *sannyāsi*.

GS: But there are laws in physics.

K: Of course there are. This is anyhow a madhouse, and we are trying to find an answer within it. This is a fact. I have to accept it as it is. Then my question is: Is there an action which is not of this? Here all action is fragmentary: you are a religious man; I am a scientist. In this everything is in a state of fragmentation.

GS: Fragmentation carries laws.

K: Of course, but these laws have not solved human problems. Apart from being a physicist, you are a human being. Take the problem as it is—that human beings live in fragments, that society is broken up. Thought is responsible for this.

GS: Thought is also responsible for all other things.

K: Surely. It is responsible for the inventions, the discoveries, the gods, the priests, the yogis—everything. So that is what actually is. The problem is how to live here and find something else. You cannot. The question is not how to integrate the various fragments, but how it is possible to live without fragmentation.

GS: To the extent to which it is possible, you have no questions. At that point it ceases to be physics; at that level I am no longer a physicist.

K: Of course. If you are first a human being, a non-fragmentary human being, your action can then be non-fragmentary.

GS: For the non-fragmented person, physics does not exist.

K: What is the importance of an artist?

GS: He transports people into states which they themselves are not able to reach—still fragmentary, but different.

K: Being fragmented, he needs self-expression; and his self is part of the fragmentation. So would you deny the artist his function? Now the physicist is important, but he does not come before the universe, before the human heart, before the human mind; he is as important or unimportant as the artist.

GS: There is a difference in the quality. The artist is usually not clear.

K: The artist is clear in his feeling, but the expression goes wrong because he is conditioned to objectivism, non-objectivism and all that. So, can I live in this world non-fragmentarily—not as a Hindu, Buddhist, Christian or Communist, but as a human being?

GS: Why not just live; why the word 'human'?

K: The way we live is not human at all. It is a battle—country, wife, children, the boss. We live that way, at war with each other.

You call that living. I say that this perpetual struggle is not living.

GS: Life is not a perpetual struggle all the time.

K: But most of the time it is. The window is closed.

GS: But why the word 'human'?

K: Sir, I did not use the word 'individual'. Do you know the meaning of the word 'individual'? It means 'one who is indivisible'. Man is not. So one realizes this fact of fragmentation, and of time: the constant battle for position, power, prestige, success, domination, and the effort to escape from all this to reach enlightenment through the mantra, through yoga. How is this everlasting chattering to come to an end? Is it at all possible not to be fragmented? How is it possible for the brain cells themselves to be quiet? Because that is the mechanism of time, put together slowly over years, which we call evolution. This is the central question.

GS: And that is rightly so. You bring the problem back to physics, because physics talks about the external universe but it does not talk about the brain cells. If you had only a fragment of reality, then you would not accept it as consistent. If it is consistent, then it is fiction. Could the fragment be self-consistent?

K: I would put it this way: Is it possible for a human being to be a physicist and be self-consistent without fragmenting himself? I see that time is the central factor here. Thought is the response of memory; thought is time.

GS: For the experiencer.

K: The experiencer is the experienced, the observer is the observed. But the observer separates himself through conclusions, images, formulas, etc., and so creates space and time, and this is one of the major fragmentations.

Can one look without the observer who is the maker of time, space, distance? After all, sir, how do you as a physicist discover anything?

GS: I am peculiar, I invent.

K: There must be a period in which the invertor is silent.

GS: Yes.

K: If he is constantly in movement, there is continuity. But there must be a break in which he sees something new. The observer sees through the image, and the image is continued in time. And so he cannot see anything new. If I look at my wife with the image of years, and I call that relationship, there is nothing new in that.

So is it possible to see something new without the observer? The observer is time. Can I look at 'what is', the fragmented, without the observer that is time? Can there be a perception without the perceiver?

GS: There is no perception without the perceiver, but the perceived is sort of waiting to be perceived.

K: The tree is there all the time without the perceiver, and the perceiver is looking at it through fragmentation, through the censor. Can the censor be absent and, yet, can there be observation?

GS: Certainly not. Perception is a single act. There is no possibility of breaking it up.

K: Who is the censor? Who is the perceiver? Who is using the verb 'to perceive'?

GS: When you are perceiving, you do not talk about the perceiver.

K: I look at the tree with knowledge. Can the observer observe without the past? Who is the thinker, the examiner?

GS: When you perceive, you do not need all this.

K: There is the tree. Can I look at it without the observer?

GS: Yes.

K: There is only that. Then the perceiver comes into operation. So the image-maker can look without the image. Otherwise you cannot invent.

GS: We were talking about communication. If time itself is the product of thinking, then how can thinking be imprisoned in time? Then what makes time common to all people?

M: Different people have the same notion of time.

K: I wonder if they do. Why do you want a concept of time? You look at the watch, you have no concept about it.

GS: The idea of time as movement is associated with the watch.

K: Within the rising and setting of the sun, there is numerical time, but is there any other time that is psychological, inward?

GS: There is another time when you think of action in the future.

K: So time is the movement of the past through the present to the future.

GS: Time is part of thought.

K: Time is thought; time is sorrow.

GS: How can thought transcend itself? What is the significance of saying that thought cannot transcend itself?

K: But it is all the time trying to do so. Let me put it this way: What validity has time? I have to go from here to there, from this house to the other house, from one continent to another continent; I want to be a manager of this factory—all that involves time, which is being put together sequentially or non-sequentially.

GS: There is a great limitation to this. Time is single but experiences are not single. Time is one dimensional, one string with beads collected on it. Experiences connected together give you an impression of time, but time itself is one dimensional, a single string. You can think of different strands and scales of time; they are a string of time. The connectivity of things can be complex. We do not experience the multiple connectivity of things. We can, of course, experience several things together; for example, I am listening to you, part of my mind may be thinking of something else, I may be shaking my toe while my understanding is functioning. I watch all that. I see a series of pictures but I do not live anything.

K: That means the self is absent.

GS: There is no single self.

K: That is, there is no centre.

GS: There is no centre which has time in it.

K: That means in oneself there is no fragmentation at all. At the very core of one's being, there is no fragmentation.

GS: Put that way, one sees that there is a state in which there is no fragmentation.

K: Can one find out a quality in which there is no fragmentation?—Which means the ending of thought that breeds fragmentation, of thought which is time.

Look, sir, when you go through the world there are separate actions—social, political, communal, the action of the hippies—all of which are fragmented. Is there an action which is not fragmented, but which will cover all that?

GS: You use the word 'action', but action is associated with time.

K: I mean the active present.

GS: Yes, it is.

K: It means that there is a quality of mind in which there is no fragmentation at all. It is the active present all the time.

What relationship has all this with love? Love has been reduced to sex and all the morality around it. If love is not, fragmentation will go on. You will be a physicist, I will be something else, and we will communicate, discuss—but these are mere words.

GS: How do you communicate? There has been some communication after you have talked. How do I understand that? How is it that I understand it?

K: What does the word 'communication' mean? You and I have something in common, which implies sharing.

GS: How is it possible to share?

K: Wait, we are using time to communicate. Having something in common implies that both of us want to understand, examine, share an issue together—I am not giving, you are not receiving. We are sharing. So a relationship of sharing is established. You are not sitting on the platform, and I on the ground. What really happens when you share a problem like sorrow in human beings? It is tremendous.

GS: At the time you are sharing sorrow, you do not see the person.

I can understand that with regard to deep personal emotions, but with an idea it is not possible.

K: What is the point of sharing ideas?

GS: We share insights.

K: Which is understanding; but ideas are not understanding. On the contrary, formulas about understanding prevent understanding. Sir, when you share together, what takes place? Both of us have the same intensity, at the same time, at the same level. That is love. Otherwise there is no sharing. After all, sir, to understand something together, I must forget all my experiences, prejudices, and so must you. Otherwise we cannot share. Have you ever discussed with a Communist, with a Catholic?

GS: I try to understand him.

K: But he will not understand you. That is simple. Take Chardin, he may have travelled extensively, covered a wide canvas, but he was fixed as a Catholic. You cannot share with a man who is fixed. Sharing implies love. Can a man who is fixed in a certain attitude love?

GS: He can have mystical experiences.

K: Because he is conditioned, he sees Krishna, he sees Christ, he sees what he wants to. The question is whether the mind can uncondition itself—not through time, for when the mind uses time to undo time, it is still within time. Real understanding is out of time. There is so little of love, of sharing, but of the other there is plenty. (*pause*)

Sir, here we ask the question: What is meditation? Can the mind be free of all its content, because consciousness is made up of the content?

M: Most often when you talk of understanding you think of one individual. To have communication you must have two minds. Also there are some thoughts which arise only when two people are together.

GS: M says that there are situations when two people have ideas together which neither could have had independently.

K: When two people come together, what takes place? You

express something verbally, I hear it, translate it and answer; that is verbal communication. And in that process certain other factors enter. You do not quite know what you are saying, I hear it, partially understand and partially answer. So communication remains broken. If you say something very clearly and I listen to you without any reaction, there is immediate communication.

May I put it this way? Because I do not know what love is, I want you to love me. But when I know what love is, I can communicate with you. I do not want anything.

But you are asking a further question, and that is: Is there a necessity at all for communication?—necessity in the sense that through communication I uncover something more, I discover something new. It is like a man who plays the violin, and uses the instrument for himself or uses the instrument, and there is nothing beyond it.

GS: Neither for good nor for evil.

K: Yes, like a flower—take it or leave it. Through communication we discover something together. Without communication, can I discover anything without verbalization? When you and I have a common interest and intensity at the same level and at the same time, then communion is possible non-verbally. I do not have to tell you that I love you.

I think we are caught so much in words, in linguistic, semantic inquiry. The word is not the thing; the description is not the described.

GS: And since this high level of communication is not a technique or a skill, the question arises: How does one learn anything? A child is able to learn.

K: Is learning a process of accumulation? That is what we do—I learn Italian, store up the words, then I speak. This is what we call learning. Is there learning which is non-accumulation? The two are totally different actions.

GS: May I ask something? It may be totally irrelevant but you will understand. Is there the 'other'? Are there other people?

K: It all depends upon what you mean by the 'other', what you mean by 'the other people'.

GS: Most times there is multiplicity—but there is also aloneness.

K: Obviously.

GS: Since aloneness is real—

K: Why do you call aloneness real and the 'other' unreal? We know loneliness, resistance, the dual movement of action—defensive or aggressive. Being caught in thought brings greater isolation—we and they, my party and yours. Now, can the mind go beyond isolation, beyond resistance? Can it be completely alone, without being isolated? It is only then that I discover something new, something which is real.

GS: I have experience of that state, but you caught me at that point when you asked: Why do you divide? There are two situations—states when I do not see multiplicity, and states in which I see multiplicity. I have a feeling that the states in which I see multiplicity are falling off.

K: Be careful, sir, you are caught. When you say, 'falling off', what do you mean? Falling off is time. Anything that you can get rid of slowly is time. Whereas the other does not involve time at all. So do not get caught, sir. (*pause*)

So is there a perception and an action without time? I see physical danger, and there is instant action. I do not say: I will gradually withdraw from danger. Is there a perception, a seeing-the-danger-of-it completely? The very seeing is the getting rid of it.

GS: If you see the whole thing completely, there is no falling off. It is not there.

M: Which means that there is no preparing for it.

GS: This statement is at variance with my experience. I have experienced timeless moments. I loved it. I have a memory of it.

K: Leave it alone, sir.

GS: When I hold it, then it is pleasure.

K: That is what it is. Pleasure is our one main ruling principle.

Madras
3 January, 1971

TRADITION AND KNOWLEDGE

Dialogue 13

A: I belonged to the self-preparation group of the Theosophical Society in 1923 and 1924. In that group there was a preparation for understanding which followed the traditional approach—of *viveka* (discrimination), of *vairāgya* (detachment) and love. A change came about when you said: Let us break away from all organizations, from all disciplines.

In the book *At the Feet of the Master*, *śama* is translated as 'control of the mind' and *dama* as 'control of the body'. Traditionally *śama* seems to have been neglected; less attention is paid to it than to *dama*, control of the body. And yet the word *śānti*, which is a one-word symbol for inner peace, is derived from *śama* as the past participle. By implication, if *śama* is not understood, *śānti* is also not understood.

K: What does the word *sādhanā* mean to you?

J: To practice *sādhanā* is to acquire discipline.

A: You neglect *śama*, the process whereby the rising impulse of the mind subsides.

K: What do you mean by 'process'? A process implies a movement —from here to there; a process involves time.

A: The process of observing the ways of the mind involves time.

K: Time is involved in a process, in a discipline, and is also necessary in order for one to arrive. Time and also space are implied in all that. From here to there implies space, and that space is covered through time.

J: Ramana says that it is pathless, free of 'process', free of time.

A: Even when we realize that it is not good to suppress the arising and ending of desire, that realization is still a process; and the process is in time.

K: What do we mean when we say that we live in time? What does 'living in time' mean?

A: The mind is geared to yesterday, today and tomorrow.

K: The mind also lives within chronological time—I come here at such and such a time. Is there any other time?

A: There is psychological time which is created by the mind.

K: What do you mean by 'time as created by the mind'?

A: The mind has a way of prolonging pleasure. My movement in chronological time is influenced by my mind.

K: What is this mind?

A: Memory.

K: What is memory? You were in Bangalore yesterday and today you are in Madras. You remember Bangalore. Remembrance of a past experience is memory. The experience has left a mark, painful or pleasurable—that is irrelevant. Why has experience left a mark? And what is the substance on which it leaves a mark?

A: On the censor.

K: What do you mean by the 'censor'? Yesterday's experience has left a mark. On what has it left a mark?

J: On the mind, which is consciousness.

K: Which consciousness? The content of consciousness is consciousness; without a content there is no consciousness—the two are not separate. Find out on what memory leaves a mark.

A: On that part of the mind/brain which carries the residue.

K: Marks are left on the brain cells. See what happens—unfinished experience leaves a mark on the brain cells which hold memory. Memory is matter—the brain cells are matter. So every incomplete experience leaves a mark which becomes knowledge. The brain as accumulated knowledge has received information, and information is knowledge. Its weight makes the mind dull.

A: How does one cope with a challenge?

K: What is coping with a challenge? If you respond according to past information, you do not know how to deal with the new problem. Experience leaves a residue as memory on the brain cells, which become the storehouse of knowledge. Knowledge is the past. So the brain, put together through time which is the past, acts, responds, functions, according to the residue of the past. And so a mind crowded with knowledge is not a free mind.

J: Because its responses arise out of the known.

A: At a certain level knowledge is essential.

K: Of course, half our lives are that. We see that the brain, which is put together through millennia, lives with the experience of the present and the past—the racial past, the familial past and the personal past are all weighted down there. We call this progress. We know technological progress—from the bullock cart to the jet. The brain says that it can only function within its memories; and thought says that it wants to get out of the prison of memories. So thought moves into the future which is enlightenment. So enlightenment is also a movement of thought. See what we are doing.

A: We apply the principle of the bullock cart and the jet—that the mind through acquired knowledge, through discipline, through control of desires, can move to freedom.

K: I do not think we are clear yet. We accumulate knowledge, which is experience, memory, and through knowledge we try to find a way out.

A: Yes.

K: The traditional approach to freedom is through knowledge. But can knowledge bring about freedom? If it can, discipline, control, sublimation, suppression are all necessary. Because that is all we know. That is tradition. 'Tradition' means 'to carry over'.

A: I clearly see that it is not possible. Then why do we not stop?

K: I clearly see that knowledge which is the accumulation of centuries is a prison. I see clearly that this is a fact; it is not an assumption or a theory. And yet the mind cannot drop it.

A: My understanding is verbal; it is based on words.

K: Is it based on words? You hit me. I have physical pain. The remembrance of the pain is in the form of words, but the pain is not verbal. Why has the mind translated the pain into words? Watch it, sir.

A: For the sake of communication.

K: Watch it. You hit me; I am in pain. That is a physical fact. Then I remember it. The remembrance is in the form of words. Why has the fact been translated into words?

J: To give continuity.

K: Is it to give continuity to the pain, or to give continuity to the man who has inflicted pain?

A: He has to reap the consequences.

J: It gives continuity to the man who receives the pain.

K: Look. You hit me. There is physical pain. That is all. Why do I not end it there? Why does the brain translate the pain into words and say: He has hit me? Why?—Because it wants to hit back. If it did not want to do that, it could say: He has hit me—full stop. But the brain remembers not only the physical pain, but also the man who causes the hurt, which becomes the psychological mark.

R: Who remembers?

K: The brain cells.

A: The 'I' process.

J: What is being recorded in the cells is the image of the man who hit me.

K: Why should I remember the man?

J: Even if I forgive him, it is the same.

K: What happens is this. The moment you hit me, I translate the fact into words. The 'I' says: He has hit me, how could he? What have I done?—All these are waves of words.

The traditional approach to enlightenment is also through knowledge: you must have knowledge to arrive, to achieve freedom. And I ask whether that is so. The experience of being hit is knowledge. Now, what is the traditional approach to the problem of pain, of suffering, of being hurt? Why has tradition maintained that knowledge is necessary as a means of enlightenment?

A: That is an over-simplification. The verbalization of pain is only one part of knowledge, there is a larger field of knowledge which is racial. The word is the essence of knowledge.

K: Is it?

J: No, it is not so.

K: So we have to see what knowledge is, what it means to know. Is knowing in the active present or, is it in the past?

A: Knowledge presupposes the past—what has been known.

K: Tradition says that knowledge is essential to freedom, to enlightenment. Why has this been maintained?—for there must have been people who questioned this. Why did not the gurus, the *Gītā*, question knowledge? Why did they not see that knowledge means the past, and that the past cannot possibly bring enlightenment? Why did the traditionalists not see that discipline, *sādhanā*, comes from knowledge?

J: Is it because they felt that memory must be maintained?

K: Why did the professionals not see that knowledge is the self, when they talked everlastingly of wiping away the self?

A: So long as the communication is verbal, you cannot wipe away the self.

K: Do you mean to say that according to the professionals you can never look at anything without the word?

A: The word is compulsive, non-volitional.

K: You hit me; there is pain. I see that. Why should that be built up as memory? You are not answering my question. Why did the professionals not see the fact that accumulated knowledge can never lead to freedom?

A: Some of them did.

K: Why did they not act? The professionals are you—which means, you have not dropped tradition. Why cannot you therefore drop it? Personally, I see a very simple fact: You hit me: there is pain. That is all.

A: What about pleasure?

K: The same thing.

A: There is effort involved in dropping pleasure.

K: Then you enter the same circus—naming, which strengthens the knowledge that you hit me. You hit me. That is a fact. My son is dead. That is a fact. To become cynical, bitter, to say: I loved him and he is gone—all that is verbalization.

A: So long as the mind continues to chatter—

K: Let it chatter. Look. The fact is one thing and the description of the fact is another. We are caught in descriptions, in explanations; we are not concerned with the facts. Why does this take place at all?

When the house is on fire I act, as I must. What is the action when you have hit me? There is only complete inaction, which means no verbalization.

A: This happened to me when my brother died.

K: Then what takes place? Why do we get caught in knowledge and make it so extraordinarily important? Why has the capacity to reason, to argue, become so extraordinarily important? The computers are taking over that function. Why have the professionals been caught in this trap?

So, can the brain cells, which are put together through time as knowledge, function with knowledge when necessary, and yet be completely free of knowledge?

A: When I have pleasure, I say: How wonderful! I do not drop pleasure.

K: I have had an affair which gave me pleasure. Then thought comes along and says: I would like to repeat it. So it begins—affair, memory, reaction to memory as thought, thought building images, demanding images. All this is part of tradition, the carrying over of yesterday into tomorrow.

A: There is also joy.

K: The moment you reduce joy to pleasure, it is gone.

A: Is there more to knowledge than pleasure and pain?

K: We cannot answer that unless we understand pleasure, pain and knowledge. The professionals have been blind, and they have made millions of people blind. The monstrosity of it! This country, the Christian world—they are all the same.

The questions which next arise are: Can the brain function at one level with complete objectivity, with knowledge which is sane, without bringing in the pleasure principle?—pleasure through prestige, status and all that. And can the brain also realize that freedom is not in knowledge? That realization is freedom. How does this happen?

J: One point here: When thought craves to die, it continues.

K: What would the professional's answer be to this question? Why does thought cling?

J: I stay in *samādhi* and come back.

K: There is no meaning in that. Do the brain cells see themselves as a repository of knowledge? Do they see for themselves—and not as a superimposed realization—that when the principle of pleasure acts, mischief begins? Then there is fear, violence, aggression—everything follows.

A: When the field of knowledge is distorted by pleasure and pain, the mischief starts.

K: Why did the traditionalists, the professionals, the scriptures, the spiritual leaders, not see this? Was it because for them authority was tremendously important?—the authority of the *Gītā*, of the scriptures. Because man is a result of all this. So you have the man who says: I have read the *Gītā*, I am the authority. An authority on what?—On somebody else's words, on somebody else's knowledge?

A: We can know various traditions without becoming involved with them. Knowing the tradition does bring you a certain clarity. We know how the professionals worked and how you work. You say that knowledge is entirely of the past.

K: Obviously. If I am tethered to a post, I cannot move.

A: Then why did the professionals not see this?

K: They were after power.

A: You do not understand. You say that they wanted power, but that is not so.

K: Look at what is taking place in each person. We see something very clearly for a moment; this perception is translated into experience as knowledge. There it is. I have seen it. It is finished. I do not have to carry it with me. The next minute I am watching.

J: Why is there a watcher?

K: Look. Why does the brain insist on a continuity in knowledge? Why does the brain continue in the multiplicity of knowledge? Why does it keep on adding, multiplying: She was so kind; I did this yesterday. Why is this going on?

Look, sir, the brain cannot function in a healthy way, sanely, if it is not completely secure. Security means order. Without order the brain cannot function; it becomes neurotic. Like a child, it needs complete security. When a child is secure, when it feels at home, it is not frightened. Then it will grow up into a marvellous human being. So the brain needs security, and it has found security in knowledge. That is the only thing it can be secure in: experience as knowledge, which acts as the future guide. So the brain, needing security, finds it in knowledge, in belief, in the family.

A: The traditionalists provide that security through knowledge.

K: The mind wants security. If the professional said: *I really do not know*, he would not be a professional.

A: And yet security at a certain level is essential.

K: One has to negate the *Gītā*, the *Bible*, the guru—the whole thing. One has to negate all the constructions that thought has put together. One has to wipe all that away and say: *I do not know; I do not know a thing*. One has to say: I will not say a thing I do not know; I will not repeat a thing somebody else has said. *Then* you begin.

Madras
4 January, 1970

CONFLICT AND CONSCIOUSNESS

Dialogue 14

A: You say that memory is the function of the brain cells. Do the brain cells, as a source of the intellect, have any valid part to play in their own silencing?

K: We were talking yesterday of why knowledge has been made important as a way of enlightenment. Apparently every religious teacher has insisted on knowledge, not only in the East but also in the West. And as tradition is so strong in this country, it is really necessary to find out what part this whole systematized thinking plays in attaining enlightenment. What part does environmental conditioning play in enlightenment? How does culture, the conditioning by culture, come into being? You must cover the whole field. Take a traditional outlook like that of Nāgārjuna or Śaṅkara, and approach it from there.

A: The traditionalists say that all action, all activity, arises from causes, and that these causes are known.

K: You are making an incorrect statement: from a fixed cause to an effect. There is no such thing.

A: It starts with this *sūtra*: All these manifestations of behaviour, it is the Buddha who has given you the source of all these manifestations. If you know the cause, you can eliminate the cause. This is a statement of the Buddha. By understanding the cause you get rid of it, and he has told you the cause. All manifested thought or behaviour is within the field of cause-effect.

K: I question this. We see that what was the cause becomes the effect and what was the effect becomes the cause. The acorn produces an oak tree. We think that *karma* operates on this principle of cause-effect. But, if there were a fixed cause, everything would be fixed. Then there would be no explanation or inquiry possible. Now, is there a fixed point at all, or is there only a constant movement which the mind and brain are incapable of following, of living? And, so, the mind says that there is cause and effect, and the mind is held in that pattern.

A: Is there such a thing as cause-effect? If there is a chain of cause-effect, at any point you can hold it. To hold the chain at the point of the cause, at the point where the effect becomes the cause, that is the key to this.

K: Who is to hold it? You insulted me yesterday, that is the cause. The insult may have been the result of my previous insult to you, and in reacting again there are a series of actions, modifications going on all the time. You insult me; at that moment, if the mind is totally aware, there is no cause-effect at all. You insult me. The response to that insult is from the old brain which has divided itself and which has been functioning in a pattern. At the moment of insult, for the old brain not to respond, there must be complete attention. In that moment of attention there is no cause-effect.

A: If there is no attention, the response becomes the cause of another chain. Therefore, where an effect germinates itself into a new cause, it is there that action which is different comes.

K: I do not think so. I insulted you because of my unconscious neglect of you. It has hurt you, and you want to hurt me. The cause of my not greeting you may have been that I was interested in the birds, in the movement of their wings. I am an artist and I wanted to look at a bird in all its movements. So I failed to greet you. Where is the cause and where is the effect?

J: The cause is in oneself.

K: The observation of the movement is not in oneself.

J: Insult arises within me, not within you.

K: I have unintentionally given cause to insult you.

J: What makes me feel insulted is within me; cause and effect are within me.

K: You are saying: Though I did not greet you, the very fact of that insult was born in you; it was not given to you. I am not at all sure.

A: If I have affection for you and I see you watching the bird, I will understand, but if I do not have affection, then I will blame you. So causation is always within.

K: I see what you are saying.

A: It is not always a one-to-one relationship. Instead of saying that this cause arises within this person, the general law is as follows: Thus the whole thing arises within a matrix of not-knowing, *avidyā*. You now come to the focus of the 'I'. For in *avidyā* there are *saṁskāra*s, (tendencies) of all that man has done. From that there is consciousness, and out of consciousness naming arises. These lead to the body and the six senses. Then you see. But one cannot start from the point of 'I-see', and start only from there. Cause is used in a broad cosmic sense.

J: Śaṅkara says that you cannot say how ignorance began, and he denies causation. Cause-effect can be ended. Before you go any further you have to exhaust the intellect.

K: Is this part of Zen?

A: No sir, it is not. The awakening of intelligence is not *sui generis*.

J: You cannot bypass the intellect. We do not know how the process began, but we can end it.

K: From the unitary cell untill man appeared, it moves on.

A: The biologist does not go beyond manifestation. To assume it is wrong.

K: There is ignorance, and there is also perception, sensation.

A: *Saṁskāra* is that which is 'put together'.

K: Put together in time, which means evolution.

A: Then you come to the next point, *vijñāna*, which is consciousness.

K: Is consciousness different from *saṁskāra*? That which has been put together is consciousness.

A: No sir, it is the matrix. Within that matrix there is your consciousness, my consciousness.

K: Let us find out.

A: The matrix is common to all of us.

K: *Saṁskāra*, you say, means something put together.

A: Literally it means 'tendencies'.

K: I am asking: What is consciousness? Consciousness is made up of its content. Without the content, is there consciousness at all? The content of consciousness is consciousness; the content has been accumulating for centuries.

A: Is content all or is it a segment of consciousness?

K: I see that all my conditioning makes for consciousness.

A: Man has existed for many, many years. Before his consciousness came into being, the matrix was already there.

K: Thought began with the unitary cell. Man has lived for more than thirty-five thousand years; during that time he has collected all kinds of experiences. All that is consciousness.

A: Out of this has come consciousness.

K: I do not separate the two. There is no separation of the two. If there is no content, there is no consciousness. In consciousness there are many fragments; it is not one solid content. There are different levels, activities, attitudes, characteristics—all that is total consciousness. One part of that total consciousness, a fragment, assumes importance. Then it says: I am consciousness, I am not consciousness; I am this, I am not this.

A: You have made a distinction between consciousness which has different levels and that point at which it says: I am different. At that point it becomes different.

R: 'I and not-I'—the division is there.

A: Then there is a difference between the matrix and the self.

K: Look, the content of consciousness is consciousness. Without the content there is no consciousness. The content is made up of various divisions—my family, your family, and all that; it is made up of fragments. One of the fragments assumes importance over all other fragments.

R: The classical way of saying this is: The reflection imagines it is the prototype.

A: The moment there is the focus, individualization starts.

K: Be careful. This is very important. The word 'individual' means 'one who is indivisible in himself; one who is not fragmented'. So one fragment assumes the authority, the power to criticize; it becomes the censor—all within the area which we call consciousness.

A: In the case of consciousness as the not-identified, what happens?

K: I don't know a thing about identification.

A: The significance of identification is that I begin to identify myself with the part. That is the point of separation.

K: Do not assert anything. The content of consciousness is consciousness; when there is no content there is no consciousness. In that content there are tremendous factors of conflict, of fragmentation: one fragment assumes authority; one fragment feels insecure, it does not identify with any fragment; another does identify itself when it says: I like this and I don't like this. There are such vast conflicts there.

R: What is that 'I'?

A: It is my own past.

J: 'I' is the fragment.

A: Buddha said that the 'I' is the totality of all impressions; it is the complex of impressions which has created an identity for itself, but which has no true identity.

R: There is consciousness, and it has immense diversity.

K: There are many fragments. How is it that one fragment becomes important, and the importance then goes on? (*pause*) I see something. In this whole field of fragmentation which is consciousness, when does the 'I' come into being?

A: Is it not implied in the field of consciousness itself? The 'I' which comes out of it is latent in it.

K: There are all these fragments. Why does the mind not leave them alone? I see that my consciousness is made up of various fragments. Why does it not leave them alone? What takes place?

A: Identification.

K: There is fragmentation, contradiction and there is conflict. Within that conflict is the desire to end conflict.

A: Where there is conflict, if I am not identified, it does not affect me. At that point it does not become conflict.

K: There is only conflict, opposition, contradiction in consciousness. Where there is opposition, contradiction, that is the field of conflict. Where there are fragments, each fragment will produce conflict, pain, pleasure, sorrow, agony, despair. That is the field. Then what takes place?

A: I want to end it.

K: Here this whole structure of consciousness is a battlefield.

A: Why do you say so? Consciousness is full of irreconcilables. The moment I use the word 'conflict', I have identified myself.

K: This field of consciousness, being divided, is the source of conflict—India and Pakistan; I am a Hindu and you are a Muslim. The fact is that division inevitably brings conflict.

A: That is so till you come to the point of naming; naming changes the quality.

K: Look at the field of conflict. There is division. Where there is division there must inevitably be conflict—my family, your family; my God, your God.

A: Does every divided fragment become aware?

K: I see the fact that where there is division there must be conflict. In this consciousness where there are so many fragments, there must be conflict. In the phenomenal world he is a Hindu and I am a Muslim, and that is breeding war and hatred. This is a simple, straight phenomenon. We all talk of unity and keep on with our divisions.

See, sir, what takes place. In this field there is conflict, contradiction, fragmentation, division. When the conflict becomes acute, then comes the 'me' and the 'you', otherwise I leave it alone. I float along in this conflict, but the moment conflict becomes acute there is war. In the Hindu-Muslim war, I am a Hindu and you are a Muslim. And so identification takes place with something which I think is greater—with God, with nations, with ideas.

So long as the conflict is mild, I leave it alone. Observe the world around. Everybody goes along walking as if in a dream, and then Pakistan attacks; you are identified.

My point is, as long as there is no conflict, there is no 'I'. We are saying, therefore, that conflict is the measure of the 'I'. There was no conflict yesterday, there is conflict today, and I hope there will not be conflict tomorrow. This movement is the 'I'. This is the essence of the 'I'.

A: There are many other facets.

K: Is the tree different from the branches, even if it has ten hundred branches? The structure of consciousness is based on this conflict. We are not discussing how to end conflict.

R: The traditional view is: Division is the 'I', and the separation from the conflict is also the 'I'.

A: As long as conflict is hidden, not observed, the 'I' is not.

R: Does this all begin here, or does the arising of the 'I' go deeper?

K: Is there a self, the 'I', which is to be studied, or is the 'I' a movement?

A: You say that the 'I' begins as a movement in consciousness.

K: No. There is an assumption that the 'I' is static. Is it so? Is the 'I' something to be learnt about? Or is the 'I' a movement? Do I learn *about* something or do I learn in movement? The former is non-existent; it is fallacious; it is an invention. So the central fact is division. It is the source of all conflict. The conflict may take different shapes, exist at different levels, but it is the same. Conflict may be pleasant—I may like to be bullied, to be beaten by my wife; but that pleasure is a part of the structure of conflict.

R: The nature of consciousness is conflict.

K: It is not its nature; consciousness *is* conflict. If I have no conflict, what happens to me?

A: You say that there is no 'I' if there is no conflict. Does that mean that the state of non-conflict is non-consciousness?

R: The state of non-conflict is beyond conflict. The dimension in which we live is conflict.

A: Sir, I said that the intensification of conflict includes naming.

K: All naming is included in this. The average man swims along till a conflict becomes acute.

A: When conflict becomes acute, then naming starts.

K: What is naming? Why do we need naming at all? Why do I say: My wife? Why? Investigate it.

A: At one level it is for communication, at another level it is subtle.

K: Why do I say: She is my wife?

A: Because I want a continuity in that.

K: Sir, why do I say: *My* wife?

A: Because of security—I want to hold on to her.

K: Look, I say the word is not the thing; it never is. The word is only a means of communication. The fact is not the word. The fact that she is my wife is legally true, but what have I done when I say it? Why have I named it?—To give continuity, to strengthen the image that I have built? I possess her or she possesses me—for sex, for comfort and so on. All these strengthen the image about her. The image is there to establish her as mine. In the meanwhile, she is changing, is looking at another man. I do not acknowledge her freedom, and I do not acknowledge freedom at all for myself. So, what have I done when I say that she is my wife?

A: You are saying that we do not like movement, that we like everything static.

K: I want to possess her, and that is why I need her. The brain cells establish a pattern of habit and refuse to leave habit.

A: I want to understand what you are saying—that our entire consciousness is words, is knowledge.

K: Knowledge is put together; it is a process. A process implies time. Time implies thought. So through thought, through knowledge, through time, you are trying to find something which is out of time, which is not knowledge, which is not thought. You cannot.

A: The whole process which we have described must also be non-verbal.

K: We use words to communicate, to share together something common between two people. The common factor between human beings is despair, agony, sorrow. Can this be dispelled through time or can it be dispelled instantly? Is this process to be ended with words or without words? The word is not the thing. You may describe the most marvellous food, but the description is not the food. The word is not the thing, but we have to use the word in order to understand the thing. Why do we make words so important?

A: In order for communication to take place, there have to be words.

K: When does communication, the sharing together of a common problem, take place?

A: It can take place non-verbally.

K: To me, communication means sharing together, thinking together, creating together, understanding. When are we together? Surely not on the verbal level alone. We are together to share the problem when we are tremendously vital, passionate at the same level with the same intensity. When does this happen? It happens when you love something. When you love—it is finished. I kiss you, and I hold your hand; it is finished. When we lack *that thing*, we spin around with words. I am sure all the professionals miss that.

So our problem is how to meet, to come together at the same time, at the same level, with the same intensity. That is the real question. We do that when there is sex which we call love. Otherwise you battle for yourself, and I battle for myself. This is the problem. Can I, who am in sorrow, say: Let us come together, let us talk it over, and not talk of what Nāgārjuna, Śaṅkara and others say?

Madras
5 January, 1971

THE NATURE OF EXPLORATION

Dialogue 15

A: All our lives we have been thinking in terms of causes, and operating on causes, finding out the cause and trying to control the cause. But even when we know the cause, we cannot operate on it. This is a part of our experience. However, the Buddha discovered the cause of suffering and was liberated from suffering. Now, you say that the cause is the effect and that the effect is the cause, and you also point out that in this, in cause and effect, time is inescapable. But even after listening to you, the impact of causes and the operating on causes is still an integral part of our thinking. Can we go into it?

K: What is the question?

A: To explore the validity of the cause-effect sequence in respect of understanding.

K: What does it mean—'to explore'? What is the state of the mind which explores? You say that all action has a cause, that cause effects action, and that without understanding causes, do what you will, action will always be limited. So you say: Explore the cause of action, understand it and, thereby, bring about a mutation in action.

I do not know the cause of action. There may be obvious causes, and there may be other causes which cannot be discovered by the conscious mind. I can see the superficial causes, but these superficial causes have very deep roots in the recesses of one's own being.

Now, can the conscious mind not only examine the superficial, but also uncover the deeper? Can the conscious mind ever examine the deeper layers? And what is the state of the mind which explores? These three questions are important. Otherwise discovering the cause has no meaning.

R: You explore when you do not know.

K: We first asked the question: What is the quality of the mind which is exploring? Before I begin to explore, I must find out the state of the mind which explores. You say that the Buddha said this, and that somebody else said that, but I say that you must first find the quality of the mind that has the capacity to explore. What is the 'I' which explores? Is it crooked, far-sighted, myopic? Have you a mind that is free from conclusions? Otherwise you cannot explore.

A: We have unconfessed postulates and we see and drop them.

K: What you are doing is analysing step by step. What takes place when you analyse? There is the analyser and the thing which is being analysed. The analyser has to be extremely clear-sighted in order to analyse. If his analysis is twisted, the analysis is not worth a straw. The analytical process implies time. In inquiring through time, distorting factors enter. The way of analysis is entirely wrong; there has to be a dropping away of analysis.

J: I am confused.

K: Yes, it is a fact that we are confused. We do not know what to do and we begin to analyse.

A: The process of analysis is to us something concrete. You said: When you operate on a cause, some other factors enter. Does it mean that the analysis of the problem becomes inconsequential?

K: I think the whole process is wrong. I am concerned with this action which is put together by a series of analytical examinations and analytical implications in which time is involved. By the time I find what I sought, I am either exhausted or dead. It is difficult to examine, to analyse the hidden layers with the conscious mind. So I feel that this whole intellectual process is wrong. I say this without any disrespect.

A: The intellect is the only tool of examination that we have. The intellect has the capacity to collect, to recollect, to foresee, to analyse. It is only a fragment. Therefore, the examination of the mind by a fragment can only bring about a fragmentary understanding. What can we do?

R: I cannot do anything.

K: You say that the intellect is the only instrument one has with the capacity to examine. Has it? Has the intellect the capacity to examine? And, if so, does it not do so only partially? I see that the intellect, being partial, can examine only partially. I see the truth of that—not as a conclusion, not as an opinion, but I see it as a fact. Therefore I no longer use the intellect.

A: Such a mind can lapse into belief. You are saying that the mind senses this. When the mind superficially turns away from analysis, it falls into other traps. So this has to be done rigorously, with the intellect.

K: Analysis is not the way.

A: With what instrument do we explore? Our reason must corroborate what you say.

J: You arrive there by some path which is not analytical. We see the logic of it.

K: I tell you that analysis is not the way of understanding. Using reason, I give you the logical sequences—all that is only an explanation. Why don't you see the truth that analysis is not the way of understanding?

A: What you say is logical.

K: Somebody tells you that your approach is false because it is based on the intellect which is partial, and that partial examination is no examination at all. What you have done is to come to a conclusion based on logic; we are not talking of logic. Logic has led you to analysis.

A: It is partial analysis.

K: It is like saying that I love my wife partially.

A: We are using the same instruments here that we have developed in order to understand the outer environment, to understand nature. But they are inadequate in this area.

K: They are not adequate. The analytic process involves time. As it involves time, it must be partial. The partial is brought about by the intellect, because the intellect is part of the whole structure.

A: What is the instrument which explores when you put the question? When we put the question, we go back to the intellect.

K: You began by saying that the intellect is the only instrument of examination. I say that the intellect is partial and, therefore, your examination will be lop-sided. Therefore, your examination is invalid.

A: It is very clear that the intellect is partial and cannot see, but it starts working through habit.

K: A began by speaking of cause-effect, effect-cause—those are processes of analysis. Analysis implies time, and in such analysis there is the analyser and the analysed. The analyser must be free from past accretions, otherwise he cannot analyse. As he cannot be free of the past, analysis has no validity.Seeing that, I say it is finished. Therefore, I am looking for another way.

A: This is the shortest summary—with logic, logic is wiped out.

K: I see that analysis is not the way. That perception frees the mind from a false process altogether. So the mind is much more vital. It is like a man walking with a heavy burden, and the heavy burden is removed.

A: But with us the burden comes back.

K: The moment you perceive something to be true, how can it return? The moment you see that the snake is dangerous, you do not go back to the snake.

A: Nāgārjuna says: If you see what I am saying as a concept, you are finished.

J: Is there some other way?

A: You say something. The moment you say something, the instrument stops operating, because that instrument is not going to say anything more.

K: But that instrument is very sharp, very clear; it abstains from partial action.

A: If it is constantly watching, it can operate.

K: No, sir, the whole analytical process is finished.

A: When we have gone through this—

K: No, we are not exploring. I am showing you how to explore.

What you have done is to use the intellect, a partial instrument. And you thought that was the complete answer. See how the mind has deceived itself, how it says: I have analysed all this. But it has not *seen* how partial it is and, therefore, how valueless. The intellect has itself become valueless as an instrument of examination. I am asking myself: If the intellect is not the instrument of examination, what takes place?

A: One feels the need for support, for help, for some prop when one comes to this point.

K: The fact is that the intellect is an incomplete instrument and cannot understand a movement which is total. Then what is examination? If the intellect cannot explore, what is the instrument that can explore? What do Śaṅkara, Nāgārjuna, the Buddha say about this? Do they deny the intellect?

A: They say: Explore with the help of the *terra firma*.

K: That is, with partial vitality, partial energy, explore the whole energy. How can this be? Why have they said this?

R: The Vedāntic concept is that you cannot see with the intellect; but with the *ātman* or the Self, which is of the very nature of perception, you can see.

A: As our minds have been heavily conditioned, when we find a support we hold on to it.

K: We find that analysis and the way of the intellect are not exploration at all. It is like going partially into a tunnel. What is the quality of the mind if the intellect is not an instrument of exploration?

A: When the intellect is put aside, the mind has nothing of the past in it.

K: Who is it that has to put aside the intellect? You are back again in the dualistic process.

A: We see that the intellect is partial.

K: That is why we ask: What is the quality of the mind, of the whole psychophysical organism, that can explore? What is the quality of that mind which sees that any partial movement is incomplete and, therefore, will not get anywhere? It sees that partial seeing is no seeing at all and, therefore, it has finished with it; it is completely over. The mind then asks: What is the nature of total perception? And, is it only such a total perception that can examine? For, it may not need to examine anything at all, because that which has to be examined is of the partial field of division, analysis and exploration.

I am asking what that total perception is. What is the quality of total perception?

A: Movement of any kind cannot be total perception.

K: What is total perception?

R: It seems as if there is no instrument, because an instrument belongs to something.

K: What is the difficulty? When you look out of the window and see these bushes, how are you looking at them? Usually you are thinking about something, and at the same time you are looking. I say that you have to look. That is all. When I look at a painting, I do not say that the painter is so and so; that he is better than somebody else. I have no measure, I do not verbalize. We said just now that partial looking is not looking at all. Therefore the mind has finished with the partial. When I look, I look.

R: The element of habit is so strong in us.

K: The mind which is caught in habit cannot explore. So we have to examine the mind which is caught in habit, understand habit. Forget exploration, causation, analysis. Let us tackle that.

A: But whatever you say with your intellect is partial.

K: See the truth of it, not the logic of it. You can supply the logic later. What you thought was the door is not the door. You will not move towards it once you see this. But you do not see.

R: What is the difference between perception and recognition? For us perception has the form of recognition.

K: Because you recognize through association; recognition is part of the habit of association. And I am saying that you cannot examine, explore with a mind which is caught in habit. Therefore, discover the mechanism of habit. Don't concern yourself with exploration.

A: Habits are grooves.

K: How have habits been formed? That is the door; I am going through that door. Now, why does the mind fall into habit? Is it because that that is the easiest way to function? Is it because that in habit there is no friction?—I do not have to think about it. I get up at six, and go to bed at nine.

A: I look at a tree. I do not think about it, and yet the mind says that it is a tree.

K: It is a habit. The mind falls into habit because that is the easiest way to live; it is easy to live mechanically. Sexually and in every other way it is easy to live that way. I can live life without effort, without change, because in habit I find complete security. In habit there is no examination, no searching, no asking.

R: I live within the field of habit.

K: So habit can only function within a very small field, like a professor who is an expert in his speciality, but functions in a very small field. Like a monk who operates within a small cell and lives in a pattern, the mind wanting security lives in a pattern, without change. All this is partial examination; it does not free the mind from pattern. So what shall I do?

A: Having seen this, knowing that partial understanding is no understanding, how does the mind totally free itself from habit?

K: I am going to show you.

A: We have examined habit, but the mind does not get out of it.

K: You will never go back to the analysis of habit; you are no longer going to examine the causes of habit. So the mind is free of the burden of analysis, which is part of habit. So you have got rid of it. Habit is not only symptomatic of something, it is psychosomatic. When we have examined it in the way we have, it is over.

A: We are still not free of habit.

K: Because you are still insisting that the door is there. You started out saying: I know. There is a certain sense of arrogance in that. You do not say: I want to find out.

What is total perception when the mind is free of habit? Habit implies conclusions, formulas, ideas, principles. *Habit is the very essence of the observer.*

R: It is all that we know of the 'I'.

K: I go to the book to find out. And that is where the damage is done, the damage established by other people—the Śaṅkaras, the Buddhas and all the rest. I prefer this guru, I prefer that one; I argue; I will not let go because my vanity is involved. Do you know the cartoon which is captioned: My guru has more enlightenment than yours?

Therefore, sir, humility is necessary. I know absolutely nothing. And I am not going to repeat a word of anything which I have not found for myself. I really do not want to know anything more. That is all. The door which I thought was real is not the door. What happens then? I do not move in that direction; I will find out.

Madras
7 January, 1971

ORDER AND IDEATION

Dialogue 16

A: The greatest hindrances to perception are ideas. What is the difference between fact and the idea about the fact?

K: How do the professionals regard perception, the seeing—the act?

R: In Vedānta, it is said that consciousness acts through the sense organs. Consciousness takes the form of the object, like water taking the shape of the vessel. That is perception.

K: What is perception, the seeing, to you? You see the chest of drawers; you have the image of the chest of drawers, therefore, you recognize it as the chest of drawers. When you see that piece of furniture, do you have the image first or do you see first, have the image and then recognize?

R: Instantaneously the image arises, then we call it a chest of drawers.

A: There is seeing, and immediate naming.

K: So I do not have the image first. There is seeing, association, recognition, naming. I do not start with the naming, the image. That is fairly easy. I see you this morning. I saw you yesterday and, therefore, there is an image of you. So that image is you. Is there a difference between the physical object of perception and its mental image?

A: There is a difference between the two. In the case of an object, there is an image of a shape; the other is an image created by reactions which are not merely of form and shape.

K: Take a simple example like a snake, the brain cells are conditioned to snakes; they know that snakes are dangerous. The brain is conditioned from childhood to the danger of a snake and so it reacts. The child, not realizing the danger, may not react, but the mother comes along and tells it. When you name something, a picture is formed in the brain. The brain becomes conditioned and, in a certain environment, the name is called up.

A: The question therefore is—before seeing the fact, the idea about the fact arises, which may not necessarily be factual.

K: Are you saying that when one feels angry, the naming of the feeling strengthens it?

A: I have quarrelled with my brother, and I am on my guard whenever I meet him. So I am unable to really see him; I only see an idea I have of him.

R: The brain cells carry the image of the hurt.

K: There is anger. At the moment of anger, there is no naming. A second later, I call the feeling 'anger'. To name the feeling 'anger' is to record the fact of anger and to strengthen the past, the memory which has recognized that feeling as anger.

R: This is different from naming.

K: We are coming to that. I see a person with whom I'm angry and then the emotional reactions set in. At the moment of anger there is no naming, but it is there a second later. Why do we name? Why do we say: I am angry? Why is there the need to put it into words? Or, is naming merely habit, an instant response?

A: A defence mechanism starts to operate. The recognition itself is creating a situation which says: I do not want to get into conflict.

K: Naming as a process of self-defence is one part of it. Why does one name a particular reaction?

R: Otherwise one would not feel that one existed.

A: If I did not name, there would not be continuity.

K: Why does the mind give it continuity?

R: To feel that it exists.

K: What exists—the feeling of anger? Why has naming become so important? I name my house, my wife, my child. Naming strengthens the 'me'. What would happen if I did not name the anger I feel? The anger would be over.

Why should there be continuity? Why does the mind operate in continuity? Why is there this constant verbalization?

A: Verbalization establishes a residue.

K: But why do we do this? Giving continuity to the feeling of anger, not ending the feeling may be a habit. It indicates that the mind needs occupation. Now, why does the mind demand to be occupied?—with sex, with God, with money. Why?

A: The mind needs stimulating. If there is no stimulus, it will fall asleep.

K: Is that so? Is this constant preoccupation not putting the mind to sleep?

A: Then why does not the mind slacken when it is not occupied?

K: On the contrary, the moment we begin to inquire why there is this necessity for constant occupation, the mind is already alive.

A: Mere absence of occupation is not sufficient to keep the mind alive.

K: Of course. There are many who get duller day by day without any occupation. But the question is: Why does your mind want to be constantly occupied? Is it because it will go to sleep if it is not? Or, is it the fear of emptiness that makes the mind want to be occupied?

I am inquiring. It is only the mind which is not occupied that can inquire. In inquiring, the mind is awake. Most of us fall into habits which prevent looking: I am a Hindu, and for the rest of my life I remain a Hindu; you are a Muslim, and for the rest of your life you are a Muslim. But if I ask myself why I am a Hindu, I open the door to the inquiry. Naming may be part of this fear of not knowing what to do.

A: Fear of not leaving the shore of the known.

K: So, can the mind observe the reaction called anger, not name it, and so be finished with it? If the mind does that, then there is no carrying over of the anger. When the reaction which I have named 'anger' arises next, it has quite a different meaning, a different quality.

A: Our difficulty is that we meet anger with ideas.

K: Why do we have ideas and formulas? Let us begin again. We know the conditioned response, the naming and so on. Now we see that naming is a factor which gives continuity to anger. I see the truth of that. So I do not name. Just as I see the danger of the snake and do not touch it, I do not touch this either. So naming is finished, and anger undergoes a change.

R: It seems as if during the moment when we are capable of observing anger, anger disappears. Anger exists in the moment when we are not capable of observing.

K: No. You call me a fool, and I get angry because I do not like your calling me a fool. I see that. I see the falsity of naming. So where is the response? Instead of naming, this happens instantly. Therefore there is no hurt at all. We first have ideas and then we perceive and act.

A: Instead of the one act of perception we have our deep conditioning. Cultural, sociological, and anthropological conditioning together create a ready frame of reference which gives us security.

K: Why do you do this, sir?

R: We have been brought up that way.

K: That is not good enough. Do you know why we do this? We know that it is economically and sociologically beneficial. Tribalism still persists; it is tremendously important. Step out of the patterns, the formulas—of Hinduism, of Islam—and you will see what happens. Personally I have no formulas. Why do you have them? Find out.

Formulas, which are patterns, give us safe conduct in action. We lay down the line according to which we act, and in that there is safety. So fear of insecurity must be one reason why we have formulas, ideas. The mind wants to be certain; the brain cells function perfectly only when there is complete security. I wonder whether you have yourself not noticed that the brain cells function only when there is order. And there is order in a formula.

A: Do you mean that physiologically we have an in-built need for order?

K: Even physiologically speaking, the organism rebels if you do not have a certain type of order. Order is essential. Have you not noticed that before going to sleep the brain tries to establish order, saying: I should not have done this; I should not have said that? And, unless you establish order before going to sleep, the brain creates its own order. These are all facts.

Formulas are one of the safest ways of conducting one's life without disorder. They are necessary for a mind that wants order, that hopes to find order. What happens to the mind which finds safety in gurus or in various forms of tribalism?—the Brahmin tribe, the Hindu tribe, or the Indian tribe. To call yourself an Indian is to be safe. To belong to Jehovah is to be treated as one belonging to a group. As long as I belong to some sect, to some guru, I am safe. What happens when I have my formula and you have your formula, when I am a Hindu and you are a Muslim? There is division; therefore insecurity.

The brain demands order, it demands security; otherwise it cannot function properly. It uses formulas as a means to order. Seeking order through formulas creates division and disorder. Once I see the real danger in all this, what happens? Then I do not seek security in formulas; then I inquire whether there is safety in any other direction, and whether there is any such thing as safety at all.

A: But the brain needs safety.

K: The brain must have order.

A: Order is not safety.

K: Order is safety; order is harmony. But the very search for order ends in disorder. Seeing this, I drop all formulas: I am no longer a Hindu, a Buddhist, a Muslim. Drop all this. The dropping is intelligence; in the very act of dropping, the mind has become intelligent. Intelligence is order. I do not know if you see this.

In enlightenment there is order. The brain functions in a perfect condition, and relationship has a different meaning.

The brain is seeking order in disorder. It does not see the nature of disorder. When the brain rejects formulas, when it rejects tribalism, in that very rejection there is intelligence. And intelligence is order.

Madras
8 January, 1971

OBJECT, KNOWLEDGE AND PERCEPTION

Dialogue 17

A: I think we should go into the question of the perception of beauty. You said the other day that the tradition had ignored the field of beauty. We need to explore this.

K: So, what is the question? What is the perception of beauty? Do you mean perception and then beauty? Surely it is not perception and beauty, but perception. What would be the traditional approach to this?

R: One source of tradition maintains that beauty is the sense of happiness which comes when there is the ending of the desire or the thirst for experience.

K: Is this a theory or a reality?

R: The writer expressed what he felt; after all, he wrote a long time ago and only fragments of his writings remain.

A: Kālidāsa says that the experience of beauty is new every moment.

R: Both in India and Greece there was this feeling that ultimate perceptions are perceptions of beauty, truth and goodness.

K: Are we discussing beauty or perception? We will start with perception. What is the traditional approach to perception?

R: They talk about it at length, and there are many contradictory viewpoints.

A: Perception is *pratyakṣam*—seeing the self-nature of things, their essential quality.

K: Seeing the essence of something is perception, is that it? I am not talking of what you see, but of the act of seeing. Do they talk about the act of seeing and not of what is seen?

R: They speak about valid knowledge and about knowledge which is not valid.

K: Seeing is one thing and seeing something is another. Which is it that they are talking about—seeing *per se* or seeing something?

A: I think it is seeing. They are concerned with the constant danger of seeing wrongly.

K: No. We are not talking of seeing rightly or wrongly, nor of what you see—the chair, the rope, the snake—but of what perception is.

A: Is there a difference between seeing and knowing?

K: Seeing, knowing and seeing the object. Seeing the object through the image, through the symbol, is entirely different from seeing. What do they say about seeing?

R: They do not discuss it this way.

K: Hunger is in itself; it is not related to food. You eat food because you are hungry, but the nature of hunger is hunger. What is seeing, perceiving to you?—not seeing the object, but the quality of the mind that perceives. Seeing the object with the eyes is one thing, seeing with knowledge is another. I am talking about seeing in itself. Is there a seeing without knowledge, without the object? I see that cupboard. Seeing that is with the word and with knowledge; the word being associated with the cupboard. So we have a seeing which is the seeing of an object through knowledge, through the image, through the symbol, through the word, that is, through the intellect. Now, is there a seeing without knowledge and the image, that is, a seeing without the object?

A: What is seeing without an object? One can see without knowledge, as you say. There is a cupboard. Even if we had no image of it, it would still be there—a cupboard. Which means, it is an object.

K: There is the little sapling and, whether I see it or not, it will grow into a tree. It is independent of my seeing. I can call it 'a mango' and, therefore, associate it with the species mango; but the mango will grow even if I do not see it.

R: Its existence has nothing to do with seeing—

A: The object exists without our seeing, but can such a perception exist without the object?

K: That tree continues to exist.

A: In Buddhist meditation they have referred to the sky when they talk about perception without an object. The sky is an object and yet not an object.

K: The dictionary meaning of 'perception' is 'to become aware of; to apprehend'. You see the cupboard, you have a preconception of it; and the mind identifies it as a cupboard. Is there seeing without preconception?—To look without the previous accumulation of prejudice, of memories of hurt, pleasure and pain. Only the mind that has no conclusions can see; the other cannot.

Is there a looking without an object, without the knowledge of the object? Of course there is. A film director came to see me once. He described how he had taken LSD, and they had taped his reactions. He sat back on a chair waiting for the effect. At first nothing happened. Then he moved his position a little. Immediately the space between him and the object disappeared. Previously there was a space between him, the observer, and the thing he observed, which happened to be a flower. The moment space disappeared, it was not a flower but something extraordinary. This was the effect of the drug. But here it is different. The observer is the holder of knowledge, it is knowledge that recognizes the cupboard, and it is the observer who sees the cupboard. See what happens: The observer with his knowledge recognizes the cupboard; recognition implies previous knowledge. So the observer is knowledge as the past. Now we are asking if there is perception without the observer, that is, without knowledge, which is the past—perception *per se*, not about something.

R: If the knowledge of the past is not there, the observer is not there. If the observer is not there, knowledge of the past is not there.

K: Therefore, it is possible to see without the observer. I am saying 'possible'. The possibility becomes a theory. We should not deal with theories, but *see* that the observer is the residue of the past and, so, cannot possibly see except through the screen of the past; therefore his seeing is partial. For perception to be, the observer must not be. Is that possible?

R: What happens to an artist? Obviously he perceives with a perception which is not the ordinary perception which we have.

K: Now wait a minute. Is perception intellectual?

R: No; the intellect is the past.

K: Therefore, it is not the seeing of an artist or the non-artist that is at issue here, but the seeing without the past. The artist may see for a moment without the past, but he translates his perception.

R: It is a momentary perception.

K: Is there an act of perception without the observer? 'Act' means immediate action, not a continuous action. And the word 'act' means 'doing', not having done or will do.

Perception is action. It is not action in terms of the actor acting in accordance with his knowledge. Are the professionals concerned with action, or are they concerned with knowledge and action?

R: I do not know. There are some texts in which they have said that the perception of beauty is that moment when time, name, form and space do not exist.

K: We are not talking of beauty. Perception implies action. I know what action is when the observer acts—the observer, having learnt a particular language or technology, having acquired knowledge, acts.

A: Does perception mean direct contact between the sense-organ and an object?

R: Traditionalists talk about mediate and immediate perception. Mediate perception is through the instrument, through a medium, whereas immediate perception does not require the sense-organ with which to see. Perhaps immediate perception is nearer to what you are talking about.

K: You see that perception through knowledge is an action of the past. It is different from perception which is action.

A: Perception itself is action, so there is no time involved.

K: The time interval between action and knowledge—the knowledge is the observer—comes to an end. This action is not time-binding; the other is. So this is clear. Then what is beauty in relation to perception?

R: It is the ending of the desire for experience. This is what the traditionalists say.

K: Put aside goodness, love, truth. Now, what is beauty?

R: It is not mere perception, because perception can be of anything, even of that which isn't beautiful.

K: Do not bring in the ugly. Perception is action; perceiving is acting—leave it at that. We are talking of beauty. You have stated what the professionals have said about it. Let us forget what others have said. I want to find out what beauty is. We see a building or we read a poem, and we say: How beautiful it is. So we recognize beauty through an object.

Now put aside the object. If beauty is not in the expression, nor in the object, where is beauty then? Is it in the beholder?—the beholder is the observer. The observer with his past knowledge recognizes something to be beautiful because his culture has told him it is beautiful; his culture has conditioned him.

A: The woman who gives pleasure is beautiful, and when she does not give pleasure, she is no longer beautiful.

K: I discard expression, I discard the created object, and I discard the idea that beauty is in the eyes of the beholder. I have discarded everything that people have said about beauty, because I see that it is not in anything they have said. What has happened to the mind that has discarded thought—thought which is the creator of objects? What is the quality of the mind which has discarded all the ideas of the beautiful that have been put together by others? Obviously such a mind is very sensitive; it was carrying a burden before, now it is lighter.

R: You say that you have discarded the object and the thought which has created the object.

A: Thought is knowledge.

K: Thought is knowledge; it is accumulated through knowledge and through culture. Thought is the response of memory which has created the object. I discard all ideas about beauty—about beauty as truth, goodness and love. Perception is the action of discarding, of putting away—not, I-am-putting-away, but putting away. So the mind is now free. Freedom does not imply freedom from something; freedom is freedom. Then what happens? The mind is free, highly sensitive, no longer burdened by the past. In that mind there is no observer at all, which means there is no 'me' observing. The 'me-observing' is a very, very limited affair, because the 'me' as the observer is the past.

See what we have done. There is the object, there is knowledge and there is perception: through knowledge we recognize the object. We are asking the question: Is there perception without knowledge, without the observer? So we discard both the object and the knowledge. In perceiving is the act of discarding.

Again we ask: What is beauty? Beauty is generally associated with an object created by thought and by feeling. And we discard that.

Then I ask: What is the quality of the mind which discards? It is really free. Freedom implies a mind that is highly sensitive. In that act of discarding, the mind has brought about its own sensitivity. This means that in that act there is no centre. And without a centre as the observer, the sensitivity is without time. It is an intensely passionate state.

R: When both the object and the knowledge of the object are gone, there is no focus.

K: Do not use the word 'focus'. The mind, discarding what it is not, is free. The act of perceiving what it is not has released the mind, and the mind is free—not free from any object, but free.

A: The act of perceiving and discarding knowledge are instantaneous and simultaneous.

K: That is freedom. The act of perceiving has brought freedom—not freedom from something. When the mind is sensitive, there is the total abandonment of the self as the observer; there is no centre, no 'me' in it. Then the mind is full of energy because it is no longer caught in the divisions of pleasure and pain and sorrow. It is intensely passionate. And it is such a mind that sees what is beautiful.

I see something—that suffering is a partial activity of energy. Human beings have divided energy into fragments: energy as pleasure, energy as pain, going to the office, learning something.

When I hate somebody and I love somebody else, both involve energy. This fragmented energy, acting in opposite directions, breeds conflict. So all our ways of living are fragmented; each is fighting the other.

When there is no activity of the fragment, there is a complete focussing of energy. That energy, when it is a harmonious whole, is passion. That energy is the mind that is free, sensitive; in it the 'me' as the past is completely dissolved. That is beauty.

Madras
11 January, 1971

ENERGY AND FRAGMENTATION

Dialogue 18

A: After listening to yesterday's talk, I wonder what is meant by energy. In observing all the fields of my activity, I see that I know only fragmented energy, and I do not know what you are talking about.

K: There is physical energy, intellectual energy, emotional energy; there is the energy of anger, of greed. All these are forms of energy. Traditionally it has been said that sexual energy must be controlled.

A: Traditionalists hold that unless all dissipation of energy is halted, we cannot know the 'other'. It does not seem to be that way. There is no relationship between suppression and the negation you talk about. But the truth is that I only know fragmented energy.

K: The traditional approach may hold us to a particular pattern, to that energy which is fragmentary.

A: It may be because every form of energy we know is destructive: our intellectual energy creates systems and patterns; our emotional energy is a reaction against other individuals.

K: Did the speaker not say yesterday that all energy springs from one source of energy?

A: What you are saying comes from a different source. You say that the function of the intellect is to see that the intellect itself is fragmentary and, therefore, inadequate. When the intellect sees its inadequacy, that is the highest truth the intellect can perceive. And it is only when you come to this that there is the 'other'. All that we seem to know is fragmentary, and you are speaking of something else.

K: What will you do? How will you stop the fragmentation of energy?

A: I would not say 'how', because that action is itself a part of the process of becoming.

K: Then what will you do? How do the professionals, the traditionalists, approach this problem—that various forms of energy, contradicting each other, contend for power; that one form assumes the role of dictator and tries to control or suppress the rest? Do they introduce the *ātman* as a way out of the problem?

A: Nāgārjuna introduces *śūnyatā* or voidness. When fragmentation is eliminated, there is a void. In the void is everything. Did you come to this spontaneously?

K: What else do the professionals say?

A: Śaṅkara says: Acquire learning and the prestige that goes with learning—so what? Acquire wealth and the power that goes with it—so what? Visit many countries, feed and entertain your friends, help the poor and the sick, bathe in the Ganga, give alms in vast quantities, repeat mantras by the million, and so on—so what? All these are of no avail unless the Self is realized. And Śaṅkara ends by saying that the man who discovers that all these forms of prestigious action are bereft of significance for self-knowledge alone is capable of self-realization.

K: How has the question of fragmentation in consciousness been tackled by the professionals?

A: They distinguish the *citta* from *caitanya*; the common root here is *cit*.

N: *Cit* is consciousness.

A: Do they go into the fragmentary nature of the mind, or do they say that the activities of the mind are unreal?

K: What is the question we are trying to explore?

A: We only know the various fragmented expressions of energy. Is it possible to see the entire field? Or is this a wrong question?

K: If one fragment or many fragments exist, what is the entity that is going to observe the totality of energy? Are our minds so conditioned that we cannot break ourselves from the conditioning?

A: We are so conditioned.

R: The other day at the discussion you said that if someone slapped me, I'd feel hurt. But that if attention were given at that moment, then I would not feel hurt; there'd be no recording of it. But the fact is that reaction is instantaneous. When reaction is instantaneous, how is it possible to give attention at that moment?

K: (*pointing to the carpet*) There is this little bit of carpet which is a part of the whole carpet. I have been seeing only this fragment, and you say that this fragment could not exist without the whole carpet. My life is spent observing the fragment. Then you come along and say: This is part of the whole, this would not exist if the other did not exist. But I cannot take my eyes off this fragment. I agree that this can only exist because of the whole carpet, but I have never, never looked at the whole carpet. I have never moved away from this. My attention has been fixed on this little bit, and I do not know how to remove my eyes and look at the whole. If I could look at the whole, I would see that there is no duality, no contradiction. But if I say that I must suppress the fragment in order to see the whole, there is duality.

R: That much is intellectually clear.

K: First, I have to understand intellectually what is being said. The intellect, however, is only a part of the whole. You know that as long as perception is focussed on a fragment of the carpet, there is no perception of the whole carpet. You say that you can understand this intellectually, but then you have already moved away from the whole. You also see that the intellect is a fragment: you are looking at the whole with different parts. Therefore, deny the intellect. (*pause*)

You see, we are used to reading in straight lines. Therefore we always think in straight lines. If we read vertically like the Chinese do, then our thinking would be vertical. But whether we think horizontally or vertically, thinking itself is a linear process and, so, a form of fragmentation. So, what is the question? (*pause*) Is there a perception which is non-linear and, therefore, non-fragmentary?

How do you see something totally? What is the perception that sees the whole structure of human life, the whole field at a glance? Look, there is the whole field of life: the physical, the emotional, the intellectual, the psychosomatic. In that field of existence there are various contradictions: sex, no sex; God, no God; communism and so on; there is also sorrow, anxiety, guilt, humility, pride. Now, how does the mind see the whole of this field? If it does not see the whole field, but tackles merely one problem in the field, it will create mischief.

A: The seventy-five thousand years of human history has produced this; there is no going back.

K: First listen. There is the whole field of existence, which we have described. There are other factors also. Now, how do I look at this whole map with all its little bridges, hamlets and towns—all that—at one glance? I cannot go up in an aeroplane—the *ātman* is an aeroplane invented by thought.

You come along and tell me: Look, if you try to answer the whole problem of existence through one fragment, you will only create more confusion. You say to me: Therefore, see the whole of it. You say that and disappear. It is now my job to find out. How do I set about doing it? I do not know what this total perception is. I see the beauty, the logic and the sanity of what you say. How am I to proceed?

A: There is a very great intensity, and passion in all this because I feel it is a precipice. It is all there at this moment.

K: You have this problem; the baby is left in your lap. What are you going to do? You must answer. What is it that prevents total perception?

A: Intellectually, I realize that I cannot see the whole thing.

K: Leave it there. What is it that prevents the total perception of this vast, complex field of existence? Have you an answer? Find out. (*pause*) Look, when I enter a room, one object, a lovely bedspread, catches my eye. I look only casually at the other things in the room. I say that the colours and the design of the bedspread are beautiful; they give me great pleasure. What has happened? The eye catches one thing in this whole field. What is it that prevents my seeing other things? What is it that makes them shadowy and distant? Just listen.

R: The observer.

K: Go slowly. That one thing is beautiful, but my observation of everything else is vague; I catch one thing, the rest recedes. Why is it that one thing becomes important? Or, why has perception focussed merely on it? Why is the eye attracted to this only?

R: Because it is pleasant.

K: What does this element of pleasure mean—that in this whole field only one thing attracts me? It means that I translate the field into pleasure. In this vast field of existence, the one thing I seek is the maintenance of pleasure.

A: For most people life is painful.

K: It is painful because we think in terms of pleasure. The principle of pleasure is the central factor which prevents me from seeing the whole; I see the whole field of life, with all its complexities, in terms of pleasure or in terms of wanting pleasure. Doesn't that prevent total perception?

A: Śaṅkara says that the fear of pain is the thorn in the bush.

R: It is very complex. Here is the fragment. Our attention is on it. What is giving attention is a fragment, and what is wanting pleasure out of it is also a fragment.

K: We have said all this.

R: So, pleasure is a fragment.

K: No, no. I want pleasure through everything: through money, sex, position, through prestige, god, virtue and ideas; I want pleasure throughout my life. And I do not see that pleasure is the thorn. I do not see that. My drive is pleasure; therefore I create a society which will bring me pleasure. And that society has its morality which is always based on pleasure. Pleasure is the guiding factor in life—my perceptions are guided by it. And if that is so, how can I see the whole field which pleasure has brought about?

What is the salient factor of pleasure?—That it is always personal: my pleasure not yours. I may sacrifice my pleasure in collective work for the greater pleasure, but it is still pleasure. And pleasure is always personal. How can the mind see the whole field of existence when life has become a movement of pleasure?

A: Pleasure gives validity to everything.

K: It is important to see the whole, not merely the particular. As long as the mind is pursuing pleasure as the 'me', the particular exists. So how can I then see this whole thing?

There must be an understanding of pleasure; I must understand pleasure, not suppress or deny it or cut it off with the intellect.

A: It cannot be cut off.

K: What religions have taught, and what man has done is to cut off pleasure. What tortures the saints go through—the burning, the mutilation. That is the traditional way.

So, I see the central fact that when one thing in life becomes all-important, I do not see the whole. Then the question arises: Why is there this pursuit of pleasure? What do the professionals have to say about this?

A: They say that every pleasure leads to pain; to concentrate on pleasure or to concentrate on pain is the same thing.

K: Why has man pursued pleasure at any cost?

A: Because our biological needs are deeply ingrained.

K: There is nothing wrong with that. We need clean food, a clean floor to sleep on. What is wrong with that? But see what happens. Today's biological needs become tomorrow's pleasure when you say: I must have all this tomorrow. This happens when thought takes over. So thinking is the factor that one has to understand, not pleasure.

A: We have come to see that pleasure is transferred to thought.

K: Now you have got it. So before you do anything about pleasure, understand thinking.

A: The movement of thought as pleasure has to be understood.

K: No. It is thought itself which sustains this movement. The concern has always been: What shall I do with thought? How do I stop thinking about sex or food? How? That's all they have done: If you see a woman, think of her as a sister, or a mother, or as a diseased woman. Murderous crowd, really!

A: We started with energy. At this point it becomes fragmented.

K: Thought in essence is the maker of fragments. Tradition has talked about suppressing thought. Act, and forget it. Do not carry it over.

Madras
14 January, 1971

FREEDOM AND THE FIELD

Dialogue 19

A: You were saying that the brain cells themselves are conditioned by the past—the biological and historical past; and you said that the structure of the brain cells could change. Could we go into that? The brain cells seem to have an activity of their own.

K: I was going to ask, this morning, whether the professionals have ever talked of the brain cells.

R: The Indian philosophers do not mention the brain cells.

K: Why? Is it because that when they speak of the mind, they include the brain cells?

A: They say that the mind is matter. They do not go further.

K: Everything is recorded in the brain cells; every incident, every impression is imprinted in the brain. One can observe the vast number of impressions in oneself. You ask how it is possible to go beyond, to make the brain cells quiet.

A: Normally you would think that the brain would be an instrument of the intellect.

K: But is not the intellect the instrument of the brain rather than the other way?

A: Is it?

K: Let us investigate it. The capacity to reason, to compare, to weigh, to judge, to understand, to investigate, to rationalize and to act are all part of memory. The intellect formulates ideas and, from that, there is action.

A: The materialistic view is that thought is to the brain what bile is to the liver, and that the phenomenal manifestation is the result of the movement of the non-phenomenal. What the traditionalists say is that at death there is the complete cessation of the brain, but that the complete cessation of the brain leaves, in a subtle way, a residue.

K: A thought?

A: The residue exists independently of the brain which has become dead. Therefore, it creates another focus. Out of its activity, something new emerges.

K: The brain cells are the repository of memory. The reaction of memory is thought. Thought can be independent of memory. It is like throwing a stone, which is independent of the hand which throws it. Whether that thought incarnates is another matter.

A: I have a mug full of water; I pour the water into the bucket and then I take the water out again. But it is not the same water I threw in; it is much more than what I put in.

K: This is fairly simple. What are you trying to say?

R: The brain cells and their activity are not the ultimate source of all this false movement.

A: You bring us to action. Now, we are all the time involved in activity. In discussing with you, we see that activity leads to mischief. To see this is the beginning of action. Are we going to take it at the level of the brain cells or at the level of the residue which triggers the activity of the brain?

R: The traditional description is: I eat with my hands. There is a smell of food. I wash my hand, but the odour remains. So the experience during life leaves a residual impression. The body dies, but the odour of experience remains, which seeks more experience.

A: You were saying that the intellect itself is the result of the activity of the brain. But with the intellect I see what effect the accumulation of the past, as memory, has left on me. Even when the intellect sees this, the activity of the brain cells is in motion.

K: Are you trying to say that the brain cells are receiving all the time, that they are recording all the time, in the state of sleeping and in the state of waking? This recording is an independent movement. That independent movement creates the capacity to think, to rationalize. The intellect can then observe the operation of the movement of thought; it can observe how thought has created itself. And that is again part of the whole structure of the brain cells. What is the question?

A: How is the structure of the brain cells to change?

K: That is quite a different matter. The brain cells are recording all the time. Perception, design, colour—everything is being registered. One element assumes tremendous importance. And the brain cells, receiving impressions all the time, consciously or unconsciously, are building the capacity to think, to rationalize. The instrument of this rationalization is the intellect. The two are not separate.

A: Without the intellect, would there be rationalization?

K: Is the capacity to rationalize independent of the brain cells? Or, being a part of the brain, can it ever be independent? You cannot rationalize independently, because the brain cells and the intellect are part of cause-effect.

Can the intellect observe the background of memory, which is the brain? I believe modern scientists are trying to isolate the various cells which contain memories and to explore the cells, to investigate them under the microscope.

If the intellect is the product of the brain, the intellect must always be conditioned by memory, by knowledge. It can project very far, but it is still tethered. The intellect can seek freedom; it can never find it. It can be free only within the radius of its own tether; in itself it is limited. And freedom must be beyond the capacity of the intellect; it must be something outside the field.

Now, what is it that is aware of this whole phenomenon—that the intellect can never be free? It can think it is free and it can project an idea, but that is not freedom, because that is the product of the brain cells which are the residue of memory. What is it that is aware that the intellect cannot go beyond the range of its own radius? I do not know if you understand the question.

A: The intellect itself can be aware of this.

K: I do not know; I am asking.

R: The intellect is a fragment.

K: There is no freedom within the field. Therefore the intellect says that there must be freedom outside the field. It is still rationalizing and, therefore, its search outside is still within the field. Then what is it that is aware of the whole field? Is it still rationalization?

A: No.

K: That record has created an instrument which you call the intellect; it has the capacity to investigate, to explore, to criticize. The intellect sees that there is no freedom within the field and that freedom lies outside. So the intellect seeks freedom outside itself; it thinks it moves outside its own field.

A: The Buddhists say that this process, which has come into being with a cause, has an end, (namely, the perception of it as a dead-end.) They maintain that to see that nothing is permanent, to see that rebirth is a product of ignorance of the true nature of the *pudgala* (ego), to observe all this without any attachment, is the perception of the dead-end. All that one is to do is to contemplate, without attachment, the impermanence of everything which has a cause. The Buddha himself saw disease, old age and death only once. Seeing it once he never turned back. The boy Krishnamurti also never looked back. The Buddha said: See the impermanence of everything; in that seeing there is no effort. Krishnamurti just says: See.

K: Then what is the question? How are these recording instruments with their own capacity, their own movements, to switch off and enter a different dimension, even for a short period? You cannot go back to the *Upaniṣads*. In that is authority.

A: We come to the point where the intellect realizes that whatever it does is within the field. What follows from that?

K: You see, the dead-end man says that, and then stops there. But another dead-end man says: I must have something more; and so the *ātman* comes in.

A: The Buddhists said: There is no soul; that which putrefies will end; it will terminate. Do not get attached. That is all that you can do. The position leads to the void, or *śūnyatā*.

R: The Vedāntins also said the same thing.

A: They invented *māyā* (illusion) which absorbed the whole of their reasoning.

K: The distinction between the two is non-existent. The intellect itself says that its own movement is within this field. Is there any other movement? It does not say that there is or that there is not. It cannot rationalize, because if it says that there is, it is back in the same field—the positive or the negative.

The question then is: Is there a movement other than this movement?—For otherwise there is no freedom. A thing that functions from a centre, within its own radius—however wide—is never free. (*pause*) What is freedom?

A: When it is the intellect which asks the question whether there is another movement, I cannot know if there is.

K: I know this is a prison; I do not know what freedom is.

A: You have taken away one confusion, namely, that all is *māyā* (illusion). Tradition has made that a conclusion.

K: My question is: Is there freedom at all? Tradition would say: Yes, there is *mokṣa* (liberation). It is all so immature.

A: Faced with this question, I have absolutely no instrument now to deal with it.

K: No, you have the instrument of rationalization, which is the intellect. I am asking whether there is any validity in this inquiry. If there is no freedom within the field, then what is freedom?

A: The intellect can never know.

K: Do not say that it cannot know. The intellect can only know freedom within the field, like a man who knows freedom within a prison. It then asks: What is freedom? If this is not freedom, then what is? Is there such a thing at all? And if there is no such thing, let us make the best of this. As man can never be free, let us make the interior of the prison more perfect—more toilets, more hangers, more rooms.

But the intellect rejects the possibility that there can be no freedom, because it is inconceivable that there is no way out of this prison. The clever brain invents *māyā*, the *ātman*, *brahman*.

Now, I am asking myself: If there is no freedom, is the mind everlastingly condemned to live within this field? What is the point of it all? The communists, the materialists say that you cannot get out. (*pause*)

I have got it: I am not concerned whether the brain cells change or not. I see that this concern about freedom, freedom which is not a formula, which is not a conclusion, is not freedom. Right?

Then the mind says: If this is not freedom, what is freedom? Again it says: I do not know. But it sees that in that not-knowing there is an expectation to know. When I say: I do not know what freedom is, there is a waiting and an expectation to find out. The mind does not really mean that it does not know; it is waiting for something to happen. I see that and I discard that. (*pause*)

So I really do not know; I am not waiting, I am not hoping that some answer will come through an outside agency. I am not expecting a thing. There it is. There is the clue. I know that there is no freedom here. There is reformation, but no freedom. Reformation can never bring freedom.

Man revolts against the idea that he can never be free, that he is condemned to live in this world. It is not the intellect which revolts, but the whole organism, the whole perception. Right? Therefore he says: As this is not freedom, I really do not know what freedom is. *I really do not know*.

That not-knowing is freedom; knowing is prison. This is logically correct. I do not know what is going to happen tomorrow. I am therefore free of the past, free of the field. Knowledge of the field is prison; absence of knowledge of the field is also prison. So the mind that lives in a state of not-knowing is a free mind.

The traditionalists went wrong when they said: Don't be attached. You see, they denied all relationship; they could not solve the problem of relationship and, so, broke away from all relationships and withdrew into isolation. To live within the knowledge of this field is prison; not to know the prison is also not freedom. So a mind that lives in the known is always in prison. That is all. Can the mind say: I do not know? Which means that the yesterday has ended. For it is the knowledge of continuity which is the prison.

A: To pursue this requires ruthlessness.

K: Do not use the word 'ruthlessness'. On the contrary, it requires tremendous delicacy. When I say: I do not know, I really do not know. Full stop. See what that means. It means that there is a sense of real humility, a sense of austerity. Then yesterday has ended. The man who has ended the past is really beginning again. He has therefore to be austere. *I really do not know*—what a marvelous thing that is. I do not know if I will die tomorrow; therefore there are no conclusions, at any time; which means never to have any burdens. The burden is the knowing.

A: Can one come to this point and stay there?

K: You do not have to stay anywhere.

A: The mind has a way of switching back; words take you only to a point.

K: Go slowly. Do not put it that way. You see the man who speaks of detachment and the man who invents the *ātman*. I come along and say: Look, both are wrong. In this field there is no freedom. Then you ask: Is there freedom at all? I say: I really do not know. It does not mean that I have forgotten the past. In the I-do-not-know there is no inclusion of the past, or the discarding of the past, or a utilization of the past. All that it says is: In the past there is no freedom; the past is knowledge; the past is accumulation; the past is the intellect—there is no freedom in all that. When a man says: I really do not know, to the question: Is there freedom at all?—that man is free of the known.

R: But the structure of the brain cells remains.

K: They become extraordinarily flexible. Being flexible they can reject, accept; there is movement.

A: We can never reject activity. The normal day-to-day activity must go on.

K: Are you asking what action is to a man who does not know? The man who knows acts from knowledge, so his action is within that prison which is the field of the known. He projects that field into the future. Now, what is action to the other man who does not know? He does not even ask, *because he is acting*. He will have his meal in the afternoon; he will go for an evening walk—apart from that, all other action is total inaction to such a man.

You are missing something, which is, not to know whether there is a tomorrow. You see, the activist is committed, he is involved; his action is always mischievous. Action-in-relationship in the field of the known, is attachment-detachment, dominance-subservience. And life is relationship. Have the professionals talked about relationship?

R: No.

K: To them relationship meant attachment and, therefore, they said: Be detached. That may be the reason why the Indian belief in detachment has made the mind so repetitive and stupid. But one has to live in this world. Even in the Himalayas I need food, which people bring me; there is relationship.

A: In his first sermon the Buddha said that both detachment and attachment are ignoble. The two represented the Hindu idea of running away from the world.

K: Why did they not consider relationship? When the *sannyāsi* renounces the world, he cannot renounce relationship. He may not sleep with a woman, but he cannot renounce relationship. I am asking myself: If I deny relationship, doesn't action become meaningless? What is action without relationship? Is it something mechanical?

A: Action is relationship.

K: Relationship is the primary thing. Otherwise what exists? If my father had not slept with my mother, I would not exist. So relationship is the basic movement of life. But relationship within the field of knowledge is deadly, destructive, corrupt. *That is the worldly*.

So, what is action? We have separated action from relationship: social action, political action, but have not solved this problem of relationship. We discard it because it is too dangerous to discuss. If I discussed my relationship with my wife, untold things might happen. So I do not want to discuss it. All that I say is: I must be detached.

If we accept that all living is relationship, then what is action? There is the mechanical action of technology; to act mechanically is to reduce relationship to turning a wheel. And that is why we have denied love.

A: Can we examine our relationship with nature?

K: What is my relationship with nature?—with the birds, with the sky, the trees, the flowers and the moving waters. That is my life. We are discussing our relationship to everything, not just the relationship between man and woman. All this is part of life. I am talking of the relationship to everything.

I can be attached to the word, but not to the waters. You see, we miss the whole thing because we confuse the word with the thing.

A: Is it a question of re-awakening sensitivity?

K: No. The question is: What is relationship? What is it to be related to everything? Relationship means care; care means attention; attention means love. That is why relationship is the basis of everything. If you miss that, you miss the whole thing. Yes, sir, this is the prison. To know is the prison, and to live in the knowing is also the prison.

Madras
January 16, 1971

THE MATRIX OF TRADITION

Dialogue 20

B: In Buddhism they mention three categories of people in the world: the ordinary, worldly man who has his pleasures, pain, etc.; the path-winner, the person who has a glimpse of the direction; and the *arhat*. The worldly man might perform rituals, but he is still a worldly man till he has an experience, a glimpse of the direction. The path-winner wanders away but always comes back, till such time when there is no more going back to the first stage.

K: A man who is of the world has a glimpse of the path—how does he have it? And once he is on the path he may wander back and forth, wander and come back to the path and, finally, settle down and reach the state of being an *arhat*. Are you asking how the worldly man is to have a glimpse?

C: There is the concept of *sādhanā*, which is a method of attaining the spiritual goal.

K: Methods or systems imply a process in time.

C: It may not necessarily imply time.

K: If I have to go through the gate to attain a goal, then going through the gate implies a process of time. All *sādhanās* imply a process of time.

C: Tradition also says that *sādhanās* are useless.

K: Most people insist on *sādhanā*. Though they say it is not necessary, it has become part of the tradition.

B: They say that it is better to go through *sādhanā*, but they do not guarantee that you will reach the goal through the *sādhanā*.

K: The word *sādhanā* implies a process, and a process means things put together. And the putting together implies time. Even the most scientific concept of time recognizes that time is the putting of things in a horizontal or vertical position. So, *sādhanā* implies time. What is the question, sir? What does the tradition say?

B: The Buddhist tradition says that when a man in sorrow has a glimpse of the path, he is a path-winner. When he works out his salvation, he becomes an *arhat*.

C: They say that when you attain the non-dual state, there is no going back.

K: How do you come to it?

C: Since it is not a process, they do not say how you come to it. They put it negatively: You cannot come to it by studying, by listening to people, by ritual or by *sādhanā*.

K: Is it a question of duality? Being in the world implies a duality; there is then a glimpse of a non-dualistic state and again a getting back to the dualistic state.

C: They say that in reality there is no duality, but that the intellect creates a duality. Once non-duality is realized, there is no question of worldliness creeping in.

K: Living as they do in duality, will the negation of ritual get human beings to a state of non-duality? Does the tradition claim that there is a level in which there is no duality at all; and that a mind which is caught in a dualistic state will come to 'the other' by negating beliefs, rituals and so on?

Shall we approach this problem in a simple way? Human beings live in a state of duality in which there is sorrow, there is pain, there is conflict, and all that. And man asks how he can get out of it. The non-dualistic state is merely a theory, second-hand information, which he might have read about but does not know. Therefore it has no value. Disregard what others have said. I know only the state in which there is sorrow and pain. That is a fact, and that is from where I start.

C: Some people have conflict and misery and realize that the dualistic state is the cause of the trouble. So they want to get rid of it. Some do not start from this, but they feel discontented and read and, having read, they start imagining the non-dual state.

K: It is a theory. The fact is one thing and the idea about the fact is another. We are not concerned with the man who supplies a conclusion derived from a specialist. We are only discussing the man who is in conflict and who is discontented with that conflict. How does he get out of it?

C: The traditional way is to explore through books. Man attains by negating and resolves by knowledge.

K: Proceed step by step. I am in conflict. Now, how do I resolve it? You say by knowledge. What is knowledge?

C: The realization of conflict is knowledge.

K: I do not have to realize it; I am in conflict. I know I am in conflict, in pain, in sorrow. What do you mean by 'knowledge', and what do you mean by 'conflict'? To know that I am in conflict—is that knowledge? Or, do you call knowledge knowing what I should do about that conflict? When you use the word 'knowledge', what do you mean by that? What is the Sanskrit equivalent of that word?

C: *Jñāna*.

K: What does that mean? Knowledge about what? Is it the knowledge about the cause of conflict?

C: *Jñāna* will apply to the nature of conflict and also to how it arises.

K: How does it come into being, and how does it work? What is the nature and structure of it? To know the cause is to know the structure and the nature of pain. Do you call that knowledge?

C: Sir, *jñāna* has been divided as that which pertains to the phenomenal world and that which refers to the non-phenomenal world.

K: What do you mean by conflict?

C: Conflict is duality.

K: We know what the word 'knowledge' is. What do you mean by the word 'conflict'?

C: *Dvandva*—conflict between the two—hot and cold, pleasure and pain, happiness and sorrow.

K: So let us proceed. I am in conflict: I want to go out and I want to stay here; I am unhappy and I want to do something which makes for happiness. I acquire knowledge about it by seeing the cause, the nature, the structure of this conflict. The understanding of the cause, the nature, the structure of this conflict is knowledge. And knowing that, having this knowledge, will it free the mind from conflict?

Are you saying that knowledge will free the mind from conflict? Now, I know that I am jealous because my wife looks at another man or because you have a better job than I. I know why I am jealous. I know the nature and structure of jealously, which is: I would like to be in your place; I would like my wife not to look at you. I know the cause, I know the effect; the reaction of all that is—I am jealous. I see the full structure of it as an engineer sees a structure. Does this knowledge free me from jealousy? Obviously it does not.

C: Knowledge which will resolve conflict is the kind of knowledge in which there is no duality.

K: How do you know—because somebody else has said it?

C: By looking into why jealousy arises. Why should I be jealous?

K: That is analysis. Does analysis free the mind from conflict?

C: Analysis alone will not.

K: Knowledge is the result of analysis. I analyse. I see why I am jealous: I was angry with my wife and so on, and she has left me. Does this knowledge free me from the fear of living alone without her?

C: The feeling of jealously does cease.

K: How do you propose to end jealously? I have analysed myself till I am sick, and the next minute I am jealous again.

C: That means by analysis you have not ended jealousy.

K: Analysis is part of knowledge. I have accumulated knowledge because I have analysed. I am jealous because I have tried to possess my wife. The realization of this is knowledge. And I want to possess her because I am afraid to live alone—and this is also part of knowledge. And you are saying: Through analysis there is an accumulation of knowledge, and that knowledge is going to free you from jealousy. Does it?

C: No, sir. I may analyse my jealousy; I may also say: What does it matter if my wife has gone to another man? It all depends on the individual response.

K: That is all intellection, which is part of analysis. All knowledge is intellectual. And knowledge will not make you free.

C: *Jñāna* is not an intellectual process. The intellectual process ends with the *manas* (mind) and *buddhi* (intellect).

K: So you are saying that there is another factor which is beyond the intellect, beyond knowledge. Analysis and the accumulation of knowledge through analysis is one kind of knowledge, and there is some other factor beyond that.

C: Which enables the *buddhi* to see, to discriminate.

B: How is knowledge acquired? Let us take the first step.

K: I have been on that road many times, and I have acquired knowledge. I have seen that person often, and I have talked to him. He has been friendly or unfriendly. I have accumulated through experience, through analysis, through incidents, through information; and that is called knowledge.

C: What makes that knowledge possible? What makes experience possible?

K: Experience is possible only when there is the experiencer. You say something which I do not like, and that hurts me. That is an experience, then that experience becomes knowledge. Will that knowledge end conflict?

C: No.

K: Then what will end conflict? Do they say that it is that entity which realizes the experiencer and that has gathered this knowledge which will end conflict? If so, then there is a superior entity.

C: There is a principle through which all these disparate experiences of the individual are made possible. How do I know I am the experiencer?

K: Because I have experienced before. I know I am the experiencer because you have hurt me before. The previous knowledge makes the experiencer.

B: I see the sun rise. I feel that my experience of having seen the sun—

K: Having seen the sun rise once and seeing it day after day, the accumulation of that knowledge makes the experiencer.

C: They postulate an entity which does not experience.

K: The postulated entity is another opinion which I have acquired from somebody else. It is fairly simple and clear. First, I am aware, I get to know I am in conflict. I analyse it. Through analysis I acquire the knowledge that I am jealous. All that is simple. Analysis, observation, watching, have given me information as to why I am jealous. That information is knowledge. And that knowledge apparently cannot get rid of jealousy. Then what will get rid of it? Do not invent another superior self. I know nothing about it. I know only conflict, analysis, knowledge; and I see that knowledge does not get rid of conflict.

B: What is the substratum of all experience? What is that out of which all experiences arise? What is the matrix?

K: Is it an accumulation of experience? The matrix is things put together; the matrix of experience is experience; the matrix of the carpet is the warp and the woof. Are you asking, sir, what is the thread that makes experience, or are you asking what the matter is upon which the experience leaves a pattern?

C: Traditionalists consider that knowledge as the gathering of experience, memory, belongs to the realm of the *manas* and *buddhi*, and that this is made possible by the *ātman* (higher self), which sheds light; without the *ātman*, the *manas* cannot function.

K: What is the material upon which experience leaves a mark? Is there such material? Obviously it is the brain; the brain cells are the material on which every incident, conscious or unconscious, leaves a mark. The brain receives information all the time: I see that flower, and it has already registered. The brain is constantly recording; the racial inheritance and the personal inheritance all leave a mark on the brain.

B: The mind is energy.

K: The registration of the brain is part of energy. The whole thing is energy. The brain is the repository of all recording—sensory as well as non-sensory. That is the tape which has been collected for centuries; and that is knowledge. If you did not know where you lived, you would not be able to go home. Because you have been there, you know the way.

Knowledge does not necessarily free the mind from conflict. We see that. Without introducing the *ātman*, which is part of the traditional knowledge that I have acquired, what will free the mind? Though I may call it the *ātman*, it is the same field of knowledge.

C: How is the *ātman* within the field of knowledge?

K: Unless I think about it, there is no *ātman*.

C: Thinking about it is not realizing it. It is not within the comprehension of thought.

K: Thinking about something is still within the field of thought. A man who thinks about the *ātman* is still within the field of thought.

C: The men who talked of the *ātman* never thought; they realized it. The only argument that they cite is: When you wake up after a sound, deep sleep, how do you remember that you have had a sound sleep?—for in deep sleep the mind does not work.

K: How do you know when it does not work? The brain cells are working day and night. Only when you get up the next morning do you know that you are tired or that you have had a good sleep. They are all the functions of the brain. So the *ātman* is within the field of thought. It must be. Otherwise you would not use that word. We are saying that the *ātman* is part of the brain. Because thought cannot solve the problem through thought, it therefore says that there must be the *ātman*.

C: But they have said that the *ātman* is outside experience.

B: Explain the material of experience.

K: I see the flower, I name it. The name, the form, the verbalization is the memory; because the flower has been seen before, the brain says: That is a flower.

B: Does it operate if I close my eyes?

K: Of course. Shut your eyes and close your ears. You can still think. Thinking about God is within the field of thought. The man who has not thought at all, to him there is no God. The ancient ones, thinking about something superior, wanting something greater, said that there was God. That was the product of thought. So that was within the field of knowledge.

C: Not much importance is given to God in the *Upaniṣads*. According to their conception, God and *brahman* (universal spirit) are the same.

K: Someone who is not a Hindu comes along and says: God is Jesus, and you, with your culture, speak of the *ātman*. What is the difference? He has been brought up in his culture, and you in yours.

C: We speak of both. God is personal; the *ātman* is not personal.

K: They are all the products of thought. Look how deceptive the mind has become, caught in words. I have accumulated knowledge about suffering, and suffering does not end. Not knowing how to end it, thought says that there must be some other factor. It thinks about it. So it invents the *ātman*. Otherwise the *ātman* would not have come into existence. But the *ātman* does not end suffering either, because it is part of knowledge. Knowledge about suffering has not ended suffering.

C: But they themselves have said that thought will not solve the problem.

K: But the *ātman* is the product of thought.

C: The *ātman* is experienced by sages; it is their personal experience.

K: When they say that they experience the *ātman*, what does it mean?

C: They say that it cannot be described.

K: Of course it cannot be; but it is part of thought.

C: To them it was not part of thought; they realized it.

K: How do I realize anything? I must recognize it, must I not? What do I recognise?

C: Recognition means seeing a thing without the process of thought.

K: I recognize you because I have met you yesterday. If I did not, I would not know you.

C: That is not the process by which you recognize *brahman*.

K: Be simple. Let us talk logically. What is the process of recognizing something new? To recognize a flower, a yellow one say, I must have already known it before. So recognition implies knowledge. In order to recognize the *ātman*, I must already have known it. It is, therefore, within the field of experience. So when they say that you cannot 'experience' the *ātman*, what do they mean?

The fact is that I suffer; and I say: I want to end suffering. So, why do I bring in the *ātman*? It has no value at all. It is like describing food to a man who is really hungry.

C: I agree that whatever they have said does not help.

K: On the contrary, they have destroyed the mind by introducing a factor which does not help.

C: Is this possible?

K: See it. Say: I will never talk about the *ātman*; it does not mean a thing. So, how do I face this? How can the mind resolve the factor of sorrow?—not through the *ātman*; that is too childish. It can only resolve it, not through knowledge, but by looking at it without knowledge.

C: Is this possible?

K: Do not introduce the *ātman*. Try it. Test it out. The other you cannot test. Put it away completely. Then what happens? Then how do I look at suffering—with knowledge or without knowledge? Do I look at it with eyes which are filled with the past and, therefore, translate everything in terms of the past?

B: We cannot use the past as a means to free ourselves from suffering.

K: When you say that you see what suffering is, you are directly in relationship with suffering—not the observer observing suffering.

I look at suffering without the image. The image is the past. The image from the past may be the *ātman*. Of course it is. Test it. Test the image as you would test it in the laboratory. In the same way, test this. The *ātman* which I see is part of thought. There is no testing there at all; here there is testing. I am looking at this sorrow with past experience: my past experience divides the past from the present; there is duality. The present is sorrow and I am looking at the present through the past, and translating it in terms of the past. If the mind could look at it without the past, there would be a different meaning altogether. So I have to test it. Can the mind look without past memory? Can I look at that flower without past knowledge? Test it; you can either do it or not do it.

Rishi Valley
21 January, 1970

THE GURU, TRADITION AND FREEDOM

Dialogue 21

K: Could we relate the whole field of tradition to what we are talking about to see the divergences, contradictions and similarities, and also to see if there is anything new in what we are saying? Let us discuss this, questioning it back and forth.

A: Let us start with the traditional four *puruṣārthas* (aims of life): *dharma* (duty), *artha* (wealth), *kāma* (pleasure) and *mokṣa* (freedom). The traditional approach to living begins with the fact that existence has these aspects, and that each of them is vital for the development of understanding.

K: Should we not start with the meaning of it all?

A: The traditionalists started with the four aspects as the meaning.

K: Should we not inquire what human existence, human sorrow and conflict mean? How do the professionals answer this question?

SW: In the tradition we find two clear directions—the orthodox direction which goes by the verbal interpretation of facts and the breakaway tradition, as seen in *Dattātreya* and the *Yoga-Vaśiṣṭha*. The seers who broke away said: No guru. We have discovered it for ourselves; we will not swear by the *Vedas*. The whole of nature, the whole world is our guru. Observe and understand the world. In Buddha also, there was a breaking away. His teaching represents the core of the breakaway pattern. Those who broke away were closely linked with life.

If you read the *Yoga-Vaśiṣṭha*, it says that the mind is full of thoughts, conflicts; and these conflicts arise because of desire and fear; unless you are able to resolve them, you cannot understand. It talks of negative thinking. Max Müller and some others misinterpreted the word *nirodha*. The word does not mean suppression; it means negation.

A great deal is said about gurus. The *Yoga-Vaśiṣṭha* says that giving initiation and other such actions are meaningless. The awakening of the disciple is in right understanding and in awareness. That alone is the primary and responsible fact. These essentials are the core of the breakaway tradition.

R: And yet there are many places in the *Yoga-Vaśiṣṭha* where it says that without a guru you cannot find anything.

A: Breakaway from what? If it is a breakaway from the social system, then the breakaway tradition also continues the social system.

SW: To the problem of understanding, tradition gives a formal and verbal approach. In the breakaway tradition, this is not so. The break is not away from society. Both traditions exist. In the *maṭhas* or monasteries, they talked of the Vedas but what they said has nothing to do with life; there were others who related all that they understood to life. But whatever was said had nothing to do with society.

R: How is it that the guru tradition has become so important?

K: Shall we discuss this question of the guru? Shall we begin with that? What does the word 'guru' mean?

SW: *Desika* is the right word, not guru. *Desika* means 'one who helps to awaken the disciple; one who helps the seeker to understand'. The word means 'one who learns'.

R: The disciple is called a *śiṣya*. A *śiṣya* is one who is capable of learning.

SW: Guru means 'vast, beyond, great'.

K: If the guru is one who is great, beyond, one who is profound, then what relationship has he to a disciple?

SW: In the *Upaniṣads*, it is one of love and compassion. The *Upaniṣads* maintain that compassion is the contact between the guru and the disciple.

K: How has the tradition now become authoritarian? How has a sense of discipline, of following, of accepting whatever the guru says been introduced into the relationship? The authoritarian, compulsive, destructive relationship comes in the way of real thinking; it destroys initiative. How has this relationship come into being?

SW: It is difficult to say. The two approaches must have existed for a long time. In one tradition, the guru is taken as a friend, as a person the disciple loves; in that the guru is not authoritarian at all. The other tradition exploits. It wants authority, followers.

A: Swāmiji's main point is that there has not been a homogeneous stream. There is the outsider and there is the conformist. A non-conformist is one who rejects society; he is outside society.

R: We come back to your first question: What is it all about? Apart from the gurus, what is the fundamental answer to life?

K: I wonder if we could find out. Could you dig into it? Could you dig everything out of me? Do you understand what I mean? You come to a well and you get water according to the size of your bucket; whatever vessel you carry, that is the amount of water you get. You have read a great deal of the ancient literature, you have practised, you have read what we have talked about. You are well equipped from the traditional point of view, and you know what is happening in the world. Now, you and I meet. Dig out of me as much as you can. Question me about everything, from the beginning to the end. Question deeply as a conformist and as a non-conformist, as a guru and as a non-guru, as a disciple and as a non-disciple. It is like going to a well with tremendous thirst, wanting to find out everything. Do it that way, sir. Then I think it will be profitable.

SW: Then can I be absolutely free?

K: Break all the windows, because I feel wisdom is infinite; it has no limits. And because it has no frontiers, it is totally impersonal. So, with all your experience, knowledge and understanding of tradition and the breakaway pattern, which also becomes tradition, with what you know and what you have understood, from your own meditations, from your own life, you come to me. Do not be satisfied by just a few words. Dig deep.

SW: I would like to know how you came to it yourself.

K: You want to know how this person came upon it? I could not tell you. You see, sir, he apparently never went through any practice, discipline, jealousy, envy, ambition, competition. He did not want power, position, prestige, fame; he did not want any of them. And therefore there was never any question of giving up. So when I say I really do not know, I think that would be the truth. Most of the traditional teachers go through, give up, practise, sacrifice, control; they sit under a tree and come upon clarity.

SW: In your teachings, sensitivity, understanding and passive awareness are factors that must saturate all one's living. I would like to ask how you came upon all these.

A: You may have had nothing to give up and, therefore, no discipline, no *sādhanā*, but what about people who have something to give up?

K: I really could not tell you how I came upon all this. I wonder why you bother about it. How is it important?

SW: It is curiosity, it is joy.

K: Let us go beyond that.

SW: The moment you say awareness, attention, sensitivity, one is so full of wonder, appreciation. How did you come to this? How is it that this man is able to talk like this? And when we analyse what he says, it is so scientific, rational and so full of meaning.

K: You know the story of how the boy was picked up, how he was born in the most orthodox Brahmin family, that he was not conditioned either by tradition or anything in life—as a Hindu or a Theosophist. None of it touched him. And I do not know why it did not touch him.

A: This question which he asks may be put in another idiom. How did it happen that a person who was in the midst of an environment which laid maximum stress on phenomenal life did not get caught in that life?

SW: K came by it. He is not able to explain, but he talks and he uses certain terms, and the whole logic of it is there. It is a wonder to the listener how, without anything, he has come to it.

K: How is it that a man like K, not having read the sacred books of the East or of the West, not having gone through the whole gamut of experience—of giving up, of sacrifice—says these things? I really could not say, sir.

A: You gave the answer a minute ago when you said that wisdom is not personal.

K: But he asks how he came upon wisdom without all this.

SW: I am not asking how he came upon it, but I find a cogency and a rationality in his talks that I find beautiful. It is in his heart.

K: When you say that it has come because it is in his heart, I do not know how to respond. It comes—not from the heart or from the mind. It comes. Or would you say, sir, that it would come to any person who is really without the self?

SW: Perfectly so, sir.

K: I think that would be the most logical answer.

SW: Or is it that you saw the misery of mankind and then got it?

K: No. To answer this question properly one has to go into the whole thing. There was that boy who was picked up and who went through all kinds of things—he was proclaimed the Messiah, he was worshipped, large properties were given to him, he had a great following. None of this touched him: he gave up land as easily as he accepted it. He did not read any sacred books; he did not read philosophy or psychology; he never practised anything. And there was the quality of speaking from emptiness.

SW: Yes.

K: You understand, sir, that there is never any accumulation from which he speaks. So the question: How do you say such things? involves the larger question of whether wisdom, or whatever you might like to call it, can be contained in any particular consciousness, or whether it lies beyond all particular consciousnesses.

Sir, look at this valley. Look at the hills, the trees, the rocks—the valley is all that. Without the content of the valley there is no valley. Now, if there is no content in consciousness, there is no consciousness—in the sense of the limited. When you ask the question: How is it that he says these things?—I really do not know. But the question can be answered: When it happens, the mind is completely empty. This does not mean that you become a medium.

SW: I derive from this that infinity is beauty, rationality, logic. It is full of symmetry in its expression.

K: Sir, having said all this, what do you want to find out? You have capacity, you have read a great deal, you have knowledge, experience, you have practised and meditated—from there, ask.

SW: Consciousness is bondage. Only from emptiness can one have entry into it.

K: So you are asking: How can a human being empty his mind?

SW: There is the traditional idea of the *adhikāri*, the person who can learn. And the traditional idea is that there are levels or differences among the people who can receive or learn. What we can learn depends on that difference. There are three levels. In the orthodox texts they are mentioned as *sattva*, *rajas* and *tamas*. Those who belong to the first category—*sattva*—can have understanding by listening to a teacher. The *rajas* category have to listen and recollect when they face a problem of life. The *tāmasic* ones cannot learn because their minds are too gross. In order to make the mind subtle, there are many methods or *upāsanās*. Yoga starts with breath control, meditation, standing on the head. Even so, they say that *āsanas* (exercise postures of yoga) are meant as a cleansing. It is said: Be passive, observe 'what is'.

K: You say that, as human beings are constituted, there are levels or gradations of receptivity. Is it possible for all people who are still in the process of becoming to come upon this?

SW: That is one part of it. The other is that for most people there are moments of understanding. But these slip away, and there is a constant struggle. What are such people to do?

K: Knowing that there are levels, is it possible to cut across these levels?

SW: Is that a question of time?

K: Can we cut across these levels or are there processes by which we can transcend the levels?

R: Tradition says that a long process of time is necessary.

SW: I do not agree with that.

R: One must have the competence to understand.

A: I say that my life is a life of becoming. When I come and sit with you, you say that time is irrelevant. I say, 'Yes', because it is clear.

But I am soon back again in the field of time, effort etc., and this thing which I feel I understand, slips away.

K: The question is fairly clear. The question is: When I listen, I seem to understand, but when I go away, it is gone. And the other question is: How is one who is not bright, who is not rational, to break through his conditioning and come upon it? What is your answer to this?

SW: My answer which is based on experience, and which is also the traditional answer, is this: Let such a man practise some form of meditation which makes the mind more alert.

K: That is, do certain practices, do certain exercises, breathing, etc., untill the mind is capable of understanding. And the other man says: When I listen to you, I understand, but it slips away. These are the two problems. First of all take a mind that has no capacity, how is it capable of seeing? How is such a mind capable of seeing, understanding, without practice, without the time process? Time implies a process, right? Without time, how is such a mind to come upon this?

My mind is dull. My mind has not the clarity to understand this thing immediately. So you tell me to practise, to breathe, to eat less; you ask me to practise all the methods and systems which will help to make my mind sharp, clear, sensitive. All that involves time and, when you allow time, there are other factors which enter into the mind. If I have to go from here to there, to cover that distance takes time. In covering that distance, there are other factors which enter during the voyage so that I never reach there. Before I reach there I see something beautiful and I am carried away. The way is not a straight, narrow path on which I walk. Innumerable factors are present. These incidents, happenings, impressions are going to change the movement of my direction. And that thing which I am trying to understand is not a fixed point either.

A: The point that it is not a fixed thing should be explored.

K: I say that my mind is confused, is disturbed; I do not understand. You tell me to understand by doing these things. So you have established understanding as a fixed point, but it is not a fixed point.

SW: True, it is not a fixed point.

K: Obviously. If it is a fixed point, and I am going towards it, there are other factors which enter in my journey towards it, and these factors are going to influence me much more than the end.

A: That end is a projection of the unknowing mind.

K: That way is not the way at all. First see it. It is not a fixed point, and it can never be a fixed point; therefore, I say: That is a false thing altogether. Then, as it is not the way, I deny the whole thing; I wipe away a tremendous field—all practices, all meditations, all knowledge. Then what have I left? I am left with the fact that I am confused, that I am dull.

Now, how do I know I am dull? How do I know I am confused?—Only through comparison, because I see that you are very perceptive. I see through comparison, through measurement that I am dull.I do not compare, and I now see what I have done through comparison: I have reduced myself to a state which I call dull. And I see that that is not the way either. So I reject comparison. Am I dull then, if I do not compare? So I have rejected the system—a process, a fixed end which you have evolved as a means of enlightenment through time. I say: Comparison is not the way; measurement means distance.

SW: Does it mean that this understanding is not a matter vitally connected with capacity at all? We started with capacity.

K: I listen to you, Swāmiji, but I do not understand. I do not know what it is that I do not understand, but you show me—time, process, fixed point, etc. You show it to me, and I deny them. So what has happened to my mind? In the very rejection, in the very denial, the mind has become less dull. The rejection of the false makes the mind clear; and the rejection of comparison, which is also the false, makes the mind sharp.

So, what have I left now? I know I am dull only in comparison with you. Dullness exists in my measuring myself with what is called brightness. And so I say: I will not measure. Am I dull then? I have completely rejected comparison, and comparison means conformity. What have I left? The thing I have called dull is not dull; it is what it is. What have I left at the end of all this? All that I have left is: I will not compare any more; I will not measure myself with somebody who is superior to me; and I will not tread this path which is beautifully laid down for me. So I reject all the structures which man has imposed upon me to achieve enlightenment.

So, where am I? I start from the beginning. I know nothing about enlightenment, understanding, process, comparison, becoming. I have thrown them away. I do not know. Knowledge is the means of getting hurt and tradition is the instrument by which I get hurt. I do not want that instrument and, therefore, I am not hurt. I start with complete innocence. Innocence means a mind that is incapable of being hurt.

Now, I say to myself: Why did they not see this simple fact that there is no fixed point? Why? Why did they pile all this on the human mind so that I have to wade through all this, in order to discard all this?

It is very interesting, sir. Why go through all this process if I have to discard it? Why did you not tell me: Do not compare; truth is not a fixed point?

Do I flower in goodness through comparison? Can humility be gained through time, practice? Obviously not. And yet you have insisted on practice. Why? When you insist on practice, you think that you are going to a fixed point. So you have deceived yourself, and you are deceiving me.

You do not say to me: You know nothing, and I know nothing; let us find out whether all the things that human beings have imposed on other human beings are true or false. You say: Enlightenment is something to be achieved through time, through discipline, through the guru.

Let us find out why human beings have imposed upon human beings something which is not true. Human beings have tortured themselves, castigated themselves to get enlightenment—as though enlightenment were a fixed point. And they end up blind. I think that is why, sir, the so-called man of error is much nearer the truth than the man who practises to reach the truth. A man who practises truth becomes impure, unchaste.

Rishi Valley
January 21, 1971

FREEDOM AND THE PRISON

Dialogue 22

K: I wonder if we could discuss this morning what perception means. Apart from what the traditionalists, the professionals and the commentaries have said, what is perception? What is it to perceive? Is it merely an intellectual process, is it merely visual or is it a combination of both? The mind takes in more than the eye sees. So when we talk about perception, what do we mean? Does it involve an intellectual process, a verbal comprehension? Does the eye see in a linear or a horizontal dimension?

B: You mean the eye as the sense organ here?

K: Yes.

SW: Is the perception of the eye, the visual, sensory perception of the eye, not uniform? We come to this room, and I see the design of the carpet. Very soon I am both seeing and not-seeing. The physical eye also does not, all the time, see in a uniform state. There must be some factor other than the contact of the object and the senses in the awareness that is 'I see'. The first awareness of inattention comes to me that way.

K: I have not come to that point; I am not speaking of attention and inattention. I am trying to understand what perception means. All I know is that I see: I see you sitting there; there is a sensory perception. The intellectual capacity of thought and the sensory perception then hold the image. That is what we generally call perception, is it not? Where does attention or inattention come into all this?

A: I see an object. There is a sensory image of that object. Then there is the memory of that image. When I see something else, the whole process begins again.

K: Everything that is recorded—conscious as well as unconscious sensory impressions, various images, conclusions, prejudices—is involved in perception. I see you, and the various images that have been built through perception, through association, and through prejudice, emerge. Thousands and thousands of images are recorded and held in the brain cells. When I meet you, I turn on attention and the images emerge. That is what we call perception, isn't it? This is the ordinary process of perception. Where does the trouble begin?

A: Are not sensitivity and its varying degrees vital elements in perception? My perception of squalor is different from yours. Can you separate perception from the degrees of sensitivity?—Perception is not the same to you and to me.

K: When I have all these accumulated—conscious and unconscious—images, my mind is loaded. Where is the place for sensitivity?

A: Perception is not a passive act of memory. There is something new with every new perception, with every new response. And degrees of sensitivity are inherent in all these responses. I do not understand why there are these degrees and from where they come, because ignorance is imponderable.

B: Even the seeing here is like a camera which sees its shutters, not the object.

A: If I look through ideas there is really no seeing.

K: The mind is crowded with impressions and information about the object it sees; it is never empty. It looks through this burden of associations, with pleasure and pain, with jealousy. What is wrong with that?

R: I am never face to face with all this. There is sensory perception, then the images, then my likes and my dislikes. My likes and dislikes are also facts, but they are facts which I do not realize.

K: They are facts; they are as much facts as it is a fact that you are sitting here. Which means that I see you each time through a screen. What is wrong with that? Isn't it a natural process?

SW: In that state I do not see at all.

K: First I want to be clear about all this. There are thousands of impressions, thousands of perceptions, thousands of conclusions. Let us cover all that with the word 'conclusion'. I look at the world through these conclusions; each sensory perception thickens my conclusions; they never disappear. This is the process which is going on all the time, all through my life.

Image-making and conclusions are of the past. Sensory perception is immediate and the conclusion becomes the past. I am looking at you through the eyes of the past. That is what we are doing; it is a fact. Now what is wrong with that? Why shouldn't I look at you that way? What started with perception is not perception at all. But do not condemn it yet. That is what we are doing all the time. I want to be sure before we proceed any further.

Go slowly. Everything perceived is translated in terms of conclusions. That is a fact we all know. That is tradition; it is experience. Experience, knowledge, tradition are implied by the word 'past'and by the word 'conclusion'. The brain cells retain the memory of the past. And so, experience, knowledge, tradition determine the structure and nature of the brain cells. The brain cells are the past. They retain the memory of the past because in that there is safety. There is safety in the retaining of biological processes as well as in the retaining of psychological accumulations. In all that there is tremendous safety.

SW: How is there safety in the past? Am I really safe?

K: Do not question it yet. Look at it. Without memory you would not know your name, you would not know how to go to Bangalore, or recognize your husband or your wife. There is the feeling of complete safety because in tradition, in knowledge and in conclusions there is nothing new, therefore nothing disturbing.

SW: There is nothing to disturb.

K: Anything new is disturbing and, as the brain cells need order, they find order in the past.

A: But to come back to your question, what is wrong with that?

K: There is nothing wrong in that. I am inquiring into the nature of sensory perception, into the operations of the brain, the mechanism of thought, and how the mind operates. There is safety in sensory perception, image, conclusion, the past. All that is tradition. In tradition there is safety. In the past there is complete security.

SW: Security implies struggle.

K: Security implies the sense of not wanting to be disturbed. I do not know if you have noticed that the brain needs order. It may establish order in disorder—which is neurosis. It needs order and, therefore, it will find order in disorder, and become neurotic. Do you see this? The brain demands order because in order there is security.

SW: That is perfectly clear.

K: In tradition there is order. In continuity there is order. The brain, seeking order, creates security, a harbour where it feels safe. And K comes along with revolutionary ideas and tells you: This is not order. And so there is conflict between you and him. You reduce the new into terms of the old, and there find safety, security. Why does the mind do this? The Russian Revolution and the French Revolution upset the whole established structure, but soon the brain created order out of disorder, and there was an end to revolution.

A: We have discovered something—that the moment I see something new which creates a disturbance, perception is the instrument by which I convert the new into the old.

K: That is the biological process of the brain. It is a biological necessity for the brain, because in that it finds the most efficient way of working.

A: Will you examine the in-built incapacity of the brain to see and its tendency to distort the new?

K: Wait, sir. Unless the danger of seeking security in the past is understood, the brain cells will not see anything new. If they see something new, they will translate it in terms of the old. Therefore, the brain cells have themselves to see the immense danger of looking for security in the past.

A: Which means a total change.

K: I do not know a thing. I only see sensory images, conclusions, and safety in conclusions. It may be a new conclusion, a disorderly conclusion, but there is safety there; however neurotic it is, in that neuroticism there is safety.

See the beauty of it. This is the truth, and that is why it is beautiful. How is the brain, which is insistently demanding security, to see that in the past there is no security, but that security is always in the new? The brain cells are seeking security, both in disorder and in order. If you offer a system, a methodological order, the brain accepts it. That is the whole biological process and the whole traditional process: security in the past, never in the future, never in the present—the absolute security of the past. And that is knowledge: biological knowledge, technological knowledge and the knowledge which has been gathered through experience. In knowledge there is security, and knowledge is the past. So what is the next question?

SW: There is a modified continuity in this process. This creates a feeling of progress.

K: Knowledge can be continued, modified; but that is still within the field of knowledge—the whole thing is there. What is wrong with this?

SW: All that you say is a fact. However, there is another factor; this is not the whole thing. There is something radically wanting in this.

K: What is wanting in this? Go step by step. This is the structure. What is the something which is not quite right? Find out. I will show it to you.

SW: There is no permanency.

K: What are you saying? Knowledge is the most permanent thing. I see that knowledge is necessary, and also that knowledge is the past; thought is the response of the past; and so the mind is always living in the past. So the mind is a prisoner. (*pause*)

What does a prisoner talk about? Freedom? Why did you not see it? Being in prison, he talks about freedom, *mokṣa*, *nirvāṇa*. He knows his prison is not freedom, but he wants freedom, because in freedom there is joy, there is beauty. Because his present life is a repetitive, mechanical continuity, he has to invent an ideal, he has to invent *mokṣa*, a heaven. And then there is safety in the future. He invents God, he pursues truth and enlightenment, all the while remaining anchored in the past. This anchorage is a biological necessity. So, can the brain not only see that knowledge is essential, but also see the dangers of knowledge? Knowledge brings about division. Is not knowledge the factor which divides?

SW: Yes, of course.

K: Don't agree. See. Can the brain cells seek security in knowledge, and also see that in knowledge there is the danger of division?

SW: To see both at the same time is difficult.

K: See it at the same time; otherwise you will not see it.

A: How is knowledge divisive?

K: Knowledge, the division between the known and the unknown, is itself divisive. The divisions of yesterday, today and tomorrow: the today, modified from yesterday's knowledge, which is the past, modifying the future, is divisive. Knowledge is also my image of you and my conclusions about you—my sense that I *know* you, when you in the meantime may have changed. My image of you divides us.

Knowledge also gives security. So can the brain cells realize that at one level knowledge is necessary, but that at another level it is divisive and, therefore, dangerous? The building of images is the divisive factor in knowledge. Can the brain cells see that in order to be physically secure knowledge is necessary, and also, at the same time, see that knowledge based on images derived from conclusions is divisive? Then what next?

SW: There are two types of image-making. There is a recording in technological knowledge which has the form of image-making.

A: We are talking of image-making with some emotional content, in which there is a projection of freedom as an escape from the past. Technological recording does not have this emotional content.

K: The brain knows that in this there is no freedom and, therefore, it has to invent a freedom outside the prison. When you see the whole structure of knowledge, then the rest is understood.

A: There is a question which I want to ask: Is it that the mind has a capacity to verbalize something which it does not experience but would like to experience?

K: We have not finished yet, sir. The word 'knowledge' includes both technological and biological knowledge. I see that knowledge is both divisive and unifying. In knowledge there is the bondage of time. But man also knows that in this there is no freedom. And he wants freedom, for in freedom there may lie super security. That is why man has from time immemorial talked of freedom. But as freedom is not within the prison, man has always thought of freedom as lying outside the prison. And we are saying that *freedom is here*, not outside.

SW: If the desire for freedom is a biological characteristic, is not the desire for super security also biological?

K: Is there freedom in all the things which thought has built? Is there freedom in concepts of freedom? Look at it. Thought cannot find freedom in this prison. And because it cannot find freedom here, it believes that freedom must lie outside.

SW: In other words, is there freedom in knowledge?

K: Is there freedom in the past? Knowledge is the past; it is the accumulation of the millions of years of experience. Does experience give freedom? Obviously not. So is there such a thing as freedom?

SW: I do not know. I see that freedom is not outside; it is a projection. And yet there is no freedom inside.

K: I do not know. I have always thought of freedom as being outside. All the religious books and practices have thought of it as over there, but there may be absolute freedom *here*. Look. I know, the brain knows, thought is aware that it has created the prison. All that thought knows is that in demanding security it has created the prison. And it must have security, otherwise it can not function. So thought inquires: Where is freedom? Thought seeks it in a place where it is not projected, formulated or invented from the past, which is still knowledge. Freedom must be somewhere.

A: Is the discovery of freedom an act of perception?

K: Visual perception and knowledge have created all this. Both knowledge and non-knowledge are projections of thought.

R: What is non-knowledge?

A: We are thinking of the unknown as freedom.

K: Therefore the unknown is the known. It is very simple now. This is the structure of thought. So what is freedom? And is there such a thing at all?

A: We only see that whatever thought produces is not freedom at all.

K: Is there security in thought? Thought has created all this. Is there security here?

SW: It is thought which has produced all this.

K: I have assumed that there is security, but is there security? I have said that I must have knowledge, but is that security? I see divisions—between your family and my family, between what is yours and what is mine. Is there security in all this?

See what I have found: There is security in knowledge, but not in this divisiveness which is a result of knowledge. So thought says to itself: Is there security in the very structure of thinking itself? Is there security in the past? Is there security in tradition? Is there security in knowledge? The brain has sought security in all these, but is that security? The brain has to see for itself that there is no security there. So what happens? (*pause*)

I see that there is no security there. It is a tremendous discovery for me. So thought says: What next? I must destroy myself because I am the greatest danger. But now, who is the 'I' who is going to destroy itself? So thought again says: I must not divide.

SW: Slay the slayer.

K: The prison and the prisoner, the slayer and the slain—is there an ending of the self without this division? For division means a contradiction. Is there an ending without effort? In the ending is the quality of sensitivity. To come through all this to this point requires a tremendous subtlety, which is sensitivity.

So, can thought end itself? This investigation has required great attention, great awareness, a moving step by step—never missing a thing— which has its own discipline, its own order. Following its own functioning step by step, seeing its own attitudes, searching in areas which bring no real security, observing that it has sought security in division, the brain is now orderly. It sees now that in division there is no security, therefore every step it takes is a step in order. And that order is its own security.

Order is the perception of things as they are; it is the perception of what one is—not a conclusion. I cannot see things as they are if I have conclusions, for in conclusions there is disorder. Thought has sought security in conclusions, which has spread disorder. Therefore, it now rejects conclusions immediately. It functions in knowledge only when it is necessary, but nowhere else. For everywhere else the function of thought is to create conclusions and images. Therefore thought comes to an end.

Rishi Valley
24 January, 1971

STABILITY AND KNOWLEDGE

Dialogue 23

SW: I perceive a tree. Then an idea arises from memory which says: This is a mango tree. This idea comes in the way of my looking at the tree and, so, I am not able to see the fact of the tree. This screen of ideas interferes with the present, and there is no real perception.

K: Are you asking, sir, what relationship is? What is the relationship between the observed and the observer? What does it mean to be related, to be in contact? Relationship means to be related. The relationship between two people; the relationship between the concept, the ideal and the conceiver of the ideal; the relationship of the one with the many; the relationship between one thought and another thought and with the interval between thoughts; the relationship between the present and the future as death; the relationship between the world and myself—all that is involved in relationship, is it not? I may renounce the world, I may live in a cave, but I am still related to my whole background, and the background is me. I think relationship implies all that. (*pause*)

A: We always think of relationship in isolation and not as a part of the whole; relationship is always with something.

K: Can there be a relationship if there is a centre, an observer to whom you are related? When the centre feels it is related to something, is that relationship?

A: It has been pointed out that it is only when I feel related to something that the 'I' as the centre is strengthened. The centre assumes a cohesive character only through its fragmented parts.

K: How do we discuss this? Where do we begin with this vast subject?

A: Would you start with belief, because belief is the basis of all relationship?

K: What does relationship mean to you?

A: To be in communication.

K: What does relationship mean to you? When you look at me, at her, in what way are you related to me, to her? Are you related?

A: I think so.

K: Let us examine it. I look at you, you look at me. What is our relationship? Except for a verbal relationship, is there a relationship at all?

R: There is a feeling of relationship when there is a movement towards something.

K: If both of us are moving towards an ideal, going together to a point, is that relationship? Can there be relationship when each one is in isolation?

SW: The first question you asked was: Can there be relationship if there is a centre?

K: If I have built a wall of resistance, of self-protection around myself consciously or unconsciously, in order not to get hurt, in order to be safe, is there any relationship at all? Do look at this. I am afraid because I have been hurt physically as well as psychologically; my whole being is wounded, and I do not want to be wounded any more. So I build a wall of resistance, of defence, of 'I know-you don't know' around myself, to feel completely safe from further hurt. Having done that, what is my relationship with you?

A: What do you mean by relationship in our daily life?

K: Why do you ask me? Look at yourself. What takes place in your normal daily life? You go to the office; you are bullied, insulted by someone at the top; with your wounded pride you come home; your wife nags you; you withdraw further but yet you sleep with her. Have you any relationship?

A: That means that when there is a centre there is no relationship.

R: But there is ordinary goodwill.

K: Is there goodwill if I live within an enclosure, within this wall of resistance? What is my goodwill towards you then? I am polite but I keep my distance; I am always behind my wall.

SW: Even in the life of an ordinary man there are some relationships which are not always from behind a wall.

A: You say that there is no relationship; but the fact is that in life we are committed to one another; we do not act on the basis of self-interest alone.

K: You say that you are acting in the interest of the other; is that really so? I follow the leader who hopes to revolutionize society inwardly and outwardly; I follow him and I obey; I commit myself to a course of action that both my leader and I have agreed to. Is there a relationship between me and the leader who is working for the same end? Relationship means 'to be in contact with; to be in close proximity to'.

A: The basis of this relationship is utility.

K: So the basis of our relationship is utilitarian.

R: If you apply that test, then there is no relationship.

K: There is an idea, a formula, a pattern, a goal, a principle, a utopia we agree upon, but is there relationship?

A: Is relationship then merely an idea?

K: You are not addressing the deeper issue here, which is: As long as there is an observer who is committing himself to a course of action, is there a relationship between you and me?

A: Is there no relationship between two people?

K: This is really an enormous problem, sir. Am I related to that tree when I look at it? Relationship is a distance between me, as an observer, and the tree, which is the observed. When there is a distance between the observer and the observed, is there any possibility of relationship? I am married and have built an image of my wife, and she has built an image of me; the image is a distancing factor. Is there any relationship between us apart from the physical one? All of us co-operate to do something; it brings us together. But I have my own worries, and she has her own agonies. We are working together, but are we related?

A: Sir, this point of working together has been understood, but not the other.

K: Just a minute. I believe it took three thousand people working together to build the rocket, each man working to create a perfect mechanism; each man put aside his idiosyncracies and there was what is called 'co-operation' between them. Is that real co-operation? When you and I with common motives work together to build a house, we are still separate human beings. Is that co-operation? When I look at a tree, there is a distance between me and the tree; I am not 'in relationship' with the tree. That distance is not created by the physical space; it is created by knowledge. Therefore, what is relationship, what is co-operation and what is the factor of division?

SW: Images in one form or another divide.

K: Go slowly. There is that tree. I look at it. The physical distance between me and that tree may be a few yards, but the actual distance between me and that tree is vast. Though I look at it, my eyes, mind, heart—everything—is very far away. That distance is incalculable. In the same way, I look at my wife, and I am very far away. In the same way, I am very far away in co-operative action.

SW: Is the word, the image, interfering in all this?

K: We are going to find out. There is the word, the image, and the goal towards which both are co-operating. What is dividing you and me is the goal.

SW: But there is no goal with regard to the tree.

K: Just stay there. Do not jump ahead. We think that working together for a goal has brought us in contact. But, in fact, the goal is separating us.

A: No. How can you say that the goal is dividing us?

K: I do not know; I may be wrong. We are investigating. You and I have a goal; we work together.

SW: Is it a question of becoming?

K: Do look at it. I say that goals divide people; a goal does not bring people together. Your goal and my goal are separate; they have divided us. The goal itself and not co-operation, which is irrelevant, has divided us.

SW: I see one thing: where two people come together for the joy of something, that is different.

K: When two people come together out of affection, love, joy, then what is the action which does not divide? I love you, you love me, what is the action out of that love?—Not movement towards a goal. What is the action between two people who love?

A: When two people come together in affection, it may produce a result, but they are not coming together for the result. Therefore, in any such coming together there is no division. Whereas if two people come together with a goal, that is a divisive factor.

K: We have discovered something. Do go into it. I see that when people come together with affection, when there is no goal, no purpose, no utopia, then there is no division. Then all status disappears and there is only function—then I will sweep the garden because it is part of the needs of the place.

R: For love of the place—

K: Not love of the place. But love. You see what we are missing. Goals divide people—the goal being a formula, an ideal. I want to see what is involved here. I see that as long as I have a goal, a principle, a utopia, that very goal, that very principle divides people. Therefore it is finished for me.

Then I ask myself: How am I to live, to work with you without a goal? I see that relationship means to be in close contact, so that there is no distance between the two. And I also see that there is a vast psychological distance in the relationship between the flower and myself, my wife and myself; therefore I am not related at all. So what am I going to do? I tell myself that I must commit myself to the family, to the trees, lose myself in devotion to the goal, and work together. Intellectuals tell me that the goal is more important than the person, that the whole is greater than the part. So what am I doing?

I love nature, I love my family. So I commit myself to the idea that we must all work together for an end. What is happening to me? What am I doing?

SW: Isolating myself.

K: No sir, *look* at what is happening.

A: The fact is I am not related. I struggle to build a relationship, to bridge the gap between thought and thought. I have got to build this bridge between thought and thought because unless I do this, I feel absolutely isolated. I feel lost.

K: That is only a part of it. Go into it some more. What is happening to my mind when it is struggling to commit itself to everything —to family, to nature, to beauty, to working together?

SW: There is a lot of conflict there, sir.

K: I realize, as A has pointed out, that I am not related to anything. I have come to that point. Not being related to anything and wanting to be related, I commit myself, I involve myself in action; and yet the isolation goes on. So what is going on in my mind?

R: There is a constant struggle.

K: You have not moved away from that point. I am not related, but I try to be related, I try to identify myself through action. What is going on in my mind? (*pause*)

I am moving on the periphery. What happens to the mind when it moves on the outside all the time?

SW: The mind is strengthened.

A: I am escaping from myself.

K: What does that mean? Do look at it. Nature becomes very important, the family becomes very important, and the action to which I have committed myself becomes very important. But what has happened to me? Every relationship has been completely externalized.

Now, what has happened to the mind that has externalized the whole movement of relationship? What happens to your mind when it is occupied with the external, with the periphery?

SW: It has lost all sensitivity.

K: Do look at what happens inside you. In reaction to the externalizing process you withdraw, you become a monk. What happens to the mind when it withdraws?

SW: It is incapable of spontaneity.

K: You will find the answer, if you really look. (*pause*) What happens to your mind when you withdraw or when you are committed? What happens to the mind when you withdraw into your own conclusions? In place of one world you create another, which you call the inner world.

SW: The mind is not free.

K: Is that what has happened to your mind?

SW: It remains committed.

K: The mind is committed to outward phenomena, and the reaction to that is the inward commitment, the withdrawal. The commitment to the inward, to mystical experience, to your own world of imagination, is a reaction. What happens to the mind that is doing this?

R: It is occupied.

K: Is that what is going on? She says that it is occupied. Is that all? Put your guts into it. The mind externalizes its activity and, then, withdraws and acts. What happens to the quality of the mind, to the brain which is withdrawing and externalizing?

A: It does not face the fact.

R: There is a great fear. It becomes dull.

SW: It is not free to look.

K: Have you watched your mind when it is externalizing its actions, both outward and inward action? The inward and the outward movement are the same—like a tide going out and coming in. What happens to the mind which is going outward and withdrawing inward?

A: It is becoming mechanical.

K: It is a mind without any bearing, without order, completely unstable. Because there is no order in the whole movement, it becomes neurotic, unbalanced, without proportion, inharmonious, destructive.

A: It is restless.

K: Therefore such a mind has no stability: it invents external goals or it withdraws. But the mind needs order. Order means stability. The mind tries to find stability in relationships in the external world and, not finding it out there, withdraws, trying to find it within, and is again caught in the same process. Is this a fact? (*pause*)

The mind tries to find stability in co-operative action; it tries to find stability in the family; it tries to find stability in commitments, in relationship with nature. And not finding stability in any of these, it becomes romantic, which breeds further instability. It withdraws into a world of infinite conclusions, utopias, hopes, dreams, and invents an order in that. The mind which is unstable, narrow, not rooted in anything, gets lost. Is that what is happening to you?

R: That explains the cult of the beautiful—

K: The cult of the beautiful, the cult of the ugly, the hippies' cult. Is that what is happening to your mind? Beware. *Do not accept what I am saying.*

So, a mind which is not stable, that is not firm, not deeply rooted in order (not an invented order, for an invented order is death), is destructive. It goes from communism to the guru, from *Yoga-Vaśiṣṭha* to Ramana Maharṣi; it is caught in the cult of the beautiful, the cult of the ugly, the cult of devotion, of meditation, and so on.

How is the mind to be still? Action which flows from that stillness is entirely different. See the beauty of it, sir.

A: That is the dead end of the mind.

K: No, sir. I am asking myself: How is the mind to be completely stable?—not the stability of hardness, but a flexible stability. The mind that is completely stable, firm, deep, has its roots in infinity. How is this possible? I realize that my mind is unstable, and I understand what that means: I know for myself that the mind is born of instability; I know that and, so, I negate it; and I ask: What is stability? I know instability, with all its destructive activity, and when I put all that away, what is stability? I sought stability in the family, in work, and I have sought stability inwardly, in withdrawal, in experience, in knowledge, in my own capacities, and in

God. I see that I do not know what stability is. *The not-knowing is the stability.*

The man who says: I know, therefore, I am stable, has led us to this chaos, as have the people who say: We are the chosen ones. And all the vast numbers of teachers and gurus have said: We know. Rejecting all that, rely on yourself, have confidence in yourself. When the mind puts away all this, when it has understood what is not stable, and realized that it cannot know true stability, there is the movement of harmony—*because the mind does not know.*

The mind then moves from the truth of not-knowing. That truth is stable. The mind that does not know is in a state of learning. But the moment it says: I have learnt, it has stopped learning, and that is the stability of division. So the mind says: I do not know; and the truth is that it does not know. That is all. That gives the mind the quality of learning, and in learning there is stability. Stability is in the learning, not in the 'I have learnt'.

See what all this does to the mind: It completely unburdens the mind, and that unburdening is freedom—the freedom of not-knowing. See the beauty of it—the not-knowing, therefore freedom.

What happens to that part of the brain which functions in knowledge? To function from memory to memory is part of its function, isn't it? The brain finds tremendous security in knowledge. Biologically speaking, that security is necessary, otherwise it could not survive. Now, what happens to the brain which says: I really don't know anything apart from what is necessary for biological survival? The brain which was once tethered is now free; it is not occupied; it can act but it is not occupied. That brain has never been touched; it is no longer capable of being hurt. There is a new brain born, or the old brain is purged of its preoccupations.

Rishi Valley
28 January, 1971

THE BRAIN CELLS AND MUTATION

Dialogue 24

P: We have not dealt so far with what seems to be the essence of your teaching and that is the problem of time, the silencing of the brain cells and the processes that operated in Krishnamurti. I am putting the three together because as one observes the horizontal movement of time, that is the life of K, one sees the boy born with his tradition of Brahmanism, going through a certain preparation in the Theosophical Society, being initiated, and writing certain books like *The Search* and *The Path*, books in which enlightenment is looked upon as an end, as a fixed point. In all these earlier books there is presumed to be a state which has to be reached, and also a great struggle through centuries towards it. Suddenly a change takes place in K; he negates salvation, eternity as a fixed point, and so destroys the horizontal movement of time as such. Now what exactly took place? If we could understand and see as if through a microscope what happened to Krishnamurti, if we could examine what happened to his brain which contained this horizontal movement of time, it might be possible for us to understand time and mutation in relation to the brain.

K: I understand. Do you understand, sir?

D: Yes, sir. It is a very important question.

K: I wonder if that so-called horizontal movement was not a very conditioned and superficial movement. The young man repeated what he was taught, and at a given moment there was a break. You follow?

P: No, I do not. What is meant by a superficial movement of conditioning?

K: That is, the boy accepted, repeated, walked along the path laid down traditionally and theosophically. He accepted it.

P: All of us do just that.

K: All of us do it in varying degrees. The question is: Why did he pursue that journey?

P: No. The question is: What was it that triggered that which suddenly made him say that there is no fixed point?

K: Look at it as if K were not here, as though he were dead. How would you answer this question? I am here, and so may answer you or may not but, if I were not here, how would you answer it?

P: One way of doing so would be to examine what you have said, along with the influences which have operated on you at that time, to see at what point the break took place and what were the crises, inward or outward, that have been recorded, to produce that break.

K: But suppose you knew nothing of all that and, yet, you had to answer the question seriously now, what would you do? What you suggest would take time, investigation. How would you find out *now*? How would you find out if you were faced with this problem that there was a young man who followed the traditional path, the idea of a fixed point, the fixed goal, using time, evolution, but at a given point he broke away? How would you unravel it?

D: It is like this. We heat water. Up to a hundred degrees it is uniform, and then there is complete transformation.

K: But to come to that point takes time.

P: If I did not have the historical background, the only way of investigation would be to see whether this process is possible within my own consciousness.

D: I was driving at something else. The traditionalist would say that there is a process which, like the boiling point of water, leads to transformation. You can negate tradition, but tradition is necessary to take you up to that point.

P: If the historical data on K were not available, of K being put through various *sādhanās* and so on, and one were just given the fact of this phenomenon of K, the only way to investigate would be through self-knowing.

D: How would you explain the phenomenon?

F: You seem to be creating a relationship between the former state of development and the present state of being. Is there a relationship between the two? You say that one leads to the other, that one is before the other; you are arranging it in time.

P: We know the history of the phenomenon of K—that he was born of Brahmin parents and so on. I look at his background, I notice that up to a point K talked of time, of salvation as a final point and then, suddenly, the whole thing was negated.

K: F asks why you relate this horizontal movement to the vertical movement. There is no relationship between the two. Therefore keep the two separate.

P: When I look at K, I look at the whole background.

K: Look, but do not relate the two.

P: If what you say has to be meaningful, it is essential to understand this process of time, and the freedom from the process. I therefore ask the question: What triggered it in you? If you tell me that it just happened, I will say all right. If it happens, it happens; if it does not, it does not. I will continue my life.

F: There is no trigger.

P: A certain brain made certain noises and suddenly started making other noises, and K has been saying that the brain cells themselves are time. Do not let us get away from that. So the brain cells of K which were time, underwent some kind of mutation.

K: I will show you very simply. The cultivation of a brain, of any brain, takes time; experience, knowledge and memories are stored in the brain cells. This is a biological fact. The brain is the result of time. Now, this man at some point breaks the movement of time. A totally different movement takes place; which means that the brain cells themselves undergo a mutation. And P says that I must answer and say what took place; otherwise what happened was merely chance.

D: If it was chance, then we will accept it.

B: An answer by Krishnaji may help us to bring about a mutation in ourselves.

S: Two explanations are possible: The Theosophical explanation that as the Masters were looking after K he was untouched by experience, and the other explanation is that of reincarnation.

D: When K says that the boy K was not touched by experience, how does he know? The boy wrote *The Path*, *The Search*; I will not go into the end product where he was not touched.

K: Just leave that for the moment. How did it happen? What is your answer? Given these facts, faced with them, how do you answer this?

B: Sir, how can we account for the change which took place in you in 1927? Mrs Besant has said that the two consciousnesses could not be merged. We have no personal knowledge of this, nor the capacity to know.

K: Let us investigate it together.

F: I will put it this way. The man woke to another state. One state does not lead to the other; there is no causal connection.

P: I maintain that the brain cells themselves cannot comprehend time as other than a horizontal movement. Unless this is understood, we cannot explore, at very great depth, the problem of time.

K: Let us explore. First of all, is time involved at all? If you asked how this happened to me, I really would not know. But I think we could investigate it together. If you asked me: Did you go for a walk last night? I would say yes. Whereas if you asked me: How did this happen to you? I really could not say how. What is wrong with that?

P: In itself, it is all right. But we are trying to comprehend the essential nature of the movement in time and the movement outside time. Leaving aside the question of how this happened to you, it is important that we investigate into the nature of time—not at the level of chronological time and psychological time, for we have gone into that sufficiently.

K: Begin with perception: Is seeing involved with time?

P: What happens to the brain cells in the process of seeing?

K: The brain cells, in the process of seeing, either respond in old terms or are held back in abeyance; they hold themselves back in abeyance without the past.

P: You say that in perception which is instantaneous, the brain cells hold back. If they are not operating, do they exist?

K: They do, as the store-house of knowledge which is the past. The brain cells, we all agree, are the store-house of memories, experience, knowledge which is the past. That is the old brain. In perception, the old brain does not respond.

P: Where is it?

K: It is there. It is not dead. It is there because I have to use knowledge to think. The brain cells have to be used.

P: What operates then? If the brain cells are not operating, what is operating?

K: A totally new brain. This is simple. The old brain is full of images, memories, responses, and we are used to responding with the old brain. Perception is not related to the old brain. Perception is the interval between the old response and the response which is new, which the old does not yet know. In that interval there is no time.

F: There is a contradiction. In psychology, sensation is itself direct. In the interval between sensation and perception, memories jump in and distort. So sensation is timeless but the interval is time.

K: Let us get this clear. You ask me a question. The old brain responds according to its information, according to knowledge; if the old brain has no knowledge, no information, there would be an interval between the question and answer.

F: The interval is due to the sluggishness of the brain cells.

K: No.

F: Memory traces continue in the brain.

K: If you ask me what the distance is between here and Delhi, I would not know. No amount of my thinking with the brain cells would help. The fact is not registered. If it were, I would then think about it and answer. But there is not-knowing. In that not-knowing, there is a state in which time does not exist.

D: No amount of waiting will make me know.

K: The moment I know, the knowing is time.

P: You have said two or three things; you have talked of a new brain. The question is: What has happened to the old brain?

K: The old brain is quiet.

P: Has it existence?

K: Of course it has; otherwise I cannot speak the language.

P: The moment you say that the old brain continues to exist—

K: Otherwise, I cannot function.

P: When the new exists, the other, the old, does not.

K: Perfectly right. Hold on for a moment. Let us for the sake of convenience call them the old and the new brain. The old brain has, through centuries, collected all kinds of memories, registered every experience, and it will function on that level all the time. It has its continuity in time. If it has no continuity, then it becomes neurotic, schizophrenic, unbalanced. It must have sane, rational continuity. Now that is the old brain with all its stored memories. A brain with such continuity can never find anything new, because it is only when something ends, that there is something new.

F: Continuity of what? When you speak of continuity, a movement is implied.

K: It is adding, taking away, adjusting; it is not static.

D: There is a circular movement which is continuity.

K: First, let me see this continuity, this circular movement, as a repetition of the old. At a given point of time, I call it the new, but it is still the old. I hanker afteı the new, and invent the new within the circle.

P: There is the new which is a rearrangement of the old, and there is the new which is not a rearrangement of the old. What else is there? What is this other new which is not an invention or a rearrangement of the old? Is it recognizable? Is it perceivable?

K: It is perceivable but not recognizable.

P: So it is not an experience.

K: It is a perception without the observer.

D: But not in terms of the past.

K: Perception means something new.

F: Sensation is without the past. Sensation is not loaded with the past. It is direct.

K: The mind which has become mechanical craves for something new. But the new it craves for is always within the field of the known. You may call the movement within the field horizontal or circular, but the movement is always within the field: I want the new in terms of the old.

P's question was about the brain which is the result of time, experience, knowledge: What happens to that brain when there is a perception which is new, in which there is no experience, no observer, where perception is not an experience to be stored up and remembered to become knowledge?

F: That brain does not respond.

K: What makes it not respond? How does this happen?

P: We should leave everything and remain here, because something of vital significance is happening here. We have still not got the feeling of it. I listen to you; I am attentive. In that state of attention there is nothing else but sound and movement. In that state, can I understand what has happened to the whole weight of the past?

K: It is fairly simple. The past is in continuous operation; it is registering every incident, every experience, the conscious and the unconscious. Everything is pouring in—the sound, the seeing.

P: The brain cells act independently of whether I am conscious or unconscious.

K: Yes. Now when that brain is in operation, it is always acting from the past. First of all, what is wrong with that?

P: If you observe, it is like ripples being shown up—thought as ripples. Then suddenly I am attentive, and there are no ripples.

K: In that state of attention, there is perception; that state of attention is perception.

D: When I see the fact that my brain is registering everything, and I suddenly realize that it is going on without the observer, that annihilates me. If it goes on without me, then I am finished.

K: It is like a recording machine that is registering everything.

D: Why do I need to call it a machine? It is a wondrous thing. And I do not know the why and the how of it.

K: You have heard that noise of the horn blowing. The brain cells have registered it; there is no resistance or acceptance.

D: There is more to it than that.

K: Go slowly. This brain is a machine which registers. It is like a tape recorder that is registering everything all the time. If you challenge the brain, it will respond in terms of its likes, or of its dislikes: you are a danger, and she is not a danger. In that instant is born the 'me'. It is the function of the brain to register.

D: That is a partial statement. That it registers is a fact, but there may be something more to it.

K: You are jumping ahead. The function of the brain is to register, to record. Every experience, whether conscious or unconscious, every sound, every word, every nuance, is going on irrespective of the thinker as a separate entity. Registering that noise which is unpleasant, listening to some flattery, to some insult, wanting more or less—out of this registration emerges the 'I'.

P: When the registration takes place, I am conscious of the sound.

K: What does that mean?—that it is pleasant or unpleasant. At the moment of experiencing, there is no 'I' in it at all.

P: There is a state with the sound, and there is a state without the sound.

K: Now comes the new action. I register that noise—the hideous noise, the ugly noise—there is no response to it. The moment there is a response, that response is the 'I'. That response increases or decreases according to pleasure, pain, suffering.

Now, P's question was: How is that old brain, which is doing all this automatically, mechanically, all the time, how is that old brain, whether it is running horizontally or in circles, ever to see without the registerer or registration?

P: We have gone over this. I want to take it further from there. We listen. Sound passes through us. There is attention. In that state, for a second, horizontal movement has come to an end. What has happened to the old brain?

K: But it is still there.

P: What do you mean, 'It is still there'?

K: Look at it. See what happens. There is that child crying. The sound of the child's cry is being registered—why does the mother not look after it?—and so on.

P: Do you record all that?

K: No. I am purely listening; there is complete listening. What has happened to the old brain in that listening? Have you understood the question? We are taking the journey together. (*pause*)

Let me put it differently. What is the essential need of a brain? (*pause*) Must it not feel safe, secure, to function? One sees that the brain needs security. Then some event occurs, and the brain sees the fact that to have presumed that there was such a thing as security or comfort is not correct.

D: The brain cannot see it.

F: We take the brain as an accumulation of impressions and as a store-house of memories. But the store-house of memories is outside the brain, and the brain is only a lens.

P: Why do we not observe our own minds at this moment, instead of talking of the brain in the abstract?

K: Listen. Your brain demands security; it needs a great sense of protection, both physical and psychological. That is all I am saying; that is its function. This is the essential point.

D: What is the basic query?

P: The basic query is that when there is this horizontal movement of the mind as time, as memory, as the operation of the brain cells, what is it that makes the 'other' possible? And what takes place when the 'other' is?

K: I will tell you. The brain needs security, protection, safety in order to survive; it has survived for millions of years. Now what takes place? The mind in search of security is always experimenting, and attaches itself to a guru, to nationalism, to socialism; it gets stuck there, and has to be rooted out. Because of its basic need for safety and survival, it has invented time sequences—

horizontal and circular time. What happens when the basic need for security is granted? Is perception now not entirely different?

D: It is the demand for security that resists the question you are asking.

K: No; my brain is secure. So far, for seventy years, it has not been damaged because it has rejected security at the price of illusion. It says: Do not invent beliefs or ideas, for in them there is no security at all. Wipe them out because they are illusory. Therefore the brain is completely secure—not in anything, but secure in itself.

Previously, it sought security through something—through family, through God, through egotism, through competition—through seeking. Security through something is the greatest insecurity. The brain discards that. Therefore it can perceive. Because it has no illusions, no motives, no formulas, it can perceive. Because it does not seek any security, it is completely secure. The mind is then free of illusions. Illusion, not in Śaṅkara's sense, but just the illusion that says: I will find security in the family, in God, in knowledge—which is the past. Now what is there to perceive? It is perceiving.

F: We are as we are made; we know that we are at the mercy of the psychosomatic body and, therefore, we are very insecure. There has to be a different approach to this. It is something very vulnerable, because our bodies are so fragile.

K: So I will protect the body. There is no egotism involved in that.

F: Vulnerability is connected with the ego.

K: I will protect the body without the ego. I will wash it, look after it. We think it is the ego which protects the body. Once we grant deeply the necessity for complete survival, for protection, for safety for the brain, we will solve all the other problems.

Let us put it this way: Is perception related to the brain which demands security and survival at any price?

P: My mind does not function in this way. Therefore I find it very difficult to listen. I am trying to work at a microscopic examination of the mind, to see whether it is possible to arrive at a point when the brain cells actually cease functioning. Questions of security or insecurity have no relevance here. At this moment, if I raise these questions I am lost. Here I am before you, and I want to understand this movement of time which is horizontal, to see whether there can be a state when the brain cells cease to function. Any queries, questions, or answers away from this will only lead to confusion.

K: Are you saying that having finished with what we have said, my brain cells are in perpetual movement in one form or another?

P: I say that I am listening to you. There is no movement in my mind.

K: Why? Because you are listening with an attention in which there is no centre that attends; it is a state in which you are just attending.

P: Now, in that state I ask: Where is the weight of the past? I am asking that question to understand the problem of time, and not anything else.

K: In attending, in giving complete attention, is there time?

P: Because there is no response, how do I measure?

K: When there is attention, there is no time because there is no movement at all. Movement means measurement, comparison—from here to there, and so on. In attention there is no ripple, there is no centre, there is no measurement.

The next question is: What has happened to the old brain? It is your question. Keep it there. What has happened? (*pause*)

I have got it. Attention is not disassociated from the brain; attention is the whole body. The whole psychosomatic organism is attentive—that includes the brain cells. Therefore, the brain cells are exceedingly quiet, alive, not responding with the old; otherwise you could not be attentive. There is the answer. And in that attention, the brain can function. That attention is silence, is emptiness—call it what you like.

Out of that silence, out of that innocence, emptiness, the brain can operate; but not the thinker in terms of seeking security in something.

P: Does it mean that the whole brain has undergone a transformation?

K: No. What has taken place is mutation. The observer is not.

P: But the brain cells are the same.

K: Watch it. Do not put it that way; then you are lost. Watch it in yourself. Attention means complete attention—of the body, of the psyche, of the cells; everything there is with life—alive. In that state, there is no centre, there is no time, there is no observer as the 'me'. There is no time in terms of the past, yet the past exists—because I speak the language; I know my way to the room. Right?

Then what happens to the brain cells? They are registering but there is no 'me'. Therefore the 'me' that is part of the brain cells is wiped out.

Bombay
6 February, 1971

GOD

Dialogue 25

P: Krishnaji, at one level, your teaching is very materialistic because it refuses to accept anything which does not have a referent; it is based on 'what is'. You have even gone so far as to say that consciousness is the brain cells, that thought is matter, and that nothing else exists. Now in terms of this, what is your attitude to God?

K: I do not know what you mean by materialism and what you mean by God.

P: You have said: Thought is matter and the brain cells themselves are consciousness. Now these are material things, measurable. And, in that sense, yours would be part of a materialistic position, in the tradition of the *Lokāyatas*. In terms of your teaching, what place has God? Is God matter?

K: Do you clearly understand the word 'material'?

P: What is material is measurable.

F: There is no such thing as the material, P.

P: The brain is matter.

F: No; it is energy. Everything is energy, but that energy is not observable. You can only see the effects of energy which you call matter; the effects of energy appear as matter.

D: When she says 'matter', she probably means energy. Energy and matter are convertible, but still measurable.

K: You are saying that matter is energy and energy is matter; you cannot divide them as pure energy and pure matter.

D: The material is the expression or appearance of energy.

F: What we call matter is nothing but energy. It is only energy as apprehended by the senses of perception. There is no such thing as matter. It is only a manner of speaking.

P: You see Krishnaji, your teaching is based on that which is observable by the instruments of hearing, of seeing. Even though you may talk of not-naming, what is observable is through the instruments of seeing, listening. The senses are the only instruments we have with which to observe.

K: We know sensory observation—seeing, hearing, touching—and the intellect, which is part of the whole structure. Now what is the question?

P: In that sense, the teaching is materialistic, as opposed to the metaphysical. Your position is a materialistic position.

F: If you want to stick to facts, the only instrument we have is the brain. Now, is the brain everything or is it an instrument in the hands of somebody else? If you say that there is only the brain, it will be a materialistic position. If you say that the instrument is materialistic, then the teaching is not materialistic.

P: The Tāntrik position and the ancient alchemist position are in one sense similar to Krishnaji's position. Everything has to be observed. There is nothing that can be accepted which has not been seen with the eyes of the see-er. I now ask: What is your view of God? I feel it is a very legitimate question.

F: Can you explain what God is?

K: What do you mean by God? We have explained energy and matter, and now you ask what we mean by God. I never use the word 'God' to indicate something which is not God. What thought has invented is not God. Whatever is invented by thought, is still within the field of time, within the field of the material.

P: Thought says: I cannot go further.

K: But it may invent God, because it cannot go further. Thought knows its limitations. Therefore, knowing its limitations, it tries to invent the limitless which it calls God. That is the position.

P: When thought sees its limitations, it is still aware of an existence beyond itself.

K: Thought has invented it. Thought can only go beyond when it comes to an end.

P: Seeing the limitations of thought is not the knowing of thought.

K: So we must go into the knowing of thought and not into God.

D: When thought sees its own limitations, it practically debunks itself.

K: Does thought realize that it is limited or, does the thinker, who is a product of thought, realize that thought is limited? Do you see the point?

P: Why do you draw the distinction?

K: Thought has created the thinker. If thought did not exist, there would be no thinker. Does the thinker, observing the limitations, say: I am limited? Or, does thought itself realize its limitations? These are two different positions. Let us be clear in all this.

We are exploring. There are the two—the thought and the thinker. The thinker, observing thought, sees, through reasoning which is a material process, that energy is limited. In the realm of thought, the thinker thinks this.

D: When the thinker says that thought is limited, both the thought and the thinker become question marks.

K: No, not yet. Thought is memory, thought is the response of knowledge, thought has brought about this thing called the thinker. The thinker then becomes separate from thought; at least it thinks it is separate from thought. The thinker, looking at its reasoning capacity, at its intellect, at its capacity to rationalize, sees that it is very, very limited. Therefore, the thinker condemns reason. The thinker says: Thought is very limited—which is a condemnation. Then the thinker says: There must be something more than thought, something beyond this limited field. That is what we are doing.

We are taking things as they are. Does the thinker think that thought is limited? Or, does thought itself realize that it is limited? I do not know if you see the difference between the two questions.

F: Thought is prior to the thinker.

P: Thought can end. But how does thought feel that it is limited?

K: That is my point. Does the thinker see that he is limited? Or, does thought say: It is impossible to go any further? You see the point?

F: Why do you separate the thinker from the thought? There are many thoughts of which the thinker is also another thought. The thinker is the guide, helper, censor; he is the most dominant thing.

K: Thought has gone through all this and established a centre which is the observer. And the observer, looking at thought, says that thought is limited.

D: In fact, it can only say: I do not know.

K: It does not say that. You are introducing a non-observable fact. First of all, thought is the response of knowledge. It has not yet realized that it is very limited. What it has done, in order to have security, is to put together various thoughts which have become the observer, the thinker, the experiencer. Then we are asking the question: Does the thinker realize that it is limited? Or, does thought itself realize that it is limited? The two are entirely different.

F: We know only a state of the thinker thinking thoughts.

K: The thinker is not a permanent entity, as thought is not permanent. The thinker is adjusting, modifying, adding. This is important. It is important to find out whether the thinker sees that it is limited or whether thought as idea—idea being organized thought—thinks that it is limited.

Now, who sees this? If the thinker sees that it is limited, then the thinker says that there must be something more—there must be God, there must be something beyond thinking. Right? If thought itself realizes that it cannot go beyond its own tether, beyond its own rooted brain cells, which are the material root of thinking, then what takes place?

P: You see, sir, that is the whole point. If you were to leave your teaching at this point, I would understand. If you were to leave it at this point—that thought itself sees its own limitation or that the brain cells themselves see it, and leave it at that, then there would be a total consistency and logic in your position. But you are always moving, going beyond this, and you cannot use any words. Thereafter, call it what you like, the feeling of God is introduced.

K: I won't accept the word 'God'.

P: You take us by reason, by logic to a point. You do not leave it there.

K: Of course not.

P: That is the real paradox.

K: I refuse to accept it as a paradox.

F: The material of something and the meaning cannot be interchanged. P is mixing up the two.

K: What she says is fairly simple. She says: We see the logic of what you say about the thinker and the thought. But you do not leave it there. You push it further.

P: Into an abstraction. I say that thought and the thinker are essentially one, but that man has separated them for his own safety, permanency, security. We are asking the question whether the thinker thinks thought is limited and, therefore, posits something beyond because he must have security, or whether thought says that whatever the movement of thought, however subtle, however obviously reasonable, it is still limited. But K goes further than that, he goes into abstractions.

K: I realize that thought and the thinker are very, very limited, but I do not stop there. To do so would result in a purely materialistic philosophy. That is what many intellectuals in the East and West have come to. They are tethered, and being tethered, they may expand but remain tied to a pole which is their experience, their belief.

Now, knowing that thought is energy, thought is memory, thought is the past, thought is time and suffering, can I answer the question whether thought itself realizes its own limitations? Thought realizes that any movement of thought is the movement of consciousness. Consciousness is the content of consciousness, and without the content there is no consciousness. Now what takes place? Is that observable or not? I do not invent God.

P: I did not say that. I never said that you invent God. I say that up to this point your position is materialistic; it is rational and logical; then suddenly you introduce another element.

K: No. Look at it. Thought itself realizes that any movement it makes is within the field of time. It is not the thinker who is incapable and, therefore, posits super-consciousness, a higher self, God or whatever else it can. Then what happens? Then thought becomes completely silent. This is an observable fact which can be tested. The silence is not the result of discipline. Then what happens?

P: Sir, let me ask you a question. In that state the registering of all noise goes on. What is this machine which registers?

K: The brain.

P: The brain is the material. So this registering goes on.

K: It goes on all the time whether I am conscious or unconscious.

P: You may not name it, but the sense of existence goes on all the time.

K: No, you are using the word 'existence', but it is the recording that goes on. I want to make the difference here.

P: Let us not move away. It is not that all existence is wiped out. It would be, if thought were to end.

K: On the contrary. Life goes on, but without the 'me' as the observer. Life goes on, the registration goes on, memory goes on, but the 'me' disappears. Obviously. Because that 'me' is the limited; therefore thought as the 'me' says: I am limited. It does not mean that the body does not go on, but that the centre, which is the activity as the self, as the 'me', is not. Again that is logical, because thought says: I am limited; I will not create the 'me'—which is further limitation. It realizes it, and it drops away.

P: Having said that thought, creating the 'me', is the limitation—

K: Thought creates the 'me', and the 'me', realizing it is limited, ceases to be.

F: When this happens, why should I name what is going on as thought at all?

K: I am not naming anything. I realize that thought is the response of the past; the 'me' is made up of various additions of thought. Thought, which is the past, has created the 'me'; the 'me' is the past. And the 'me' projects the future. This whole phenomenon is a very small affair. That is all. Now what is the next question?

F: What has the state of this hopelessness to do with God?

K: It is not a state of hopelessness. On the contrary, you have introduced the quality of hopelessness. Because thought has said that it cannot go beyond itself, it is in despair. Thought realizes that whatever movement it makes, it is still within the field of time, whether it calls it despair, fulfillment, pleasure or fear.

F: So the realization of the limitations is a state of despair.

K: No. You are introducing despair. I am only saying that despair is part of thought; hope is part of thought; and that any movement I make, whether it is despair, pleasure, fear, attachment, detachment, is a movement of thought. When thought realizes that all this is its own movement in different forms, it stops. Now let us proceed further.

P: I want to ask you a question. You said that existence goes on without the 'me'. What or who proceeds further?

K: We have moved away from the word 'God'.

P: If my use of the word 'God' is very much within the field of thought, I will put it aside. Now I am moving with that. Therefore I am saying: If thought as the 'me' has ended, what is the instrument of investigation?

K: We have come to a point where there is no movement of thought. Investigating into itself so profoundly as we are doing now, so completely, so logically, thought has ended. We are now asking: What is the new factor that comes into being which is going to investigate? Or, what is the new instrument of investigation? It is not the old instrument. Right? The intellect, despite its sharpness of thought, despite its objectivity, has created tremendous confusion. All that has been denied.

P: Thought is word and meaning. If, in consciousness, there is movement without word and meaning, something else operates. What is this?

K: We have said that thought is the past, thought is the word, thought is meaning, thought is the result of suffering. And thought says: I have tried to investigate, and my investigation has led me to see my own limitations. Now, what is the next question? What is investigation then? If you clearly see the limitations, then what is happening?

P: Only the seeing.

K: No. Seeing is visual, and the sensory seeing depends on the word, the meaning.

P: After what we have said, there is only seeing which operates.

K: I want to be clear. You say that there are sensory perceptions. But we have gone beyond that.

P: When we use the word 'seeing', does it describe a state where all the sensory instruments are functioning?

K: Absolutely.

P: So if there is only one sensory instrument functioning at a time, then it is tethered to thought; when there is seeing and no listening, that seeing is tethered to thought. But when all the sensory instruments are functioning, then there is nothing to be tethered to. That is the only thing one can know. That is existence. Otherwise there would be death.

K: We agree. Then what is the next question? What is perception then? What is investigation? What is there to investigate? What is there to explore? Right? What have you to say? You have all become silent.

P: When thought has come to an end there is nothing more to investigate.

K: When thought comes to an end, what more is there to investigate? Then who is the investigator? And what is the result of the investigation? Now, is your question what is there to investigate, or what is the instrument that investigates?

P: One has always regarded investigation as moving towards a point.

K: Is it a forward movement?

P: We are trying to investigate God, truth, but as thought has ended, there is no point towards which there can be movement.

K: Go slowly; do not say anything categorically. All that you can say is that there is no movement, no movement forward. A forward movement implies thought and time. That is all I am trying to get at. When you really deny that, you deny movement, outward or inward. Then what takes place?

Now begins an investigation of a totally different kind. First of all, the brain realizes that it wants order, security, safety, in order to function sanely, happily, easily. That is its basic demand. Now the brain realizes that any movement from itself is within the field of time and, therefore, within the field of thought. Is there then a movement at all? And is it a totally different kind of movement—a qualitatively different movement, which is not related to time, to process, to the forward or backward movements?

Now the question is: Is there any other movement? Is there something which is not related to time? Any movement, outwardly or inwardly, as far as the brain is concerned, is within the field of time. I see that. The brain realizes that though it may think that it is extended infinitely, it is still very small.

Is there a movement which is not related to thought?—This question is put by the brain, not by some super entity. The brain realizes that any movement in time is sorrow. So it naturally abstains from any movement. Then it asks itself if there is any other movement which it really does not know, which it has never tasted.

That means that one has to go back to the question of energy. We have separated energy as human and cosmic. Do you follow what I mean? Do you see it? I have always regarded the movement of energy as being within the limited field, and I have separated that energy from cosmic, universal energy. Now the battle is over. Thought has realized its limitation and, consequently, human energy has become something entirely different.

The division of energy as the cosmic and the human is created by thought. The division ceases, and another factor has entered. To a mind which is not centred within itself, there is no division. Then, what is there to investigate? Or, what is the instrument of investigation?

There is investigation, but not the investigation to which I have been accustomed—which is an exercise of the intellect, of reason, and all the rest of it. And this investigation is not intuitive. The brain now realizes that in itself there is no division. Therefore, the brain has not divided itself as the cosmic, the human, sexual, the scientific or the business brain. Energy has no division.

Then what takes place? We started by asking if thought is material. Thought is material, because the brain is matter; thought is the result of the material. Thought may be abstract but it is the result of the material. Obviously it is. Few have gone beyond.

F: The meaning of the body is consciousness; what is the meaning of existence?

K: What is the meaning of this room? Emptiness, because emptiness is created by the four walls, and in that emptiness, I can put a chair and use the room.

F: The room has meaning because P lives here.

K: Furnishes, lives, fears, hopes, quarrels here.

F: What is consciousness? You reply that it is the content, but I am asking for something more—for the meaning, not the description.

K: F is asking for something more. He is asking: What is the meaning of my existence? None at all—

F: Is there no question of your wanting to have meaning? What is the meaning of Krishnamurti? Can you negate the self? Then you are guillotined. The individual within, the censor, existence, consciousness, body—there is more besides these. And that is the abstract soul. Ultimately there is a soul around which everything impinges. Can you negate that?

K: The soul is the 'me'.

P: That is the difficulty. There is a validity in F's question because the self is the most difficult thing to negate. If you attempt to negate the ego, the self, you will never succeed. But if you proceed as we have just done, that is all that is necessary.

F: What is the meaning of all this? Why should the 'me' end? The meaning of the atoms is the organism; the meaning of the organism is consciousness. Why should it stop there?

K: It does not stop there. It stops there only when thought realizes its limitations. Let us come back. What is the instrument that is going to investigate—the instrument in which there is no separation, in which there is no investigator and the investigated? I see that thought has really no meaning. It has meaning only within its small field. Now we ask: What else is there to discover?—not as a discoverer discovering something. What is the movement which is neither inward nor outward? Is it death? Is it the total negation of everything? Then what takes place?

When thought, in which we include consciousness and its content—despair, failure, success—ends, then what takes place? That part of the brain which is registering, goes on. It must go on, otherwise it would become insane. But there is the whole of the brain, which is quiet. Thought does not enter that field at all. In fact thought enters into a very small portion of the field of the brain.

P: It is a fact that we use only a millionth part of our brain.

K: There is the other part.

F: There is no reason to suppose that the remnants of the brain which are not used can become anything more than the other parts of consciousness.

K: No. Do look at it.

F: Even biologically, you are not right. The size of the brain which is usable, determines the extent of consciousness. If you use more, consciousness will be greater.

K: The old brain is very limited. The entire brain is the new which has not been used. The entire quality of the brain is new. Thought, which is limited, functions in a limited field. The old brain is not active because the limited has ceased.

P: So you are saying that if you see the small part of the brain as limited, limitation ends.

K: No. Limitation goes on.

P: But because the part does not take over the whole, nor does it limit itself to itself, the rest of the brain, which is not used, comes into operation. Then this is again a totally materialistic position.

K: Agreed. Carry on further.

P: That is all; there is nothing more to discuss.

F: I have an objection. Even if the entire brain is used fully, it will still only be consciousness; it will be a tremendously enlarged consciousness.

K: Depending on whether there is a centre.

D: If there is a centre, then you are not using the 'other'.

F: We have been operating only within the limited. Now if you move into the 'other', how do you know that the consciousness has not a focalizing tendency?

K: Focalizing takes place when thought operates as pain, despair, success—when thought operates as the 'me'. When the 'me' is silent, where is consciousness?

F: After that it all becomes conjecture. You presume that the only factor which can project the centre is disappointment, hurt; you presume that thought is limited and projects itself. Why should the focus as the 'me' depend on limitation?

K: Focalization takes place when thought is functioning.

P: If thought with its word and meaning ceases, whatever operates then is not recognizable as word and meaning.

F: You are narrowing the field. I am still legitimately questioning the point that frustration is the only point of focalization.

K: I included everything, not only frustration, in the field of time. Now I see that the brain cells have operated in a very small field of time, and that that small field, with its limited energy, has created all the mischief. The old brain becomes quiet. What we have called quietness is limitation becoming quiet. The noise of that has ended, and that is the silence of limitation. When thought realizes that, then the brain itself, the whole brain, becomes quiet.

P: Yet it registers.

K: Of course.

P: Existence continues.

K: Existence, without any continuance. Then what? The whole brain becomes quiet, not only the limited part.

F: It is the same thing to us.

P: If you do not know the 'other', and the 'other' is not in operation, what becomes quiet in our case is only limitation.

K: Therefore, that quietness is not quietness.

P: This is something new which you are introducing.

D: What makes you say that we are not using the whole brain?

F: I am saying that my total brain is functioning, but I am not conscious of it, because I am enclosing myself within the limited field.

K: First stop the movement of thought, then see what happens.

D: When the movement of thought stops, things happen on their own. Is the inquiry of what happens afterwards necessary?

P: I want to ask one question here. You have said that the ending of the limitation of the 'me' as thought is not silence.

K: That is the beauty of it.

P: Let me get the feeling of it. Please say it again.

K: When thought with its limitations says that it is silent, it is not silent. Silence is when the total quality of the brain is still—the total thing, not just a part of it.

F: Why should the total brain become silent?

K: The total brain has always been quiet. What I have called silence is the ending of the 'me'—of the thought which is rattling around. The rattling around is thought. The chattering around has stopped completely. When the chattering comes to an end, there is a feeling of silence; but that is not silence. Silence is when the total mind, the brain, though registering, is completely quiet—because energy is quiet. It may explode, but the basis of energy is quiet. (*pause*)

Now, there is passion only when sorrow has no movement. Have you understood what I have said? Sorrow is energy. With sorrow comes the movement of escape from sorrow—through understanding, through suppression. But when there is no movement at all in sorrow, there is an explosion into passion. The same thing takes place when there is no movement—outward or inward, when there is no movement which the limited 'me' has created for itself, in order to achieve something more. When there is absolute and total silence, therefore no movement of any kind, when there is complete quiet, there is a totally different kind of explosion which is—

P: Which is God.

K: I refuse to use the word 'God'. But this state is not an invention, it is not something put together by cunning thought, because now thought is completely without movement. That is why it is important to explore thought and not the 'other'.

Bombay
9 February, 1971

ENERGY, ENTROPY AND LIFE

Dialogue 26

D: The other day we discussed God. We also discussed energy, and you spoke of human energy and cosmic energy. I will state the scientific position. Scientists have measured energy and have arrived at an equation: $E=MC^2$, a fantastic figure. This is material energy. Biologists have also proved that life-energy is anti-entropic, which means that while material energy dissipates itself, life energy does not. So this movement of anti-entropy is against the material flow of energy which dissipates and ends in dead uniformity. The human being generally moves with entropic energy and, therefore, decays. Scientists have measured even the time span of this energy. The problem therefore is: How can man, being aware of this, be part of the movement of energy that is anti-entropic?

K: One can see quite simply that that which is mechanical wears itself out, given a certain time.

D: What is measurable can be manipulated by the mind of man. An instance of this is the atom bomb. This energy, this movement of entropy, dominates the world today. How do we get out of its grip?

P: This is a very important point. If there is a movement of energy which does not dissipate itself, which does not end, decay then, from the point of view of science as well as man, it is probably the answer to all the problems of the world.

K: So what are you asking? How is the movement of this mechanical decay in which man is caught to be brought to an end? Is there a contrary movement?

D: And, what is the nature of that contrary movement?

K: Let us put that question again simply. Man is caught in material energy, in mechanical energy; he is caught by technology, by the movement of thought. Do you get the key to it?

D: No.

K: There is the whole field of technological knowledge and the movement in that knowledge; that is the field in which man lives. It has tremendous influence on him; it is really taking him over, absorbing him. Scientists have measured the energy of that movement, and that energy is an energy of decay, an energy of waste. Scientists also say that there is a contrary movement of energy in the opposite direction which is creative energy. Real human energy is non-mechanical, non-technological. Now, what is the question?

D: Modern biologists such as Huxley and de Chardin hold that man has developed from the smallest cell, and that in him there is an emergence of consciousness. Man as an entity can be conscious of the whole evolutionary process.

P: From this another very interesting fact emerges. De Chardin says that the next leap forward will come by 'a process of seeing', which is the same as the traditional *paśyantī*. I think it is important to explore this verb which has such a loaded traditional meaning in India.

K: We will come to that if we can examine the decaying process — the energy which is mechanical, which is entropic. We are also trying to find that life-energy which is non-mechanical. What is this energy?

D: Biologists say that it lies in cultural development, in the destiny of man, not in a new species emerging.

A: This question faces modern man at many levels. After the satellites went up, there was a new measurement of the cosmos. We call that the measurable infinite. But man also knows that there is the immeasurable infinite.

K: Quite. They have measured thought. They have measured memory.

F: In what sense do you mean this?

K: In the sense that the electrical impulses of thought are measured.

F: Thought is the measure of entropy.

P: Only that which has a beginning and an end can be measured.

K: So there is a movement which ultimately, in its very motion, leads to decay.

F: It also leads to radiance and that is the end of entropy. There are those two movements—a mechanical movement and an anti-mechanical movement.

A: The biologist's approach is very tentative when it comes to consciousness. Whenever he speaks of life-energy, he does not speak with the same precision as when he speaks of the other kind of energy. There is a recognition that the anti-entropic is the unknown, the undefinable. After having said that there is the 'other', the 'other' still remains unknown.

D: One fact is certain. That the life-energy does not move in the direction in which the entropic energy moves.

A: Let us take the movement of life-energy as something unknown to us. We cannot manipulate it. In the measure that man becomes conscious of the entire evolutionary process in himself, he becomes aware of consciousness.

P: I think we are going around in circles. What is observable is that man is born, lives and dies. The phenomenon of a cyclic movement, of a beginning and an ending of energy, is visible and deeply structured in our consciousness—something emerging and disappearing, which are the two manifestations of energy. Is there an energy which is not concerned with emerging or disappearing?

K: It is the same thing. Do we accept that there is a beginning and an ending of energy?

F: Individuals may begin and end, but life does not. It creates.

K: Do not bring in the individual yet. There is a movement of energy which is mechanical, which is measurable, which may end, and there is life-energy which you cannot manipulate; it goes on infinitely. We see that in one case there is a wastage of energy, and that in the other there is a non-wastage of energy.

F: I do not see the other as a fact.

K: All right. Let us see the movement of energy which can reach a height and decline. Is there any other form of energy which can never end, which is not related to the energy which begins, continues and withers away? Now how are we going to find out? I have got it. What is energy that decays?

P: Material energy decays. Why does it decay?—By friction?

D: By pressure?

F: The fact is that there is energy overcoming friction, and energy dissipating in friction.

P: You say that there is an energy which decays in friction, through friction. I say that its very nature is friction. All that movement which we call energy, in itself is friction. Show me why it is not so.

D: Energy is the biological capacity to overcome resistance; but it dissipates itself in this process.

K: As in a machine.

P: So it is manifest as friction.

K: Let us go into this. Any energy that meets resistance wears itself out. Take a car going up the hill without enough power—the energy created by the machine will wear out. Is there an energy which can never wear out, whether you go uphill, downhill, parallel, vertical? Is there an energy which has no friction in itself and, which, if it meets resistance, does not recognize resistance, does not recognize friction? There is another factor to it. Energy also comes into being through resistance, through manipulation.

P: The moment energy crystallizes—

K: Do not say that.

P: Why, sir, the human organism is a crystallization.

K: The human organism is a field of energy, but do not use the word 'crystallization'. I am keeping it very simple. There is energy that meets resistance and wears itself out. In that whole field there is the energy brought about through resistance, through conflict, through violence, through growth and decay, through the process of time. Now we are asking if there is any other energy which does not belong to this field, which is not of time.

A: Tradition calls it the timeless arrow.

F: Are you asking whether there is an energy which is irresistible?

K: No. I only know energy which is in the field of time. It may have a span of ten million years, but it is still in the field of time. That is all we human beings know. And, as human beings, we are inquiring if there is an energy which is not in the field of time.

F: Are you asking whether it is an energy which does not undergo transformation?

K: Look. I know energy, the cause of energy, the ending of energy. I know energy as the overcoming of resistance, I know the energy of sorrow, the energy of conflict, of hope, of despair; they are within the field of time. And that is the whole of my consciousness. I am asking: Is there an energy which is not time-bound, which is not within the field of time at all? Is there an energy which may go through the field of time and, yet, not be touched by time? It is very interesting. Man must have asked this question for centuries upon centuries, and not being able to find an answer, he postulated God, and put God outside the field of time. (*pause*)

But putting God outside the field is to invite God into the field of time; and therefore all that is part of consciousness. And that decays. It decays, if I may use that word, because it is of time and because it is divisible. And my mind which is divisible, which wants to find a timeless energy, proceeds to postulate an energy which it calls God, and worships that. All that is within the field of time. So I ask: Is there any other energy which is not of time? Shall we go into it?

D: Yes.

K: How do I find out? I reject God, because God is within the field of time. I reject the super self, the *ātman*, the *brahman*, the soul, heaven, for they are all within the field of time. Now you ask: Is there an energy which is timeless? Yes, sir, there is. Shall we go into it?

D: Yes, sir.

K: How do I find out? Consciousness must empty itself of its content, the content which time has created. Must it not?

P: May I ask something? Is the total emptying of consciousness not the same as seeing the totality of consciousness?

K: It is. Agreed. I do not think I have made myself clear. There is the fact of totally emptying consciousness; there is another fact which is seeing with the totality, with all the content—seeing the field of time as a total state; seeing the whole field of time now. What does that seeing mean?

Is that seeing different from the field of time or, has that seeing separated itself from the field of time? What we call perception is that seeing which, separated from the field of time, looks at the field of time and thinks it is free.

D: Right, sir. This perception presupposes a perceiver.

K: We are back to the same thing. So the question arises: What is total seeing? I see logically, verbally; I comprehend the whole consciousness of man. The whole of consciousness is its content, and this content has been accumulated through time, which is culture, religion, knowledge. Whether this content expands or contracts, it is still within the field of time. It is the movement of consciousness within the field of time. Consciousness is time itself. What do you say D, is consciousness time?

D: I have no other instrument but consciousness.

K: I am aware of that. I see that consciousness is time, because the content of consciousness is consciousness, and the content has been accumulated through centuries upon centuries.

D: Consciousness is conflict, friction.

K: We know that. How can my mind look at this total field of time, and not be of the field?—That is the question. Otherwise it cannot look. Total perception must be free of time. Is there a perception which is not of time? What do you say?

D: That is our question.

K: And if it is not of time, then perception is the life-movement. Perception itself is the life-movement.

D: Logically that would be so.

A: Can we say that perception itself is the life-movement? I do not know anything about it.

K: Can my mind which is of time, which consists of accumulated impressions of experience and knowledge gathered in time—which is the content of consciousness—disassociate itself from the total field? Or, is there a perception which is not of time and which therefore sees the totality?

P: A is right. I cannot just posit the 'other'.

A: The moment I posit the 'other', it becomes the god of the *Upaniṣads*. All that I can say is: Seeing that all consciousness is within the field of time, I can remain with it; I am it.

K: You are it. Somebody comes along and tells you that movement within the field of time is measurable, and he asks: Is there a perception which sees the totality of consciousness, which is time? He does not tell you whether there is or there is not. Is there such a perception? That is a legitimate question.

P: May I say something? I see you. I see this room. I see the interiority of my consciousness. There is no more than that. I can see. It is a concrete thing; seeing is concrete.

K: Are we wasting time?

P: We are not. We have to be concrete. This is seeing.

K: I understand P. Here I am sitting in this room. I see the content of the room and myself in it. 'Myself' is the observer who is conscious of the room, the proportion of the room, of the space of the room. I see this through the consciousness which is made up of time. The observer and the observed are within the field of time. That is all. When the observer invents something, that is still within the field of time. So any movement is within the field of time. That is all I know. That is a fact. Knowing that, somebody asks: Is there a movement which is not of time? Have you understood my question?

P: I do not know.

K: You may put the question to yourself. To put the question to yourself is legitimate.

P: Putting the question is a fact, but that does not make it legitimate.

D: Questions sometimes imply something more than facts.

K: I am proceeding from the question: Can the mind see the totality of itself? Can the mind see itself as the field of time?—Not as an observer observing the field of time. Can the mind itself become totally aware, so that it sees consciousness as time? It is all fairly simple.

P: I do not see that. What is involved in seeing consciousness as time? When I am observing thought, I see it as a flux; I see that movement: I wake up to a thought as having been, then to another thought as having been, and so on and on. And I put all this together and say: There is movement. When Krishnaji says, 'Observe this room', I observe this room—but there is no perception of time. Is it the active present?

K: What are you trying to say, P?

P: I cannot accept your statement regarding the perception of consciousness as a movement of time. If we do not allow the concreteness of the actual seeing, we move into the field of the conceptual.

K: What you are saying is that when you enter a room you perceive the proportions of the room, its shape, the colours and, also, that you perceive your own consciousness with the same tactile sense.

P: Then I perceive A speaking. I then connect the two perceptions, and thought brings in time. There is no sense of time apart from the connections.

K: If there is perception, there is no time. I look, and there is no time.

P: You asked a question: Do you see consciousness as the whole content of time? I question that; I want to examine it under a microscope.

K: My mind is the result of memory, experience, knowledge; it is the result of time. My consciousness is within the field of time. How can I see that the whole content is within the field of time?

P: Because of memory, of thought.

K: One is a formula, a conclusion, a statement; the other is a process of finding out.

P: I find it very difficult. Do you know what you are asking, sir? You are asking us to perceive an abstraction. Can an abstraction be perceived? The moment there is no thought, 'what is' becomes an idea or an abstraction.

K: Wait. You have drawn your own conclusions when you say that it is an abstraction; I have not come to any conclusions.

P: I ask myself: When I accept that consciousness is a product of time, is that a statement or is it something that I see?

K: Is it a statement with a verbal meaning which I accept and which, therefore, becomes a conclusion or, is it an actual fact, as this room is a fact, that the whole of my brain, the whole of my consciousness, is this enormous field of time?—Is it as concrete as that?

P: How can it be as concrete as the other?

K: I will show it to you in a minute. I see that a conclusion is not a fact because thought has entered into it. Thought hears this statement, accepts it, makes it into a formula and remains with that formula. That is an abstraction. A formula is an abstraction created by thought; and therefore it is the cause of conflict. It is of the very nature of conflict. I see that very clearly. Now, is there a perception which is not of thought, not of the field of time as the mind? Formulas are the most deadly things. Formulas and concepts are products of thought and, therefore, are all within the field of time.

P: Why is it necessary to make this absolute statement at all? Why is it necessary to make an absolute, finite statement?

K: I will show you in a minute. I am inquiring into the field of time. Time, we said, is consciousness. Time is the result of centuries upon centuries of experience. That is my consciousness, and consciousness is made up of all the content. I hear you state that, and thought picks it up and makes a formula of it. I see that the very formula is within the field of time, and that that very formula is the factor of friction. So I do not touch it. I have negated it. I am asking myself: Have I negated it, or am I still thinking, feeling that I have negated it? Am I still trying to find a fact which is not within the field of time? (*pause*)

I am discovering something: When thought operates, it must operate within the field of time. It must come to a conclusion; and conclusions are part of consciousness. That is all. I now ask myself: Is there any movement of thought, or am I pretending to myself that there is no movement of thought and that there is only perception? When I enter this room there is no movement of thought; I just see. When thought comes in, there is an entry into the field of time. Now I am asking: Is the mind deceiving itself by saying that it has no formulas when it is entrenched in formulas? By formulas I mean thought, which is consciousness. Or, is there a perception which has nothing whatsoever to do with thought? I only know that all consciousness is within the field of time, and that thought is consciousness.

Therefore, I am inquiring; I do not want to deceive myself; I do not want to pretend that I have got something which I have not got. I see that whenever thought comes into being, it must create a formula, and that the formula is within the field of time; the whole of consciousness is time. I hear you say this. Now, is it a formula which I have accepted or, is there the fact of the perception of the total movement of thought?

P: What is meant by these words which you use—'the total movement of thought'? You ask whether we have accepted it as a formula. I have neither accepted it as a formula nor is it a fact for me; it is neither of these.

K: But by listening, by examining, by investigating, you say that this is so. It is not a question of accepting. Now, move a step further. Is that 'it-is-so' an acceptance of an idea? Is it intellectual and, therefore, still within the field of time?

P: I will never answer that question to you or to myself.

K: I am asking it.

P: What do I answer?

K: You are not asking that question. You know nothing about it. I want to find out whether the mind, that is the result of time, on hearing that statement, accepts it as a statement, as a formula and, therefore, remains in time, or whether it sees the truth, the fact.

Then what takes place? It is a fact. Nothing more can be said when thought does not arise. I see the room, but the moment thought says that it has proportion, colour, beauty, time enters—

you follow? In the same way, this whole field of time exists only when thought operates.

Now, am I pretending that thought is completely absent or is it a fact—of which we can be aware? Then what takes place?—I am aware of this room without any interference of time.

P: At this moment what are you aware of?

K: The mind which is the result of time, hearing what you are saying, accepts that as a formula and says yes. The acceptance is a conclusion—which is the operation of thought. Therefore, I see that time is still operating in that sense. So is there an operation of perception without thought? What takes place then?

P: What are you perceiving at this moment? (*pause*)

K: (*Makes a gesture, brushing one hand over the other*) Nothing. That is it. It is logically correct.

A: Whatever we hear, becomes a memory the next moment.

K: I am not concerned about you at all. Forgive me. I am not concerned whether you see or do not see. I told you that I am going to investigate. I am investigating. You are merely remaining with the formula. I see this fact. Am I perceiving the formulas with a formula, or perceiving without a movement of thought, without a formula? Then P asks me: In that state, what is there to perceive? Absolutely nothing, because that state is not of time. That is the factor of life-energy.

F: This state which you are just now describing can be called entropy of thought, a state where no movement is possible any more.

K: You are not investigating.

F: It has not ended here. You are ending it.

P: I want to ask another question. You say that there is nothing. Is there movement?

K: What do you mean by movement?

P: The passage from here to there—

K: Which is measurable and comparable. Movement which is

measured is within the field of time. And you are asking whether there is movement in that nothingness. If I say that there is movement, you will tell me that it is measurable and, therefore, in time.

P: There is movement in nothingness then.

K: What does that mean? The movement of time is one thing. The movement of nothingness is not of time; it is not therefore measurable. But it has its own movement, which you cannot possibly understand unless you leave the movement of time behind. And that is infinite. And that movement is infinite.

Bombay
11 February, 1971

INTELLIGENCE AND THE INSTRUMENT

Dialogue 27

P: I wanted to ask you, Krishnaji, whether there was one question that needed to be asked by an individual which would open the door to reality. Could all questions be reduced to that one question?

F: Is there such a thing as a door? We cannot ask a question about that for which there can be no metaphor.

K: I think she means it in the sense of an opening or a break through.

F: From your own experience, what would you say is breaking through? There is no point of reference for us.

K: What is the question?

P: There are many things which we have discussed during the last few days. Can all these questions converge into one question?

K: I think so.

F: I would not put it that way. I come to you because in you there is an imponderable quality, a tiny seed of something which makes you entirely different. I do not look for differences in manifestation, but there is in you that 'elseness'. Now, is there a key to that? Is there a question which opens that up?

B: If I may ask: What is it that prevents one from seeing? This is our difficulty. Last evening when we heard Krishnaji's talk, we felt that there was nothing which we would not be prepared to do, if it was in us to do it. Can all that you say be held in one question? To you it is a very simple thing. You have an amazing capacity of converting diversity into a single thing. This convergence has not taken place in us. Could there be some action which would make all questions melt into one question?

P: I have a further question. During the past few days Krishnaji has been saying that there is a region where thought is necessary and a region where thought has no place. What is the instrument, the mechanism, which makes it possible for thought to operate only where it is legitimate, and not impinge into areas where it should not function, where it creates illusion?

K: Now, what is the question?

P: How does this happen? What is the instrument? We have examined our minds under a microscope. Now we ask: Under whose command do the brain cells function when thought ceases to function, when there is no evaluation, no operation of will, no doer, no one to direct or to command?

K: I thought K explained yesterday that it is intelligence.

D: It is the same thing. Intelligence is the instrument.

K: Let us keep to the word 'intelligence'. Intelligence is that quality of the mind which can use the vast field of knowledge, but which discards the use of knowledge in another field.

F: There is a difference between you and me. Is the difference the degree of intelligence, or is there another factor operating in you?

K: P asked a question: What is the essential demand in life? And she goes on further to ask whether thought can operate sanely, efficiently in the whole field of knowledge where it is necessary and not operate in another field where it brings chaos, misery. Now, what is it that can prevent thought from operating so that it does not create misery?

Can we tackle this question differently? Can the mind, the totality of the mind, empty itself of everything—of knowledge and non-knowledge? Can it free itself of the knowledge of science and language, and also of the mechanism of thought that functions all the time? Can the mind empty itself of all that? I do not know if I am making myself clear. Can the mind empty itself not only at the conscious level but also at the deeper secret chambers of the mind? From that emptiness, can knowledge operate? And, also, can it refrain from operating?

B: Is it then a question of emptiness?

K: Let us see. Can the mind empty itself of its whole content as the past, so that it has no motive? Can it empty itself? And can that emptiness use knowledge, pick it up, use it and then drop it—but always remain empty?

Emptiness is the sense that the mind is nothing. Emptiness has its own movement which is not measurable in terms of time. The movement in emptiness, which is not the movement of time, can operate in the field of knowledge—and there is no other operation. That movement can operate in the field of knowledge, nowhere else.

P: Are there two movements?

K: There are no two movements. That is why I said that movement can operate only in knowledge. Please follow. I am just investigating. You asked a question. K has spoken of knowledge and freedom from knowledge: Knowledge operates in the field of science, where there must be a certain will, a certain direction, an operative function, a design; knowledge does not operate where there is no place for thought and, therefore, for will.

F: It seems that sometimes we operate intentionally and sometimes non-intentionally. I can see that sometimes I do something without knowing. So there are these two operations: mental and non-mental. The movement of the two is not separate.

K: Watch your mind F. You see thought operating always within the field of knowledge. Knowledge helps man to live more comfortably in the environment. Right? It also brings pain, misery and confusion. That is a fact.

F: I object to your use of the word 'always'.

K: Wait. Then you and I ask: Is thought necessary? Why does thought create misery? Is it possible for thought not to create misery? That is all. Keep it as simple as this.

F: My answer is that the roots of our misery are not known to us. I am not aware of the promptings which create misery.

K: We began with the superficial layers. We must now go into the secret chambers of the mind.

P: Surely we are not positing a state of consciousness where thought will operate only at the technological level and at the day-to-day level of action, where it is necessary, and that it would be sufficient if by some trick or electric shock, all other consciousness as thought could be wiped away? We are not postulating that, surely?

K: Of course not.

P: But look sir, the moment you speak of a place where thought can operate legitimately and a place where thought has no legitimate place, you are postulating the 'other' — a state which is non-thought. If consciousness is only content, then what is the 'other'?

D: I can go into a state of constant euphoria through a lobotomy. Is that enough?

K: Then you become a vegetable.

F: I question your statement that thought is consciousness. Is thought the entirety of consciousness? Can we say that there is no consciousness beyond thought?

K: So we have to go into the question of consciousness.

B: We are retracing our steps. You used the word 'intelligence' in a different way. That word is the key, if we know what it is.

P: But this is also a valid question: If consciousness is the same as its content, and the content of consciousness is thought, will the cutting away of thought solve the problem?

K: No.

P: Then what is the 'other'?

F: Intelligence is different from consciousness. We must distinguish between the two. Intelligence is much vaster than consciousness. We can have unconscious intelligence.

P: What is consciousness?

K: What is consciousness? There is a waking consciousness of the superficial mind and there is a hidden consciousness, a total lack of awareness of the deeper layers.

P: I would say, Krishnaji, that there is a consciousness in which thought operates; then there is a consciousness where attention is and where there is seeing; and a consciousness which is unconscious of thought. I see these three states as they operate in me.

K: Wait. Wait. Memory—the operation of memory as thought, as action; then attention—a state where there is no thinker. So you are saying that there is the operation of thought and memory — having been and what will be. Then there is a state of attention and a state in which there is neither attention nor thought, but a sense of being half asleep.

P: Half awake, half asleep.

K: All this is what you would call consciousness. Right?

P: In all these states, either consciously or unconsciously, sensory perceptions are in operation.

F: Do not bring in the unconscious. Do not call the unconscious a form of consciousness.

D: I wanted to ask whether we could include dreams also in it; that is the unconscious part.

F: Dreams are dreams because they become conscious.

P: In the state in which one spends a large part of the day, images come and go; that is still consciousness.

F: My point is that consciousness is patchy; it is not a continuous phenomenon.

K: Can we start this way? I am approaching it tentatively —there is consciousness, wide or narrow, deep or shallow. As long as there is a centre which is conscious of itself, that centre may expand or contract. That centre says that it is either aware or not aware. That centre can attempt to go beyond the limitations which it has placed around itself. That centre has its deep roots in the cave and operates superficially. All that is consciousness. In all that there must be a centre.

P: Consciousness is that which registers. It is the only thing which distinguishes life from a state of death. As long as there is a registering, there is no death.

K: Are we speculating? Look, let us begin very simply. When are you actually conscious?

P: When I am awake, when I am aware.

K: I would begin very simply. When am I conscious?

P: I am conscious of this discussion.

K: Let us keep it simple. When am I conscious? Either through sensory reaction, or through a sensory shock, a sensory resistance, a sensory danger, a conflict in which there is pain-pleasure — it is only in those moments that I say that I am conscious. I am aware of the design of that lamp; I perceive that there is a reaction, and I say that it is either ugly or beautiful. Is not that the basis of all this? I do not want to speculate. I ask myself: When am I conscious? When I am challenged, when there is an impact of conflict, pain, pleasure, then I am conscious. This whole phenomenon is going on, whether there is a deliberate awareness or not; this thing is operating all the time. That is what we call consciousness.

F: The response to impact.

P: You mean there is no photographic consciousness. I see a dust bin—

K: But you are seeing it. The mind is registering it. That is, the brain cells are receiving all these impacts.

F: And in that is there no classification as pain, pleasure?

K: Impact as pleasure, pain, conflict, sorrow, conscious or unconscious, is going on all the time. There may be an awareness of all that at one moment, and at other moments there may not be. But it is going on all the time.

P: This process itself is consciousness, and the centre that observes is also part of consciousness.

K: What is the next question?

B: What is the nature of the unconscious?

K: It is still the same. Only it is the deeper layer.

B: Why are we unconscious of the deeper layer?

K: Because superficially we are very active all the time.

B: So the density of the superficial layer prevents our being conscious of the deeper layers.

K: I am making noises on the surface, which is like swimming on the surface. So what is my next question?

B: Is it possible to integrate the various layers?

K: No.

P: What is the relationship of thought to consciousness?

K: I do not understand this question because thought is consciousness.

P: Is there anything else but thought?

K: Why do you put that question?

P: Because you started by distinguishing the region where thought has a legitimate place from a region where thought has no legitimate place. And now you say that thought is consciousness.

K: Go slowly. Let us pause here. The first question was: Is thought part of this whole thing? Consciousness is thought—pain, conflict, memory. When the superficial mind is making a lot of noise, you come and ask: What is the relationship between thought and all that? Thought is all that.

P: You said just now that thought is a part of all that. Then what is the rest?

A: All that is consciousness. Thought comes into operation when the 'I' wants to localize.

K: That is right.

F: When the brain is cut off there is no thought.

K: That is, memory is held and paralyzed. All that we have described—memory and all that—is consciousness. Now thought comes into operation when I am interested in a part of this. The scientist is interested in material phenomena, the psychologist in his area; they have limited the field of investigation. Thought is used as a systematizer. P asks: What is the relationship between thought and consciousness? I think that is a wrong question.

P: Why is it a wrong question?

K: There is no relationship between the two because there are no two. Thought is not something separate from consciousness.

P: Is thought part of it or is thought all of it?

K: Go slowly. I do not want to say something which is untrue.

F: Thought is co-extensive with consciousness. Let us not subdivide them.

K: P asked F a very simple question: What is the relationship between thought and consciousness?

F: Which is the 'other'. She has no business to speak of the two as separate.

P: In everything K says the 'other' is posited: Thought has a legitimate place in the field of technology, but it has no legitimate place outside this field. And the point is not to perform an operation to wipe out thought. Therefore the 'other' is posited.

A: So, is there in consciousness a space which is not covered by thought?

P: Exactly.

K: I am not at all sure. I do not say that you are not right. So go on.

A: I say that there is a space in consciousness which is not thought and which is part of the human heritage. It is there.

K: I do not think that there is any space in consciousness.

P: I want to put another question to you. When I listen there is no movement of thought, but am I totally conscious?

K: Why do you call that being conscious? Wait, go slowly. A says that there is space in consciousness. We have to respond to that.

P: Whenever a statement like that is made, you immediately say that wherever there is space there is a boundary.

A: I may be using the wrong word here.

K: You have used the right word. But you do not see that space cannot be contained in a frontier, in a boundary, in a circle.

A: In one sense space is held within the circle, the square, and rectangle; but that is not the space we mean here.

K: Where there is a border there is no space.

D: According to the scientists, time and space are held together.

K: But when we say that consciousness has space, then consciousness has time. Space exists only when there is time. Time is limitation. Do not call that space. Space, in the sense in which we use the word, does not exist in consciousness. That space is something else. Leave that for the moment. Now what is the next question?

P: If we can take it from this point, I again ask: What is the relationship of thought to consciousness? Is thought contained in consciousness?

K: Do not use the word 'relationship'. That implies the two. Thought is consciousness. Do not put it in any other way.

P: Yes, thought is consciousness, listening is consciousness, learning is consciousness. If thought is consciousness, is thought not related to seeing as consciousness?

K: Put the question this way: Is there a state of mind when there is no learning at all? You see the question?

P: You have left us far behind now.

F: There are fields in which we operate without consciousness. Most of our relationships are beyond the reach of consciousness. I operate unconsciously.

K: I want to go very slowly, please. Thought is consciousness, listening is consciousness and learning is consciousness. Seeing, learning, hearing, memorizing, reacting to the memory are all part of consciousness.

P: So when any one of these parts is operating, and no other, what you say is understandable. Then there is no duality. Now we take the next step. When only one of these parts operates, is it consciousness?

K: I would not use the word 'part'. When thought operates within a specific field there is no duality. For instance, when I speak a few words in French or Italian, it is just that. But in the focalizing of consciousness, when thought compares that operation with another, there is dualism. I see a sunset; it is recorded at that moment as memory. And thought says: I wish it would happen again. See what has been discovered—when there is the simple functioning of thought without any motive, there is no duality.

P: Let us not take an impersonal thing like the sunset as an example. Let us take jealousy, the movement of thought as jealousy, my jealousy.

K: Jealousy is the factor of duality. My wife looks at another man, and I feel jealous because she is my wife, and I possess her. But if, from the beginning, I am aware that she is not mine, that she is as free as I am, the factor of jealousy need not enter.

P: I understand that. But when thought arises in consciousness, in itself there is no duality there.

K: There is duality only when there is a motive, measurement, comparison. In the observation of a beautiful sunset, in seeing its lights and shadow, there is no duality. The word 'beautiful' may be dualistic in the sense of implying the ugly, but I am using the word without the sense of comparison. The dualistic process begins the moment I say that I want to experience it again. That's all.

P: We have somehow moved away.

K: I will come back to where we left off. Consciousness is perception, hearing, seeing, listening, learning, the memory of all that and the responses of memory. All this is consciousness, whether focussed or not. In that consciousness there is time; and time creates space because it is enclosed. In it there is duality, conflict between 'the must and the must not'. And because that consciousness has boundaries and frontiers, which are limitations, in it there is no real space at all. Let us stop here.

A: There is another factor which I would like to include here. There are so many things being syphoned into my consciousness; there are the perceptions of the various peoples of the world —of the Africans, of the Latin Americans; there are the findings of the physicists, the biologists. How can we ignore all that? If we only take the 'I' and see the source of it, it is not enough. What is this process by which experience is syphoned into me? The movement of the 'I' as thought is something that is constantly being fed and renewed by that. Unless I see this process, I will not understand.

K: We said, sir, that the field of consciousness is a movement of contraction and expansion, a movement of information, knowledge. All that is happening in the environment, the political changes and so on, is a part of me; I am the environment and the environment is me. In that whole field there is the movement of the self as: I like the Arabs; I do not like the Jews.

A: I question that. One need not even takes sides. There are the liberated tribes in Africa which are caught up in militarism.

K: See what happens. Colonialism, freedom from colonialism, the tribe, then the identification with the tribe as the 'me' who belongs to the tribe.

A: On this wide canvas, we see thought narrowing into this focus, which we call consciousness.

K: All that is consciousness. Consciousness creates the mischief by saying: I like and I do not like. I am witness to this 'I-like-and-I-don't-like' because it is part of something over which I have no control at all.

A: That may be so, but that is not the problem. The problem is the identification which gives weight to the 'I-like-and-I-don't-like'.

K: Here I am, born in India with all its environment — the superstitions, the riches and poverty, the sky, the hills, the economic and the social conditions. The whole of that is me.

A: And there is also the entire historical and the pre-historical past. If you include all that, then choice disappears.

K: Yes sir, I am all that—the past and the present and the projected future. I was born in India with its five thousand year old culture. That is my consciousness. Choice arises when you say that you are a Hindu and I am a Muslim; when there is focalization through identification, there is choice.

P: Let us come back to what you have been saying—that it is legitimate for thought to operate in fields where knowledge is necessary, and that when it operates in other fields it brings sorrow, pain, duality. The question is: Is this other state of which you talk also consciousness?

K: Let us examine that. Let us stick to that question for the moment. Thought has a legitimate field of operation. If it impinges upon other fields it brings pain, suffering. What operated in this area is still consciousness, as we know it, with all the things we have put into it. The 'other' is not.

P: The 'other' is not what?

K: It is not thought.

P: But is it consciousness? Let me open out the problem a little more. Sensory perception continues to operate; there is seeing, listening. So why do you say that it is not consciousness?

K: I am saying that it is not consciousness in the sense that there is no conflict.

P: There is no conflict in consciousness. There is only conflict when consciousness operates as thought in the field where it has no legitimate place. Why should there be conflict in consciousness when thought is not operating?

K: There is no conflict at all there. Let us go slowly.

P: Then what is it that operates there?

K: It is intelligence. Intelligence is not consciousness.

P: Now we come to a stage where we just listen.

K: My mind has followed all this. It has seen, as A pointed out, that the whole content of consciousness contains the Indian tradition as well as the whole human heritage, and that I am all that; consciousness is all that. Heritage is consciousness, and that consciousness as we know it is conflict. My chief concern is to end that conflict—conflict being sorrow, pain. In examining that, there is a discovery that it is all a process of thought. There is pleasure and pain. And from that the mind says that it must operate in the field of knowledge and not here. It operates legitimately in one field, but not here. What has happened to my mind? It has become pliable, soft, alive. It sees, it hears. It does not have the quality of conflict in it. And that is intelligence; that is not consciousness. Intelligence is not heritage, whereas consciousness is heritage. Do not translate intelligence as God.

Now that intelligence can use knowledge, it can use thought to operate in the field of knowledge. Therefore its operation is never dualistic.

D: The language of intelligence must be different from the language of thought.

K: Intelligence has no language, but it can use language. The moment it has language, it is back again in the field. That intelligence which has no language is not personal; it is not mine or yours.

P: It may not be personal, but is it focalized?

K: No; it appears to focalize.

P: When it moves, does it focalize?

K: Of course, it must; but it is never in focalization.

P: It is never held?

K: It is like holding the sea in the fist—what you hold is part of the sea, but is not the sea.

Bombay
15 February, 1971

RIGHT COMMUNICATION

Dialogue 28

A: Sir, we have been listening to you with all the attention of which we are capable, with our minds and with all our analytical capacities. We have covered every inch of the ground, and we no longer accept anything we do not understand. Between you and us there has been a verbal communication and there has been also a communication beyond words. By ourselves we have not been able to penetrate the verbal barrier and reach that understanding which lies beyond words. When I sit by myself, I find that all communication with myself remains at the verbal level. I wonder whether we could take up for discussion the problem of communication.

Tradition has classified communication into four different states: *vaikharī*, *madhyamā*, *paśyantī*, and *parā*. *Vaikharī* is verbal communication apprehended through the auditory organ. It is subject to distortion of various kinds. It is dependent on sequence. *Madhyamā* is apprehended through the internal organ (the mind), and not by an external sense organ. In *madhyamā* there is the sequence of the mentally conceived. In *paśyantī* there is no sequence, it does not have the attributes of priority or posteriority; perception and communication are undivided. In *paśyantī* there is a transcendence of association with the diverse objects of the world, and also of time and space; such a state is free of the distinctions of the cognizer and the cognized. *Parā* is the power of self-revelation of the Absolute, which is inseparable from itself. *Parā* is the true channel of communication.

P: A is right. In investigating what Krishnaji calls listening and seeing, which are the operational part of his teaching, it might be possible to explore communication. I do not think we have gone into the question of whether communication is a process or whether it is an instantaneous light.

K: Can we start with the verbal level and work it through?

P: The question involves not just a communication between the speaker and oneself, but it involves the very instrument with which we apprehend.

K: Shall we begin slowly with this? There is a verbal communication in which both of us understand the meaning of the word. In that communication, the word is the meaning, and the meaning can be understood by me and by you. Then communication also means listening, not only to the meaning of the word but also to the intention of the speaker in using the word. Otherwise communication breaks off. When we use the word, it must have a quality of directness in which there is no double meaning, and it must also have the quality of the real urge to communicate something. In that urge there must be affection, care, consideration and the feeling that you must understand; not that I am superior and you are inferior. And, in using the word, there must be the contact of intention conveyed in the quality of the voice. That means both of us at the same time, at the same level, with the same intensity must understand the word. There must be the contact of intention, only then is there real communication.

A: This is so. Our minds, listening to you, used to set up so many obstacles. All that is over. Now there are no barriers.

K: What is important in communication is not so much the word, although the word and meaning are necessary, but to meet each other at the same time, at the same level, with the same intensity.

A: To communicate with oneself is also important. What does communication mean in that context?

K: Can one communicate with oneself?

A: Yes. It is a question of becoming coherent to oneself.

K: Communication is generally understood to be between two or more people.

A: But it need not even be two *people*. It can be between a person and a book. All this is implied when we talk about communicating with oneself.

K: I do not think one can communicate with oneself.

A: Sir, in Sanskrit they use the word *svasamvāda* for 'self-communication'.

K: I question that.

A: Why?

K: Even when you use the word 'self-communication', I do not think you communicate with yourself. You only observe what is going on. But the moment you use the word 'communicate', there is duality—in the sense that there is the division between you and the book, between you and me.

A: You said that there must be a certain sense of rapport, even for observing. I wonder if there is anything in that.

F: The message is the most important part in communication.

K: No; I can say something, and if you are not in a state of rapport you will twist it; you will twist the message. So the important thing is not the message but why at certain levels certain messages seem to be communicated to some people and not to others.

D: Why is the message you want to communicate not received by others?

K: We are talking of the quality of communication and not of what you communicate. When that quality is not there, you cannot communicate.

A: There is the communication of words, there is the communication of meaning and there is a communication that is beyond word and meaning.

F: The human race has developed certain instruments to take in messages through word and meaning, but they have no instruments to take in or to contact that which is beyond word and meaning. After all, radio and television have special instruments to receive. Do we have special instruments to receive?

D: The problem of communication arises only when the message is distorted or incomplete.

K: It is also in the meaning. You tell me something, and I twist it.

F: No. You tell me something. I listen to it with the instrument I have, and then translate it according to the instrument I have. There is no question of twisting it. We find that the reception of what you have to say remains at a lower wavelength. There is no question of twisting. What you say just does not seem to penetrate. It has nothing to do with the message.

P: Either the instruments have not been tuned or they are not there. Krishnaji, you can say what you will, but until the instruments are there, the message will not be received. Is the question one of the instruments being tuned right or of new instruments coming into being? That is the essential question.

K: A said that when we began contacting each other, there was a certain resistance, a certain intellectual objection to what was said. Now, he says, he has put all that aside, and he listens. Why should there have been resistance in the beginning?

A: We met after a gap of nine to ten years. There was conditioning—social, political, ideological; there was also the effort to understand you in terms of that conditioning.

K: P asks if there is a need for tuning the instrument.

P: Suppose you take a child and carefully remove it from all conditioning, it will still react, because conditioning is the instrument for transferring heritage. The instruments I have operate in a particular way; they are in themselves incapable of receiving in any other way but the known way.

K: Therefore, what is the question? Is the question one of taking these very instruments and making them sharp, vulnerable, sensitive or is it a question of new instruments coming into being?

D: May I say that the only available instruments we have are our eyes, our ears. They prevent us from understanding.

P: Through man's evolutionary history the sensory instruments have been perfected. They have been trained to operate along one channel; every sense organ operates singly: when there is hearing there is no seeing; where there is seeing there is no hearing. The operation of sensory perception is compartmentalized. I am asking whether it is the same instruments that are to be used.

B: A referred to two things—a stage where there was resistance and a stage where there was no resistance, but the instruments were the same.

A: In the use of the instruments man has no choice then. There might be an imperfect use of the instruments.

P: It may be either an imperfect use of the instrument or it may be that an entirely new instrument is necessary. Let us ask Krishnaji. Let us pose the question to him. Do you say that it is the same instrument or do you say it is a new instrument? If I had received what was to be communicated, I would not question, I would not be sitting here, but the very fact that I have not received that which has to be communicated means that the instruments I have, have failed.

A: My point is that there is a certain level of communication, but it remains at the verbal level.

P: Listening to Krishnaji many things have been communicated—the instruments can receive. I am certain, however, that the explosion which needs to take place has not happened. Despite the flexibility of consciousness, its capacity for receiving, despite the capacity of the instruments operating together, and the understanding of the problem of time, the explosion has not taken place.

A: Can we impersonalize it? Can we understand objectively the problem of communication?

P: Up to the *paśyantī* level that you described, we understand; *paśyantī* is 'seeing'.

A: Can we use the brain, which is our instrument, so that it does not create obstacles at any level?

K: What is the problem?

P: You have seen us through a span of time. Do you think we are able to communicate with you?

K: Obviously up to a point.

P: What is the hitch at that point?

K: Obviously, all communication is up to a point. I cannot go into this unless we begin very simply. I want to understand what the problem is. Communication implies telling you something and you listening to me, and either agreeing or disagreeing. That is, you and I have a common problem and we discuss it. We can only discuss the problem if we both see the common problem in its entirety, and if the meaning, the description each of us has, tallies. We can then say that we have understood each other.

Then the next point is: I may want to tell you something which you resist. I may be telling you something which is not accurate, and you have a right to resist. Then I tell you something which is true, mathematically true, and you say that it is not true because you have your own judgements and opinions. At that moment communication stops. I want to tell you something as between two human beings, not I as the guru and you as the disciple. I will express it as well as I can in words, but I know that what I want to say is not the word, nor the meaning of the word. I want to tell you something which can partially be described, and the rest of the meaning cannot be described. You take the description and not the other. Therefore, there is no communication. You are satisfied with the explanation and say that that is enough. I want to communicate something through the word, through the meaning, through the description, something which is not the word, which is not the meaning, but which is more than the description.

I want to tell you something which I feel very strongly, which I feel I must communicate to you. I describe, but you refuse to enter into that, and our communication comes to an end. Verbally we understand, but the 'other' cannot be communicated.

A: There is no refusal on our part; there is only incapacity.

K: I question it. Listen to what I said. I use words which you understand. You listen to the meaning, the word, the description, the explanation. But all that does not cover the thing which I want to convey to you. At first you refused to go beyond. You refused in the sense that you did not know what was being talked about. You felt that what could not be put into words did not exist.

I am not concerned with the word and the description. I want to tell you something now. How do I communicate what is not in the word or in the meaning, what is not a description, and yet is as real as the word and has as much meaning as the word? Words and explanations are not the things they refer to. That is the problem.

Now what is taking place in you and in me? Let us discuss that. I use words, my description is within the framework of words, and the words have space, they have a point of reference, a common meaning. You accept that; you follow up to that point and you stop there. You all do this in various degrees. Why? Why do you stop there? (*pause*) I think I know.

A: In this relationship of communication between us there has been a very clear understanding that one must never accept something which one does not comprehend. The mind has a capacity to manufacture beliefs, to take in what it would like to believe. I am trying to express the barrier my mind puts up. I say it will not do to take in anything that I do not understand.

K: Wait. You accept the word, the meaning, the description, the explanation, the analysis. You go as far that. Now I tell you, as between two human beings, that I want to communicate something else over and beyond the word; and you do not move. I ask myself why. Either you do not consciously want to understand what I want to communicate beyond the word, because the understanding might upset you, or you resist because your whole training, heritage tells you: Do not go near it, do not touch it.

A: That is not so.

K: I am just questioning. This is generally what happens. You listen to the word, the meaning, the description and the analysis, and you stop there because you sense that there is a danger to your image. So the image comes in and says: Stop. Communication then comes to an end.

A: I do not think so.

K: I am putting this tentatively.

P: What happens, Krishnaji, is that one can follow you, move with you, move within oneself to the point when thought stops, to a point where there is an ending of thought. At that point when thought ends, there is a total incapacity of moving in this new field.

K: I am coming to that P. I want to finish this. I ask myself consciously or unconsciously: Where is he leading me? I will not move because my image of myself is breaking down, and my security is threatened. I say that the description is good enough for me; I agree and stop there. My image of myself is more important, and so I am satisfied with a verbal understanding.

F: That is not so.

A: In the concrete instances which we are discussing, this is not true.

P: If you were to pose a question to me which threatened my image of myself, or even if I were to pose such a question to myself, there would be resistance. Yet by observing, moving step by step, there is no necessity to pose that question. If you pose the question, it is disastrous.

K: I am opening up the problem.

P: If I pose that question, everything rushes to protect the image, whereas if I move, observe step by step, then there is a fluidity that dissolves the image.

K: It dissolves only when you and I want to communicate something which is not merely words. Right? Very few go beyond that point; very few are willing to break their opinions, their conclusions, their images. In talking it over, I discover the image, you throw light on it, and I see. The very seeing is the ending of it.

There is the word, meaning, description, analysis, seeing without the image. That is real communication. Right? The difficulty comes in when we enter into something which is non-verbal. So, can there be communication about something which is beyond the word?

What is the quality necessary for both of us to understand something which is not the word?—Which means, to look at it, and not be caught in the description, in the explanation, in the meaning, in the word.

P: Look at what you have just done. You take us up to a point through analysis, thought, word. You sharpen intelligence, rarefy intelligence. You never proceed beyond that. So there is nothing, no description with which I can fill this emptiness.

K: Listen. To communicate in the sense we are talking about, that is, through word, meaning, description, analysis, all that and something more, the mind must not be caught in the word, in the meaning of words, in the description, or in the analysis. It must not be caught; it must be fluid, it must move. But you hold on to the words. The word, the meaning, the description, the analysis, is a process of thought and of memory. The word, cultivated, gathered through years, the meaning which you and I have given it, and the description through the word—all that is thought. Now you tell me something which is not the word. And I move all the time in terms of thought. I move with thought. Right? Communication is the word and communication is not the word. So the meaning, the description and the analysis—all that must be there, and the mind be so...(I do not know what word to use), so that you and I see the same thing, at the same time, at the same level, and with the same intensity. Otherwise our communication is verbal.

P: Now comes the crucial point.

K: Go slowly. We have come to this very carefully.

P: Is that movement in space a question of my feeling the movement of space in you?

K: Please, simple words, simple words.

P: Is it a question of contacting the movement of emptiness which you are communicating?

K: Wait, wait. I am not communicating any thing. I am only communicating *this*, not that. There is no communication there; there is communication only *here*.

A: You are saying that you have gone through words and descriptions, but all the while we have held the hand of thought. This is something which cannot be held by thought.

K: Do look at what is taking place between you two, A and P. You have a meaning, you have the word, the description, the analysis. You have come to a conclusion, and she has not come to a conclusion; communication has stopped. The moment you come to a conclusion and the other man has no conclusion, communication is finished.

P: Krishnaji says that he communicates through words up to a point, then there is a communication for which no words can be found. How is that to be done? Again I am putting it into my own words. I say that up to the point where the mind becomes fluid, rarefied, communication through words is possible because there is a point of reference. An instant after, I ask him whether the movement in that space has to contact or be contacted by the movement of Krishnaji in silence. Is it then not a problem of Krishnaji and me at all?

K: Not at all; there are no 'two'. What you have said is simple. Have you got it? (*pause*)

Two things can take place: The word, description, meaning, analysis and a conclusion; word, meaning, description, analysis, but no conclusion. The man who has got a conclusion stops there, and he cannot communicate with a man who has no conclusion. They cannot meet. They can go on discussing endlessly, but these two cannot meet.

Now we are asking: Is there something which is totally outside thought, which is the 'other'? And, is the 'other' communicable? Communicability implies 'two'. When you have no conclusion but I have a conclusion, there is an ending of communication. When there is a state where I have no conclusion and you have no conclusion, we both move, and we both smell the flower. Right? What is there to communicate when we are both smelling the flower? (*pause*)

F: Now I want to ask something. Is there such a thing as 'co-experience' or a 'co-state'?

K: There is no such thing as 'co-experience' when there is experiencing.

F: I am talking about communication. Communication implies two.

K: Up to a point.

F: And 'co-experience'?

K: When you and I are experiencing the sunset or sex, there is no two.

F: The instruments are two.

K: Of course.

F: The perceiver is not there.

A: Are these valid questions with regard to what we have talked of just now?

K: About what?

A: No conclusion, and them moving together. Are there any valid questions in that?

K: But we have not gone beyond the fact of coming to a

conclusion. Take a little more time over that; we are slurring over it.

F: I see that there is also the threat to the image.

K: I am committed to a certain activity and I am going to translate, in terms of my activity, whatever you say. I say that I have understood you, but I am going to translate what I have understood in terms of my activity. I am committed.

P: If there is a frontal attack on my image, and you ask me whether I have an image of myself, I would say: Of course I have an image; but it is a peripheral thing. There can be a stripping, a denudation, a breaking of the image without a confrontation with the image. You can strip, denude the image, but do not ask me a frontal question about the image.

K: I want to go a little deeper into this image-making.

P: Every movement of thought is adding to the image, and every negation is a denudation of the image.

D: The motivations which have built the image consist in our being bound to a certain mode of operation. So long as the mind refuses to let go, we are preventing communication.

P: I think that approach is totally wrong. If you are going to be caught in trying to be free of the image, you will never be free of it.

K: You are right.

P: You said that image and conclusion end communication, but you have to be confronted with this.

K: What is going on all the time, consciously or unconsciously, is that I am committed, or I shall be committed, or I am being committed; therefore communication is only up to a point and not beyond. This is what is happening all the time.

P: The image is built up of a lot of little things; it is what it is. I have tried to tackle it for twenty-two years, and now I say: Let me leave it alone; let me move, let me see whether what is static can be freed. Then it will do what it will.

A: But these million years of the past, how am I going to tackle that?

F: Can two brains with different pasts, different histories, different experience, feel the same thing at the same level? How is it possible?

K: The way you put the question is wrong.

P: I cannot break the image which has taken a million years to build. Can I break this instrument and make it flexible, moving? That is all.

A: There is one point which needs to be taken into account. There are certain accretions, and they can be dropped as they are pointed out in communication. This kind of thing happens effortlessly.

P: All of us who have participated these thirty days know, understand up to the point when thought ends. I am certain that what has to happen has to happen there.

K: Let us put the same thing in a different way. Is there a possibility of communicating or of experiencing that which is not verbal? The whole implication of experiencing is wrong.

P: Let me understand that. It is a very important statement: The whole of experiencing is wrong.

K: The conclusion or the idea that a state can be experienced by two is wrong.

A: That is correct.

K: It can never be experienced. What does that mean? Any man who says, 'I have experienced', has not experienced. Right, sir? You see how extraordinarily subtle it is. When you and I are looking at the sunset, there is only the sunset. I believe it is the same with sex. It is the same with two people who are at the height of anger; there are no two people. They do not say: We are experiencing anger.

F: What about the registering that goes on in the brain?

K: What is that? Memory?

F: In the present there is no memory.

K: But it acts in the present.

F: The memory is not yet created.

K: Do not theorize. Watch. You and I see the sunset. When it is in front of us, both of us see it, both of us are silent because it is glorious. We do not stop all movement. All movement stops. There are no two people there.

F: Are there not two separate 'I-consciousnesses'?

K: Both of us experience the sunset in its fullness; you and I do not talk about experiencing at that minute.

P: I would like to ask one question of you now, sir, because I feel it is important that your mind is also open to us. You took us through the state of the verbal; your mind was registering, and at some point the verbal ceased.

K: That means you and I were not forming any image.

P: Yes. At any moment of time, was there in you a registration of this?

K: I do not quite follow.

P: You moved in thought. You went through the whole process of communication through word, meaning, analysis. The point of flexibility came, and there was an ending of the analysis. Before the next analysis started, there was a gap. Has the brain any registration at all in this gap?

K: No.

P: Is there no part of your brain cells which bears the impact of this gap?

K: I wonder what you are talking about. I said no.

D: Is that because you are always in the gap?

K: What are you trying to say?

P: How do you know that there was no registration of the experience?

K: That is the next question. In experience, from the most trifling to the most sublime, is there not a recording?—as thought, as memory. There are the words, the description, and the analysis. This recording is a necessary process. What is not necessary, and irrelevant, is the conclusion. Then we are asking: Should the experiencing of something which is non-verbal necessarily be turned into thought, into description, into analysis, into words?

A: The process is now reversed.

K: See the subtlety of it. I started out with communication. Then there was an ending of thought. Then the feeling of *that*. The question now comes through a reverse process. Wait a moment. Am I right? (*pause*)

Now the next thing is: Do the brain cells register *that thing*, which then becomes the memory which says: I have experienced? Do you follow? Does that seeing, perceiving, the listening to something which is non-verbal, which cannot be experienced, register in the brain cells?

A: No.

K: Of course not.

P: You are saying something else. I would ask: Does seeing operate on the brain cells?

K: It is curious what happens. The brain is registering noise, it is registering impressions—everything is being registered. The brain is completely used to this; it accepts it. And that is a healthy, normal, rational state. Right? So it says: A strange phenomenon has occurred; I have registered it. Of course I have experienced it because it has been registered; it has been memorized.

A: I do not get it.

D: The moment it says that, the 'other' ceases to be.

K: Hold on a minute. Does every experience, except the ones which are useful for survival, have to register? I know I am asking the most absurd thing. I am asking: When you insult or flatter me, why should the brain register the insult or the flattery? The brain registers what is important. Why should the brain carry every superficial impact?

P: How can you ask why?

K: I will show you. You insult or flatter me. Why should I hold on to it? What is the point of holding on? Can I push it off, and, can the brain only hold things which are useful for it to survive?

F: You have introduced the word 'survival'.

K: Why should I hold your insult or flattery? Why should it register? Because if I do register the insult, then there is the effort to cut it off; there is like and dislike.

F: How can I cut it off?

K: Freedom is the emptying of all this. Freedom is not the burden of carrying insults, regrets, happiness, fears, miseries.

A: May I ask you one question? Am I capable of living outside the groove of registering?

K: No.

A: Living in the groove, it will register. There is nothing I can do to stop registering.

K: If you see this, there is a state of intelligence which refuses to register. Only the active present can help here, not the past or the future.

P: When there is attention there is no registering; not only that, but attention wipes out what is registered.

K: That is good enough. If the brain realizes that it need not carry all the burdens of everyday incidents, that is good enough.

Bombay
16 February, 1971

BIOLOGICAL SURVIVAL AND INTELLIGENCE

Dialogue 29

P: There was something which Krishnaji said in his talk yesterday; I do not know whether it will bear discussion. The question he posed was whether the brain cells could strip themselves of everything except the movement of survival, the pure biological necessity which alone makes the organism exist. It was a very startling statement. Krishnaji seemed to suggest that before any movement in the new dimension could take place, this total stripping to the bare bedrock was essential. In a sense he was back to a totally materialistic position.

D: If you have survival as the dimension of existence, there is no other dimension. Can this bear investigation? Is such stripping of every element of consciousness, as we have understood it, possible? We have always claimed that the human being is more than the urge for survival.

F: Are the brain cells not the repository of culture?

P: If you strip man of every psychological element except the urge for physical survival, how is he different from the animal?

K: We know both biological and psychological survival. But the factors for psychological survival, like nationalism, make biological survival almost impossible. Psychological fragmentation is destroying the beauty of survival. Can one strip man of the psychological factors?

P: Apart from the biological and psychological, is there anything else? You spoke of stripping yourself of all factors. I am asking you if there is any other element apart from the biological and the psychological.

K: As far as we know these are the only two factors that operate in man.

F: Is there not, apart from the physiological factor, such a thing as psychological survival?

K: Which means the survival of the psyche. The psyche is the result of the environment and of heritage. Last evening when we used the word 'consciousness', we said that the whole of consciousness is its content. The content of consciousness is conflict, pain; the whole of that is consciousness.

D: You said also that intelligence is more than consciousness.

K: Wait. We said that understanding the fact of consciousness and going beyond it is intelligence. You cannot come to that intelligence if this consciousness is in conflict. All that we know now is biological survival and the survival of psychological consciousness. What is the next question?

P: You implied yesterday that there was a necessity to strip consciousness of everything save the factors which insure biological survival.

K: Can you strip that whole content of consciousness which is psychological? In that stripping, intelligence operates. Then there remain only the factors which ensure biological survival and intelligence—there is no other.

P: You did not speak about intelligence yesterday. You said: When there is a total stripping of consciousness and nothing else remains, that operation is the biological movement of survival; it is the movement which perceives. Is there such a seeing?

K: Then the mind is not merely the survival-element, but there is another quality in it which perceives.

P: What is that quality?

K: What did K say yesterday?

P: He said that there is a stripping away of consciousness, and that there is only the movement of survival in silence. And that silence sees.

K: Perfectly true. Now what is silence? What is the nature of silence?

P: That seeing is something which we can affirm. But something else was said yesterday and, so, we cannot help asking: If man is stripped of everything which we consider the element which makes him human—

K: Which is conflict, pain.

P: Not only that, but compassion—

B: We consider that man, as opposed to the animal, is human. What are the things which differentiate man from the animal?— Intelligence, the capacity to analyse, speech.

D: Man is an animal that uses language. And this is the mark which distinguishes him from the rest of the animal world. Language enables man to say, 'I am I'. And the moment he goes beyond it, he speculates, he projects, he says, 'I am I, and in that "I" you can contain the whole cosmos'

B: And one more thing. Because of language, man has been able to evolve culture, and he cannot go back to the biological stage.

D: In twenty-five thousand years of evolution, of thinking, of speaking and so on, there is very little change in man; the environment has changed, but fundamentally there is very little change in man.

K: Yes.

P: I accept what B or D say, but still I am aware that I am. That statement is where it is.

K: B is saying very simply: Strip man of all the psychological factors, then what is the difference between animal and man?— Oh, there is a vast difference.

P: The moment you posit a difference, you are investigating something else.

B: Man is aware of himself and the animal is not; that is the only distinction.

K: Let us go back. We want to survive psychologically and also biologically.

D: I say there is something else.

K: We will have to find out. Merely to posit that there is something else has no meaning.

D: But you say that all other aspects of the human being have ended.

K: When conflict, misery, pain have ended—

P: As also fantasy, wonder, imagination—all that which has made man reach out, reach in.

K: K said both the outer and the inner.

P: It is the same movement. When you say that all this is to be stripped, what happens? Is it legitimate to ask that? Can we, in discussion, in going through this, get the feeling of that stripping, that seeing?

K: We have said that intelligence is beyond consciousness and that when the mind is stripped of the psychological elements, in the very stripping, there is the uncovering of this intelligence; intelligence comes into being in the very stripping. There is biological survival, and there is intelligence. That is all.

Intelligence has no heritage; consciousness has heritage. Within the field of consciousness, we are caught in becoming; we are trying to become something within that field. Strip all that. Empty all that. Let the mind empty itself of all that. In the very emptying comes intelligence. Therefore there are only two things left: the highest form of intelligence and survival, which is very different from living like an animal. Man is not merely an animal; he is able to think, design, construct.

P: Do you mean to say that there is an intelligence which manifests itself in the action of stripping consciousness?

K: Listen carefully. My consciousness is all the time trying to become, to change, to modify, to struggle, and so on. That and biological survival are all I know. Everybody operates within these two. And within that struggle, we project something beyond consciousness; but that is still within consciousness because it is projected.

The mind that really wants to be free from the wrangle, from the back-chattering asks: Can the mind strip itself of its own content? That is all. (*pause*) And intelligence comes to be in that asking.

P: Is emptying an endless process?

K: Certainly not. Because if it were an endless process, I would be caught in the same phenomenon.

P: Let us pause here. Is it not an endless process?

K: It is not an endless process.

P: You mean, once it is done, it is done?

K: Let us go slowly. You must first understand this verbally. My consciousness is made up of all that we have talked about.

P: Does the emptying of consciousness take time or is it free of time? Is it piecemeal? Or, is it an emptying of the whole?

K: Is the question whether the emptying is piecemeal or whether it is whole?

P: Putting the question that way reveals the whole which contains the piece.

B: Stripping has to be a joint process which includes the part and the whole.

K: Discuss it.

P: What is it that one strips? Or, what is it that one perceives? Or, is there a dissolution of that which emerges, which is thought?

D: If all these go, what remains?

P: When you say that all goes, what do you mean?

B: Only awareness remains. Is complete awareness the whole?

P: Yes.

K: She says yes, but what is the question?

P: Is the awareness of a point of consciousness, of one thing such as jealousy, the totality of consciousness?

K: When you use the word 'aware', what do you mean? If you mean aware of the implications—a state where there is no choice, no will, no compulsion, no resistance, obviously it is so.

P: So at any point this is possible.

K: Of course.

P: Yes, because that is the door—the door of dissolution.

K: No. Hold it a minute.

P: I used that word 'door' deliberately.

K: Hold on. Let us begin slowly, because I want to go step by step. My consciousness is made up of all this. My consciousness is part of the whole, both at the superficial and at the deeper level. You are asking: Is there any awareness which is so penetrating that in that very awareness the whole is present? Or, is it present bit by bit? Is there a search, is there a looking in, an analysing?

D: The yogic position is that nature is a flowing river. In that flow, man's organism comes into being. As soon as it comes into being, it has also the capacity to choose. And the moment it chooses, it separates itself from the flow, from the river. This is a process of separation from the flow, and the only thing which brings this into being is choice. Therefore, they say that the dissolution of choice may bring you to total emptiness and that in that emptiness you see.

K: Right sir, that is one point. P's question was: Is this awareness a gradual process of stripping bit by bit? Does this awareness, in which there is no choice, empty the whole of consciousness? Does it go beyond consciousness?

F: Supposing I cease to choose, is that stripping?

P: Is there an end to stripping?

K: Or, is it a constant process?

P: And the second question was: Where there is intelligence, is there stripping?

K: Let us start with the first question, it is good enough. What do you say?

P: It is one of those extraordinary questions where you cannot either say yes or say no.

D: It hangs on time or no time. If it is invited, it is time.

P: If you say it is not a question of time, then it is not a process. Five minutes later it will emerge again. So this question cannot be answered.

K: I am not sure. Let us begin again. My consciousness is made up of all this; my consciousness is used to the process of time; my consciousness thinks in terms of gradualness; my consciousness is: practise, and through practice achieve—which is time; my consciousness is a process of time.

Now I am asking that consciousness whether it can go beyond this. Can we, who are caught in the movement of time, go beyond time? Consciousness cannot answer that question. Consciousness does not know what it means to go beyond time because it only thinks in terms of time. So, when questioned whether the process can end (leading to a state in which there is no time), it cannot answer, can it?

Now, since consciousness cannot answer the question, we say: Let us see what awareness is and investigate whether that awareness can bring about a timeless state. But this brings in new elements: What is awareness? Is it within the field of time, or is it outside the field of time? Is there in awareness any choice, any explanation, justification or condemnation? In awareness is there an observer, or the one who chooses? And if there is an observer, is that awareness? So, is there an awareness in which the observer is totally absent? Obviously there is. I am aware of that lamp, I do not have to choose when I am aware of it. Is there an awareness in which the observer is totally absent?—Not a continuous state of awareness in which the observer is absent, which again is a fallacious statement.

A: The word for this is *svarūpa śūnyatā*—the observer becomes empty; he is stripped.

K: Now, is that awareness to be cultivated?—which implies time. How does this awareness in which there is no observer come into being? Is this awareness to be cultivated? If it is to be cultivated, it is the result of time, and also a part of that consciousness in which choice exists.

And you say awareness is not choice; it is observation in which there is no observer. Now, how is that to come about without consciousness interfering? Does it come out of consciousness, flower out of it? Or, is it free of consciousness?

D: It is free of consciousness.

P: Does it come about when I ask the question: Who am I?

K: All the traditionalists have asked that question.

P: But it is an essential question. Does it come about when I really try to investigate the source of the ego itself? Or, does awareness come about when one tries to discover the observer?

K: No. The moment you try, you are in time.

P: It is a question of semantics. You can strip consciousness at any point—where is the observer? We are taking it for granted that the observer is.

K: Let us begin slowly. One sees what consciousness is. Any movement within that field is still a process of time: it may try to be or not to be; it may try to go beyond; it may try to invent something beyond consciousness, but it is still part of time. So I am stuck.

P: I want to use words which are not yours. So I have rejected all your words. I have to use my own instruments. What is the element in me which seems to me the most potent and powerful?—It is the sense of the 'I'.

K: Which is the past.

P: I will not use your language. It is very interesting not to use your language. I say the most potent thing is the sense of the 'I'. Now can there be a perception of the 'I'?

F: That is a wrong question. I will tell you why. You ask: Can I perceive the 'I'? Now the 'I' is nothing but an insatiable hunger for experience.

K: P began by asking: Who am I? Is the 'I' an action of consciousness?

P: Let us look, let us investigate.

K: When I ask myself: Who am I? is the 'I' the central factor in consciousness?

P: It seems so. And then I say: Let me see the 'I', let me find it, perceive it, touch it.

K: So you are asking: Is this central factor perceivable by the senses? Is the central factor tangible, to be felt, to be tasted? Or, is that central factor, the 'I', something which the senses have invented?

P: That comes later. First of all, I see whether it can be touched.

K: When I ask the question: Who am I? I must also question who is investigating, who is asking the question.

P: I do not ask that question now. I have asked that question over and over again; I have discussed awareness endlessly. I discard it because you have said: Do not accept one word which is not your own. I start looking. Is this 'I' which is the central core of myself, tangible? I observe it in the surface layers, in the deeper layers of my consciousness, in the hidden darkness, and as I unfold it what takes place is a light within, an explosion, an extension within.

Another factor that operates is that that which has been exclusive becomes inclusive. So far I have been exclusive, now the world flows in.

K: We see that.

P: And I find that this is not something which can be touched or perceived. What can be perceived is that which has been; it is a manifestation of this 'I'. I see I had a thought of this 'I' in action, but it is already over. Then I explore: From where does thought emerge? Can I pursue a thought? How far can I go with a thought? How far can I hold a thought? Can thought be held in consciousness? These are tangible things which the individual has to completely feel for himself.

K: Let us be simple. When I ask: Who am I? who is asking the question? One finds on investigation that the 'I' is not observable. And so, is the 'I' within the field of the senses? Or, have the senses created the 'I'?

P: The very fact that it is not within the field of the senses—

K: Do not move away from that. Is it not also within the field of the senses? We jump too quickly.

P: I want to put aside everything Krishnaji has said, and I find that the very inquiry, the very investigation into the 'I' creates light, an intelligence.

K: You are saying that the very inquiry brings about awareness. Obviously I did not say it did not.

P: And, in the inquiry, one can only use certain instruments, which are the senses. Whether the inquiry is outside or within, the only instruments which can be used are the senses, because that is all we know: the seeing, listening, feeling—and the field is illuminated. The field of the without and the field of the within are illuminated. Now, in this state of illumination, you suddenly find that there has been a thought, but that it is already over. If you now ask: Is the stripping partial or total? the question is irrelevant; it has no meaning.

K: Wait a minute. I am not sure. Is perception partial? I have investigated through the senses—the senses creating the 'I', investigating the 'I'. The activity brings a lightness, a clarity. Not entire clarity, but some clarity.

P: I would not use the word 'some clarity', but 'clarity'.

K: It brings clarity. We will stick to that. Is that clarity expandable?

P: The nature of seeing is such—I can see here, and I can see there, depending on the power of the eye.

K: We said that perception is not only visual but also non-visual. We said perception is that which illuminates.

P: I would like to ask you something. You have said that seeing is not only visual but also non-visual. What is the nature of this non-visual seeing?

K: The non-visual is the non-thinkable. The non-visual does not pertain to the word; it does not pertain to thought. That is all. It is without meaning, without expression, without thought. Is there a perception without thought? Now proceed.

P: There is a perception that can see close, that can see far.

K: Wait. We are talking only of perception—not duration, length, size or breadth of perception, but of perception which is non-visual, which is neither deep nor shallow. Shallow perception or deep perception come only when thought interferes.

P: Now, in that, is there partial or total stripping? We started with that question.

F: She is asking this: In every perception, there is the non-verbal element of mere sensation; then there is the psychological super-imposition. Is there a state of mind in which super-imposition does not occur and there is no stripping?

P: That is right. Perception is perception. We are asking: Is there a perception in which stripping is not necessary?

K: There is no such thing as an everlasting perception.

P: Is it identical with what you call intelligence?

K: I do not know. Why are you asking that?

P: Because it is timeless.

K: Timeless means timeless. Why do you ask this? Isn't perception which is non-verbal also non-thought, non-time? If you have answered this question, you have answered that one also. A mind which is perceiving is not asking this question; it is perceiving. And each perception is perception; it is not carrying over perception. Where does the question of stripping or not stripping arise?

P: Perception is never carried into another thought. I see that lamp. The seeing has not been carried. Only thought is being carried.

K: That is obvious. My consciousness is my mind, which is the result of sensory perception. It is also the result of evolution and time. It is expandable and contractible. And thought is part of consciousness. Now somebody comes along and asks: Who am I? Is the 'I' a permanent entity in this consciousness?

D: It is not permanent.

K: Is this 'I' consciousness?

D: It cannot be.

K: Consciousness is heritage. Of course it is.

F: We are mixing the concept of consciousness with the experience of consciousness.

K: This is very clear—the 'I' is that consciousness.

P: The 'I' has a great reality for me until I begin to investigate.

K: Of course. The fact is that after looking, after observing, I see that I am the whole of this consciousness. This is not a verbal statement. I am the heritage—I am all that. Is this 'I' observable? Can it be felt, can it be twisted? Is it the result of perception and of heritage?

F: It is not the result of the inherited; it is the inherited.

K: And then she asks: Who is that 'I'? Is that 'I' part of consciousness, part of thought? I say yes. Thought is part of the 'I', except where thought is functioning technologically, where there is no 'I'. The moment you move away from the scientific field, you come to the 'I', which is part of the biological heritage.

F: The 'I' is the centre of perception; it is a working centre of perception, an *ad hoc* centre, and the 'other' is an effective centre.

K: Be simple. We see that consciousness is the 'I'; the whole of that field is the 'I'. The 'I' is the centre in the field.

P: I want to put aside everything and tackle it in a new way. I see that the most important element in me is the 'I'. Now what is the 'I'? What is its nature? One investigates that, and in the very process of observation there is clarity.

K: Full stop.

P: Clarity being non-eternal—

K: But it can be picked up again.

P: I say, may be.

K: Because I have an idea that perception is whole.

P: Can the question whether clarity is eternal legitimately arise in this state?

K: It does not arise in the state of perception. It only arises or exists when I ask: Is this process everlasting?

P: And what would you say?

K: You are being asked. Answer. You have to answer this question. At the moment of perception, the question does not arise. The next moment, I do not perceive so clearly.

P: If I am alert to see that I am not perceiving so clearly, I will investigate that.

K: So what am I doing? There is perception. That is all.

P: The key to the doorway is in that question.

K: Let us be simple about this. There is perception. In that perception there is no question of duration. There is only perception. The next minute I do not see clearly, there is no clear perception; it is muddled. Then there is the investigation of pollution, and so clarity. Muddle and again perception, covering and uncovering—this goes on. This is going on. Right?

F: Is it a movement of time?

P: Something very interesting takes place. The very nature of this awareness is that it operates on the other.

K: What do you mean by the 'other'?

P: Inattention.

K: Wait. There is attention followed by inattention. Then be aware of inattention, which then becomes attention. This balancing is going on all the time.

P: Now I make a statement: Awareness lessens inattention. It would be incorrect for me to say this. The only thing I can observe is that there is an action of attention on inattention.

K: Does that action on inattention wipe away inattention, so that inattention does not come again?

D: It is attentive to the inattentive.

P: I am going further than being attentive to the inattentive. I say that the nature of this attention is such that it operates on the brain cells. I am very, very hesitant when I say this. It is the nature of attention to operate on the brain cells. That which is dormant in the brain cells re-emerges when it is exposed to attention, and the very nature of dormancy undergoes a change. I would like this area to be investigated.

K: Let us begin again. If there is choice in that awareness, we are back again in consciousness. Awareness is non-verbal; it has no relationship to thought. We call that awareness attention. When there is inattention there is inattention, why do you mix up the two? I am inattentive; there is no attention. That is all.

In that inattention there are certain actions going on. And those activities bring further misery, confusion, trouble. So I say to myself: I must be attentive all the time so as to prevent this disturbance taking place. And I say: I have to cultivate attention. That very cultivation becomes inattention. The seeing of that inattention brings attention.

Attention affects the brain cells. Look what has happened. There is attention, and then inattention. In inattention there is confusion, misery, and all the rest of it. Now what takes place?

D: The dispelling of inattention has gone down in the unconscious.

P: Is it not really that you can do nothing about it?

K: I agree P, but hold on a minute. Do not say that there is nothing. We will find out. We are investigating. There is attention and there is inattention. In inattention everything is confusion. Why do I want to put the two together? When there is the urge to put the two together, there is an action of the will, which is choice: I prefer attention to inattention. And so I am back again in the field of consciousness. So what is the action where the two are never brought together? I want to explore that a little bit.

When there is attention, thought as memory does not operate; there is no thinking process in attention, there is only attention. I am only aware that I have been inattentive when the action produces discomfort, misery or danger. Then I say to myself: I have been inattentive. And as inattention has left a mark on the brain, I am concerned with the misery inattention has brought about. Then, in investigating that misery, attention comes again, leaving no mark. So what is taking place? Each time there is inattention, there is the quick and instant perception of it. Perception has an immediacy; it has no duration. It is not of time. Perception and attention leave no mark: The immediacy of perception is always taking place.

Bombay
18 February, 1971

THE MIND AND THE HEART

Dialogue 30

P: So far our discussions have been related to the mind and its problems. What we have not discussed is the movement of the heart.

K: I am glad you have raised that.

P: Is the movement of the heart a different movement from the movement of the mind? Are they one movement or two movements? And if they are two movements, what are the elements which make these two movements different? I use the words 'mind' and 'heart' because these are the two focal points around which certain sensory responses appear to focus. Are the two movements in fact one movement?

K: Let us begin. What do you mean by 'movement'?

P: Any kind of emotional response which we call love, affection, goodwill, compassion, seems to ripple, to move from a focal point which we identify as the region of the heart. These ripples affect the heart, make it physically beat faster.

K: This is the physiological movement of the brain cells.

D: Or is it the nerves which have an impact on the heart?

K: It is a response of the nerves, the heart, the brain, the whole psychosomatic organism. Now, is the movement of the mind separate from the movement of what is generally called the heart? We are not speaking of the physical heart, but of the emotions: the sentiments, the anger, the jealousy, the feeling of guilt—all the emotions that make the heart throb and beat faster. Are the movements of the mind and heart separate? Let us discuss it.

P: In the context of what we have been saying all along, that is, of stripping the mind until nothing except the movement of survival remains, the only factor which would distinguish man would be this strange movement of the heart.

K: I think this division is artificial. First of all, we should not start that way.

P: While we have been discussing with you, there has been a silencing of the brain cells, there has been a tremendous clarity, yet there has been no response from the heart; there have been no ripples.

K: So you are separating the two: There is the movement of the mind and there is the movement of the heart. Let us question whether they are separate. And also, if they are not separate, when the mind is emptied of consciousness, in the sense in which we have used that word, what is the quality of the mind that is compassion, that is love, that has empathy? Let us begin by asking whether the movement of the heart is separate.

P: What identity has anger with the movement of affection?

K: I am asking: Is any movement separate?

P: Separate from what?

K: Is any movement separate, or is all movement unitary, like all energy is unitary, though we may divide it up and fragment it? One has broken up movement into different categories, as the movement of the heart and the movement of the mind. We are asking: Is there a movement of the heart separate from the movement of the mind? I do not know if I can verbalize this: Are the mind, the heart and the brain one unit? And from that unit, movement flows, a movement which is unitary. But we divide the emotions, the sentiments of devotion, tenderness, compassion, enthusiasm from their opposites.

P: As evil, cruelty, vanity. But there is a purely intellectual movement which is neither the one nor the other—the purely technological movement.

K: Is the technological movement different from the movement of the mind?

P: I think thought has its own technology. It has its own momentum, it has its own reason for existence, its own direction, its own speed, its own motives and its own energy.

F: You cannot measure thought. Do not call it technology.

D: Thought waves have been measured. Technology implies measurability.

K: We said just now that compassion, love, tenderness, care, consideration and politeness are one movement. The opposite movement is contrary to that; it is the movement of violence and so on. So there is the movement of the mind, the movement of affection, love, compassion, and there is the movement of violence. So there are now three movements. Then there is another movement which asserts that this must be and this must not be. Has the assertion that this must be or this must not be anything whatsoever to do with the other mental movements?

D: Apart from the three there is the movement of the co-ordinator.

K: Now we have the fourth movement, that of the co-ordinator. The four movements are: the movement of the heart which has affection; the movement of violence, callousness, depression, vulgarity and all that; then the intellectual movement and, finally, the movement of the co-ordinator. Now, each one of these movements has its own sub-divisions. And each of the sub-divisions is in contradiction with its opposite. And so it multiplies. See how complex it becomes. This psychosomatic organism has many contradictions, not just intellectual and emotional movements. These movements are multitudinous and contradictory. And there is the co-ordinator trying to arrange things so that he can operate.

F: Is there not a selective mechanism, which picks out and names things 'thought', 'mind', 'heart' and so on? Is that not the co-ordinator?

K: Co-ordinator, chooser, integrator, selector, call it what you will—they are all in contradiction with each other.

F: Why do you say that they are in contradiction? Is it because each one is an independent movement?

D: In the way one lives, they seem to be in contradiction.

F: But each one is moving on its own.

P: As F says: If, at any given point, one is, then the other is not.

F: Then there cannot be contradiction.

K: When one is, the other is not. But the co-ordinator weighs these two: I want this, and I do not want that.

F: That is the whole movement of life.

P: We started this discussion by asking whether there is such a thing as a movement of the heart. So far we have investigated the movement of the mind.

B: Is the heart's movement a nourishing movement? Is it a movement of sustenance? And is it not necessary, in order that the movement of the brain does not remain sterile?

D: We are not in the field of contradiction at all.

K: There is no contradiction when one is and the other is not. Contradiction comes in when the co-ordinator says: I would rather have this and not that. Then contradiction, the opposition as choice, begins.

A: If I am full of hate, etc., I cannot take two steps beyond. The question is: Is the movement of the heart distinct from that of the mind? Or, does it have its own quality?

K: That is what P is saying. There is the movement of the mind—the intellectual, technological movement; there is the movement of the heart; and there is the movement of violence. There are multitudinous movements in us, and the co-ordinator selects one or two to sustain himself. From there, what is the next question?

P: Are these movements parallel to each other? Ultimately they are either the one movement or the other.

K: I am not sure.

P: Is the movement of the brain basically that which excites emotions?

A: Though one may not have personal hate or anger, when I read about Bengal, certain emotions come, and they are social responses; I do not do a thing about it. Whereas to have love, affection, is a definite quality of enrichment; it is a sustenance which the mind cannot give you.

D: We have already agreed that the perception of the brain is thought.

K: Let us get the meaning of the words clear. The response to various forms of stimuli is what we call emotion. Is perception an emotion?

Now what is the next question? Are the two movements with their sub-divisions parallel?

P: Parallel movement means separate movement; they never meet.

K: Or, are they really one movement, which we do not know?

P: Take the example of desire—which category, thought or emotion, would you put it in?

B: Desire is from the heart.

P: After a while desire becomes thought. So where will you put it?

A: It arises only as a thought.

F: The arising of desire as an immediate emotional response of the heart is not separate from thought: when one is angry the heart beats faster. All that is one movement.

K: Desire, hate, love are mental and emotive movements. You ask whether they are parallel and, therefore, separate. I myself am not saying that they are or that they are not.

P: I don't think that that is a valid question. The valid question is: If they are two separate movements, is it possible for them ever to come together? Or, is the very cause of our misfortune the fact that we keep them separate?

F: That which perceives the pattern is thought; that which perceives without the pattern is emotion.

P: When you make such a statement, either this is so for us and, therefore, the duality has ceased in us, or it is a theory.

K: It is a theory. Conclusions and formulas mean nothing. I say: I do not know. I know only these two movements—the intellectual or rational movement and the feeling of kindliness, gentleness. That is all. Are these separate movements? Or, does our present misfortune and confusion arise because we have treated them as separate movements? You see, P, we have divided the body and the soul. The religious tendency in both the East and in the West has been to divide. But it is really a single psychosomatic state which invents the soul. And so the question is: Are there two movements, or have we accustomed ourselves to the thought that the two, the body and the soul, are separate?

P: But how can you neglect the fact that an emotional intensity brings a new quality of being, a complete experience of what the other person feels; a sense of unspoken understanding?

K: Do not bring that in yet. We are asking: Are these two movements separate? Or, is it because we are so habit-ridden that we have accepted these two as separate movements? If they are not seprate, what is the one unitary movement that includes thought as the movement of the brain and the movement of the heart?

How do you investigate this question? I can only investigate it from fact to fact; I can have no theories about it. I see the fact of perception; I see the fact of the movement of thought; and I ask: When there is no movement of thought, is there a movement which is non-verbal? Have I explained myself?

If there is complete cessation of thinking, which is movement, is there a movement which is an emotive movement—as love, devotion, tenderness, care? Is there a movement separate from thought; thought being verbal—meaning, explanation, description, etc.? When the movement of thought comes to an end without any compulsion, is there not a totally different movement which is not that or this?

P: That is so, sir, and I am saying this very, very hesitantly. There is a state when it is as if an elixir is released, when one is overflowing; a state in which the heart is the only thing that there is. I am using metaphors. There can be action in that state, there can be doing, thinking; there can be everything. There is also a state when thought has ceased and the mind is very clear and alert, but the elixir is not present.

K: Let us stick to one thing. Just what is the factor of division?

P: What divides is an actual physical sense; it is not mental. There is a certain ripple; a ripple is very real.

K: I am not talking about that. What is the factor in us that divides one as the emotive movement and the other as the intellectual movement of thought? Why is there the division between soul and body?

D: Would you admit that the very faculty of the intellect sees that there is a movement which emerges from thought and another that emerges from the heart? It is observable.

K: I ask: Why is there a division?

D: The hand is different from the leg.

K: They have different functions.

D: There is the function of the brain and there is the function of the heart.

A: As far as my experience goes, when the verbal movement ceases, there is an awareness of the entire body in which emotional content is pure feeling. It is no more thinking, but pure feeling.

P: In the tradition there is a word called *rasa*, which is very close to what Krishnaji says. Tradition recognizes different types of *rasa*: *rasa* is essence, it is that which fills, that which permeates. But *rasa* is a word which needs to be investigated.

D: It is emotion.

P: It is much more; *rasa* is essence.

K: Keep to that word: 'essence', 'perfume'. Essence means what is. Now what happens? In observing the whole movement of thought, in observing the content of consciousness, the essence comes out of it. And in observing the movement of the heart, in that perception, there is the essence. Essence is the same whether it is this or that.

A: That is what the Buddhists also say.

K: In perceiving the whole movement of thought as consciousness —consciousness with its content, which is consciousness—and in observing it, in that very observation is the external refinement, which is the essence. Right? In the same way, there is the perception of the whole movement of the body, of love, joy. When you perceive all that, there is the essence. And in that there are no two essences.

When you use the word 'essence', what does it imply? You see, it is the essence of the flower which makes the perfume. The essence has to come into being. Now, how do you produce it? Do you distil it?—When flowers are distilled, the essence of the flowers is the perfume.

D: When the pollution goes, it is essence.

F: There is the essence of friendship, of affection.

K: No, no. I would not use 'essence' in that way—as 'essence of friendship', 'essence of jealousy'. No. No.

F: What do you mean by 'essence'?

K: Just look. I have watched what we have been doing during these discussions. We have observed the movement of thought as consciousness; we have observed the whole of it—the content of the movement is consciousness. There is the perception of that. The perception is the distillation of that; and that we call 'essence' which is pure intelligence. It is not my intelligence or your intelligence; it is intelligence. It is essence. And when we observe the movement of love, hate, pleasure, fear, which are all emotive, there is perception. And, as you perceive, the essence comes out of that. There are no two essences.

D: Here comes my question. What is the relationship between essence as you perceive it and uniqueness? I think they are interchangeable.

K: I think I would rather use the word 'essence'.

P: The great masters of alchemy were called *rasa-siddhas*.

D: 'They who are established in *rasa*', that is, those who have attained, who have their being *in that*.

K: During these days and before, one has watched the movement of thought. One has watched it, and watched it without any choice; and in that is the essence. Out of that choiceless observation, comes the essence of the one and the essence of the other. Therefore what is the essence? Is it a refinement of emotions, or is it totally unrelated to emotion?—and yet related, because it has been observed. Right?

P: So energy which is attention—

K: Energy is essence.

P: Though operating on matter, essence is unrelated to both.

K: Let us begin again slowly with essence. Is it unrelated to consciousness? I am assuming that one has observed consciousness. There has been a perception of the movement of consciousness as thought, and as the content of that consciousness, which is time. The very observation of that—the flame of observation—distills. Right?

In the same way, the flame of perception brings the essence of emotive movement. Now your question was: Having this essence, what is its relationship to the emotion?—None whatsoever; essence has nothing to do with the flower. Though the essence is part of the flower, it is not of it. I do not know if you see this.

F: 'Although it is part of the flower, the essence is not of it'—how can that be so, even grammatically?

K: Look, sir, the other day I saw them taking the bark of a tree to produce some kind of alcohol; that essence is not the bark.

F: But it is in the bark.

D: Which is realized because of the heat.

K: The heat of perception produces the essence. So what is the question?—Is essence related to consciousness? Obviously not. The whole point here is the flame of perception; the flame of perception is the essence.

D: It creates the essence and it is the essence.

K: *It is the essence.*

P: Is perception the moment of creation?

D: Do we create what we perceive?

K: I do not know what you mean by creation.

P: Bringing into being something which was not there before.

K: Is perception creation? What do you mean by creation? I know what perception means. Let us stick to that word. I do not know what the meaning of creation is. Producing a baby? Baking bread?

D: No, I would not say that. Moving from here to there is also producing.

K: Do not reduce everything to creation; going to the office is not creation. What does it mean to create, to produce something which has not existed before, say to create a statue? What is brought into being—is it essence? There are only two things which can be brought about: thought or emotion.

D: Bringing into being means 'essence manifested'.

K: I ask of you: What is creation? I do not know. Is it bringing into being something new which is not in the mould of the known?

P: Creation is bringing into being something new, something not of the old.

K: Therefore let us be clear. 'Bringing into being something totally new'—at what level? Watch it. At the sensory level, at the intellectual level, at the level of memory—where? 'Bringing into being something new'—So that you see it, so that you can visualize it? So, when you speak of bringing into being something totally new, at what level is it brought about?

P: The sensory.

K: At the sensory level? Take a picture which is non-verbal—can you paint something that is totally new? That is, can you bring something into being which is not an expression of the self? It is not new if it is self-expression.

P: If creation is something entirely new, which is unrelated to any self-expression, then probably all self-expression ceases, all manifestation ceases.

K: Wait. Wait.

P: I will say that, because there does not exist anything which is not an expression of the self....

K: That is what I want to get at. The man who discovered the jet—at the moment of discovery there was no self-expression. He translated it into self-expression. It is something discovered, then it is put into a formula. I only know that the flame of perception has brought about the essence, and now the question is: Has that essence any expression? Does it create anything new?

D: It creates a new perception.

K: No. There is no new perception; the flame is the perception.

The flame is a flame all the time. One moment there is the pure flame of perception, then it is forgotten, and again the pure flame of perception, then forgotten. Each time the flame is new.

D: Perception touches matter, and there is an explosion and mutation. Now, you cannot postulate that which emerges out of it. It is the discovery of the jet engine.

K: Let us put it this way. In that essence when there is action, there is no concern with self-expression. It is concerned with action. Action then is total, not partial.

P: I want to ask one more question. The manifestation of this—

K: Is action.

P: Has it contact with matter?

A: We go with you as far as perception.

K: No, sir, you have gone further. There is a perception which is a flame, which has distilled the essence. Now that perception acts or may not act. If it acts, it has no frontiers at all; there is no 'me' acting. Obviously.

P: That itself is creation. Creation is not something apart from that.

K: The very expression of that essence is creation in action—not new action or old action. The essence is expression.

P: Then is perception also action?

K: Of course. See the beauty of it. Forget about action. See what has taken place in you. Perception without any qualification is a flame. It distills whatever it perceives; it distills whatever it perceives, because it is the flame.

There is that perception which distills at every minute: When you say I am a fool, to perceive that. And in that perception there is the essence. That essence acts, or it does not act—depending upon the environment, depending upon where it is. But in that action there is no 'me'; there is no motive at all.

Bombay
19 February, 1971

LIST OF PARTICIPANTS

K: J. Krishnamurti
A: Achyut Patwardhan
B: S. Balasundaram
D: P.Y. Deshpande
F: Maurice Friedman
GS: George Sundarshan
J: Janardan Patwardhan
P: Pupul Jayakar
R: Radha Burnier
S: Sunanda Patwardhan
SW: Swami Sundaram